To Boldly Stay

To Boldly Stay

Essays on Star Trek: Deep Space Nine

Edited by SHERRY GINN
and MICHAEL G. CORNELIUS

McFarland & Company, Inc., Publishers
Jefferson, North Carolina

This book has undergone peer review.

ISBN (print) 978-1-4766-8540-3
ISBN (ebook) 978-1-4766-4628-2

LIBRARY OF CONGRESS AND BRITISH LIBRARY
CATALOGUING DATA ARE AVAILABLE

Library of Congress Control Number 2022018064

Front cover images: © 2022 sdecoret/Aaron Alien/Shutterstock

Printed in the United States of America

*McFarland & Company, Inc., Publishers
Box 611, Jefferson, North Carolina 28640
www.mcfarlandpub.com*

Sherry says that this one is for Larry, as always.
and
Michael says that this one, as all things, is for Joe.
And Knox. But not necessarily in that order.

Table of Contents

Acknowledgments

Sherry Ginn: I would like to thank Michael Cornelius for agreeing once again to coedit a collection with me; you'd think he would learn by now! Thank you, Michael. I also extend my thanks to our contributors for their awesome essays, especially considering we were trying to get this book together during the coronavirus pandemic. Thanks to everyone at McFarland for again accepting my writing. Larry, as usual, found a way to entertain himself while I was writing and Madison slept or ate (also as usual).

Michael G. Cornelius: I would like to thank my good friend and colleague Sherry Ginn; after swearing off any such projects for the next few years, she drew me back into her clutches with three little words: *Deep. Space. Nine.* It seems I will never learn. Thanks to our contributors for putting up with Señor Cranky Editor here, and thanks to McFarland for being great partners in the realm of academic popular culture studies. I am proud of what we have accomplished.

Introduction

MICHAEL G. CORNELIUS *and* SHERRY GINN

Although *Star Trek: Deep Space Nine* ended over twenty-five years ago, a stand-alone examination of the series has not been published to date. This seems a significant critical oversight. On air from 1993 to 1999, *Deep Space Nine* was a departure from *The Next Generation*'s depiction of the United Federation of Planets' diplomatic and scientific study of the Alpha Quadrant. Situated on a space station at the entrance of a stable wormhole near the planet Bajor, *Deep Space Nine*'s stories revolved around the uneasy cease-fire between the Bajorans and the Cardassians as mediated by the Federation. Different in style from the two previous incarnations of *Star Trek*, *Deep Space Nine* is broadly considered to depict a future shadowier and more dystopian than the vision illustrated in *The Original Series* (1966–1969) and *The Next Generation* (1987–1994). It also differed in other significant ways from its predecessors, and not just by placing the action on a space station rather than a starship; *Deep Space Nine* serialized storylines over several years of production; introduced interpersonal conflict into relationships; questioned utopian visions of the Federation's past, present, and future; and presented spirituality and religiosity as a primary plotline for the series' main character. Strange new worlds, indeed.

Star Trek creator Gene Roddenberry brokered *The Original Series* to NBC as "*Wagon Train* to the Stars," and two of its sequels—*The Next Generation* and *Voyager* (1995–2001)—followed the familiar format of "exploring strange new worlds and going boldly where no one had gone before." *Deep Space Nine*, on the other hand, placed its multiracial/multi-species characters on a stationary space station and brought the galaxy to them. Because of its location at the entrance of the wormhole connecting the Alpha Quadrant to the unknown Gamma Quadrant, Starbase Deep Space 9 provided an opportunity for exploration as well as commerce and diplomacy for the Federation. New, unknown species/races could be introduced, and familiar species could be examined in much more detail than in previous iterations of *Star Trek*, which frequently followed the more familiar "stand-alone" episodic format. *Deep Space Nine*, along with J. Michael Straczynski's *Babylon 5* (1993–1998), offered a new version of an older narrative format to the television audience: a serialized story that would span years before reaching its culmination. If the *Star Trek* motto has always been to boldly go where no one had gone before, then *Deep Space Nine* (along with *Babylon 5*) did so narratively, helping to usher in a new renaissance of serialized television that has become fairly standard in the first quarter of the twenty-first century, hallmarking series as divergent as *Lost* (2004–2010), *Game of Thrones* (2011–2019), and *Killing Eve* (2018–2022).

    Deep Space Nine also differed from its predecessors in its exploration of religion and spirituality. As a secular humanist, Roddenberry was uninterested in divine or supernatural intervention in the affairs of people, and neither *The Original Series* nor *The Next Generation* earnestly explored the issue (Pearson). Generally, any episodes that addressed religiosity directly exposed its adherents as tricksters and charlatans (e.g., *The Original Series*: "The Return of the Archons"; *The Next Generation*: "The Devil's Due"; *Voyager*: "Live Fast and Prosper"); its phenomena as explicable technobabble (*The Next Generation*: "Rightful Heir"; *Voyager*: "Emanations"); or the whole thing as the hokum, occasionally dangerous by-product of a culture portrayed as "simpler" than the Federation or Earth (*The Original Series*: "Who Mourns for Adonais?"; *The Next Generation*: "Who Watches the Watchers"; *Voyager*: "Someone to Watch Over Me"). In "Who Mourns for Adonais?" for example, Captain Kirk's (William Shatner) famous rejoinder that "Mankind has no need for gods. We find the one quite adequate" hints at the existence of some loose monotheism while simultaneously deriding the religious beliefs of another species. *Deep Space Nine*, on the other hand, takes a very earnest approach to the subject, presenting the viewer with a challenge from the very first episode: a Starfleet officer, Commander Benjamin Sisko (Avery Brooks), is revered as a spiritual leader by the Bajoran people, and rather than reject the role outright, Sisko thoughtfully navigates this new identity, fully embracing his role as Emissary and his destiny by the series' end.

    In addition to Sisko, *Deep Space Nine* featured an ensemble cast that included the commander's son Jake (Cirroc Lofton); his Bajoran first officer Major Kira (Nana Visitor); the station's human doctor Julian Bashir (Siddig El Fadil, later Alexander Siddig)[1]; the science officer and joined Trill Jadzia Dax (Terry Farrell); the shape-shifting Constable Odo (René Auberjonois); the human Chief of Operations Miles O'Brien (Colm Meaney); and the Ferengi bar-owner Quark (Armin Shimerman). However, unlike *The Original Series* and *The Next Generation*, *Deep Space Nine* also included an ever-expanding number of prominent ancillary and recurring characters, such as Quark's brother Rom (Max Grodénchik) and Rom's son Nog (Aron Eisenberg); O'Brien's wife Keiko (Rosalind Chao) and daughter Molly (Hana Hatae); the mysterious Cardassian tailor Garak (Andrew Robinson); the barfly Morn (Mark Allen Shepherd); and the duplicitous Cardassian Gul Dukat (Marc Alaimo) and Bajoran religious leader Kai Winn (Louise Fletcher).[2]

These important secondary characters allowed for the exploration of psychosocial relationships—from family dynamics to interpersonal/inter-special difference to regional conflict—that the more "work"-oriented earlier *Star Trek* series generally ignored. Combined with the serialized narrative structure, *Deep Space Nine* became the most richly complex and (perhaps) the most "sci-fi" series in the entire *Star Trek* pantheon, in so much as it used the genre to advance important conversations about race, gender, faith, and the way in which societies tell stories.

These are the seeds that germinate in this collection—explorations of race, gender, faith, and narrative—all examined through this most important (and yet under-examined) *Star Trek* series. This collection investigates those themes and tropes that were deeply considered throughout and largely trademark the seven seasons of *Deep Space Nine*, examples of which can be observed in the titles of the essays included in this collection. First, though, we feel it important to explore what made/makes *Deep Space Nine* so distinct within the *Star Trek* universe, and how this distinctiveness created the conditions for an entirely different, entirely bold, new vision for/ of *Star Trek*.

Deep Space Nine, *At Rest*

This distinction is perhaps most noticeable in the inherent, if not altogether obvious, contradictions in the titles to both this collection and the eponymous subject of the essays contained herein. The contradiction in our original working title is perhaps glaringly noticeable: *Essays on the Series that "Went" Where No Other Trek Had Gone Before* must be considered ironically when the series narrative focuses on a location that is stationary. Mobility highlights the first two iterations of *Star Trek* (three, if one counts *The Animated Series*, 1973–1974); Kirk, Picard, and their crews spend their missions crisscrossing the expanses of both the known and the unknown corners of the galaxy. The primary setting for each is a spaceship, a locale that is designed to be perpetually in motion. It was Isaac Newton who signified perpetual motion as a qualitative characteristic of force, in his first law of motion, and until *Deep Space Nine*, motion and perpetuality were, indeed, the driving forces that dominated the *Star Trek* narrative. Newton's law, after all, applies not just to force; narratives that are never at rest will never *be* at rest until some external force acts upon their situation, creating the conditions necessary for change. As such, *The Original Series* and *The Next Generation*—indeed, *Star Trek*'s entire story-telling philosophy—emerged as a restless narrative of exploration that emphasized the rush and tumult of newness. The "new worlds" and "new life" and "new civilizations" trumpeted in the voiceover monologue to both series' opening credits belies what is, essentially, a need for accumulation. Week after week of new worlds, new civilizations, new adventures, new characters, new antagonists, new technobabble—after a point of such extended and extensive accumulation, newness simply becomes novelty, and the wonder that all this newness is designed to engender simply becomes a glut of too-much-ness, so that each world may be new, and each civilization may be new, but they all seem the same, both to the characters and to the viewer. Joshua Landry suggests that such accumulative habits only reflect the propensity of Western consumers to be "obsessed with stories," and that this obsession results in narrative consumption focused on accretion, not on contemplation: "We no longer have the slightest time for lyric poetry but instead consume infinite quantities of novels and films and television shows" (497). Thus the wonder of space is replaced by a surfeit of vastness and the constancy of accrual—"more" simply results in "ever-more," with little time or perspective to ponder the meaning of it all.

Roddenberry's utopian vision ultimately has a similar stultifying effect on the series, on the characters in his series, and even on the viewers watching his series. The pointed lack of interpersonal conflict and the decidedly faultless depictions of humanity may seem, at first, a pleasant and diverting counterpoint from the all-too-often unpleasant vicissitudes and disputations that characterize any contemporary existence. There is pleasure in the belief that things—all things, *every*thing—will get better, even if such utopic visions will not emerge until centuries after one is dead. Yet the lack of interpersonal conflict suggests a narrative endpoint, the period after the climax where the resolution is wrought, the day is saved, and no more work needs to be done to perfect humanity. As such, the Enterprise's vaunted "five-year mission" almost reads like a need to seek out not strange new worlds, but new conflicts, since there are no more to be had within. A lack of internal conflict suggests the need for constant external stimulation, stimulation necessary to act as a type of cognitive motivation. Thus, the utopian world of *Star Trek* has negated humanity; bored, we reach out to and beyond the stars not to seek new knowledge, but to entertain ourselves with the conflicts of others. And when that conflict is resolved (most often through the intervention of the Enterprise crew, seeking stimulation through the problems of others), humanity can simply warp off to the next conflict. This is how narrative is sustained in the first two *Star Trek* series. Yet there is a narrative point where constant newness becomes constant sameness, where the wonder of tomorrow becomes the dullness of a future that still seems not only all-too-far away, but less and less possible by the minute, because it is so out of reach, so needlessly endless, so incongruent with what we know to be human.

Perfection is a hallmark of mythopoesis, of larger-than-life figures who seem ideally disposed to right wrongs, restore order, and steady the ship of society. These figures are characterized by personages like Sherlock Holmes and Superman and Nancy Drew, individuals whose identity is focused on improving the conditions of life for those around them, even on a planetary scale. Yet while Holmes is a perfect being whose mythopoesis ensures he will not fail in his mission, his assistant Watson is simply the dim-witted human along for the ride, the buffoonish companion who—through his utter humanity—allows us to experience mythopoesis for ourselves. If Holmes were to narrate his own adventures, then while there might be much to learn about the science of detection, there would be much loss in the wonder of the climactic moment, when the avenging angel that is the consulting detective solves the crime and restores the status quo.[3] The idea of rescue from without is far more enticing than rescue from within. It is easier and somehow more satisfying when Superman saves us from whatever peril the planet is in than doing the hard work ourselves; whether nuclear proliferation or climate change or whatever apocalyptic scenario we continually self-create, humanity has demonstrated that, time and again, we lack both the consensus and the interest to save ourselves, though we would be eternally grateful—well, maybe not eternally— if someone else were to swoop in and do all the work of rescue for us.

Yet humanity does not need rescuing in *The Original Series* or *The Next Generation*. It has already been saved. It is humanity itself that becomes a figure of mythopoesis in the philosophy of the series, dashing to and fro like a frenetic, frantic, caffeine-addicted superhero, saving the day, righting wrongs, and restoring the status quo. The solitary mythopoetic hero in any narrative is counterbalanced by a world in perpetual chaos; in *Star Trek*, mythopoetic humanity is counterbalanced by—everything, and everyone, else, a *universe* in perpetual chaos, and the narrative exegesis is thus forced into weekly "the-Enterprise-saves-the-day-again" missions, casting humanity into the role of hero, savior, and moral paragon by which all other things must be measured. Forget the arrogance of such a stance; frankly, it is simply too exhausting to be able to uphold the ethical conventions that *Star Trek* demands. It is no wonder that the Enterprise is perpetually on the move; should it ever stop, its entire *métier* must be called into question. One cannot be mythopoetic in a world that no longer needs myths, so *Star Trek* perpetually invents new worlds and new civilizations that require deliverance.[4]

What these first *Star Trek* series perhaps fail to realize is that, in embracing perpetual motion and in embracing the perfected nature of the human species, they are (in a converse manner) rejecting constructs of narrative time. As Molly Clark Hillard, citing Julia Kristeva, observes,

> According to Kristeva, the trope of linear time is imagined as a "prospective unfolding," including within its terms departure, progression, and arrival (17) … Departure, progression, arrival: narrative, which shares these characteristics of "unfolding," might be conceived of as the "natural" mode of articulation of a normative "masculine time." To impose narrative on physiological and cultural processes imposes a comforting linearity on what must have seemed disturbingly cyclic [323].

Most episodes of *The Original Series* and *The Next Generation* feature Hillard's aspects of departure, progression, and arrival, though in *Star Trek* this order is inverted: the Enterprise arrives at a planet; "progresses" through the narrative conflict while "progressing" the civilization itself (usually in line with secular humanistic, Federation-approved values); and then departs for the next adventure. In mastering this constructing/ive form of contact ("building" the Federation, as it were, whether through planetary inclusion or simply by shifting other cultures into a Federation ethos), the Enterprise crew not only leaves behind interpersonal conflict, but also personal development. As several of the essays in this collection will note, *The Next Generation* introduces personal development issues for many members of the crew—such as Data's search for humanity, La Forge's disquiet with his disabled form, Picard's inability to connect with others—that occasionally receive narrative attention (especially for Data and Picard, while La Forge's self-conflicts are largely abandoned) but which result in almost no progression whatsoever. Thus, *Star Trek* abandons personal progression for narrative progression. In shaping humanity as a species that is already perfected and one that is perpetually in motion perfecting others, it can avoid both any critique of the human species as well as the notion that individual members of humanity may require—or even benefit from—personal development. In such a scope time loses all meaning. The mission of *The Original Series'* Enterprise may have been five years, but who can say how much time actually passes? In *The Next Generation*, the totality of accumulation—the accumulation of adventures, of comings and goings, of meetings and discoveries—suggests the passage of time, but the only true marker of temporal gain is the appearance of Commander Riker's (Jonathan Frakes) beard and the evolving configurations of Counselor Troi's (Marina Sirtis) uniform. As a narrative in motion, perpetually in motion, to that point in time, *Star Trek* had demonstrated its determined desire to go everywhere and thus, ultimately, to go nowhere.

Conversely, blessedly, *Deep Space Nine* is a narrative characterized by *rest*. The stationary setting and fixed orbit of space station Deep Space 9 allows for narrative development at a discordant pace that can explore, seemingly at its whim, newness *and* sameness, and thus ensure that there is never too much of one at the expense of the other. Landry observes that, as narrative consumers, "We are deeply impatient with the static. If it doesn't move, we refuse to look at it" (498). Yet he also adds that our favorite stories are "those that feature transformation, metamorphosis, *Bildung*, whether spiritual growth or just physical improvement" (498). *Deep Space Nine* may be static, but it is hardly without progression. Yes, *Deep Space Nine* encounters new civilizations; but it also explores and develops familiar civilizations like the Bajorans, the Cardassians, the Klingons, and the Ferengi. Yes, *Deep Space Nine* seeks out strange new life; but it also seeks to uncover more about characters who soon become well known to us, creating a dynamic series of revolving protagonists and antagonists that include individuals from a wide variety of alien races. And yes, *Deep Space Nine* constantly lauds humanity; but it also critically assesses humanity, too. In the pilot episode, "Emissary," when station doctor Julian Bashir enthuses that Bajoran space is the "frontier," his declaration is not meant to truly define his setting, but clearly acts as a criticism of the human-centric view of the universe *Star Trek* had for decades enthusiastically embraced. As the series developed, critiques of the unabashedly myopic outlook of humanity only increased. In storylines featuring the Maquis, for example, *Deep Space Nine* explores a group of largely human settlers/terrorists who reject not just Federation values, but the Federation itself. In the second part of the episode "The Maquis," Sisko finds himself at odds with a former friend, Lieutenant Commander Calvin Hudson (Bernie Casey), who has joined the Maquis. In one poignant conversation, Hudson attempts to persuade Sisko to join his efforts, telling him, "These settlers, Ben, if you saw all they have accomplished without any help from the Federation, then you'd fight along with them" ("The Maquis"). When Sisko refuses to aid the Maquis, Hudson accuses Sisko and the Federation of abandoning the settlers. When Sisko provides an impassioned defense of the Federation and their treaty with Cardassia, Hudson's argument takes on a darker tone:

> Hudson: The Federation abandoned us. Told us to take care of ourselves. Well, that's what we intend to do, Ben.... Every week innocent people are being murdered by the Cardassians. I will not allow those deaths to go unpunished.
> Sisko: You don't want peace, Cal. You want revenge ["The Maquis, Part II"].

Violence, reprisal, murder—these are hardly Federation "values." And yet we are meant to both root for and against the Maquis. Commander Michael Eddington (Kenneth Marshall), another former Starfleet officer who has abandoned the Federation for the Maquis, tells Sisko that the main crime of any member of the Maquis is that they

> left the Federation, and that's the one thing you can't accept. Nobody leaves paradise. Everybody should want to be in the Federation.... You know, in some ways, you're even worse than the Borg. At least they tell you about their plans for assimilation. You're more insidious. You assimilate people and they don't even know it ["For the Cause"].

Eddington's suggestion that the rejection of Federation values is the ultimate crime is both hyperbolic and startlingly accurate. Sisko's pursuit of Eddington, when he so earnestly endeavored to help his friend Hudson, plays out as both personally vindictive as well as a desperate need to validate the Federation itself. For his part, Eddington casts himself as Jean Valjean, the sympathetic hero of Victor Hugo's 1862 novel *Les Misérables*, a man who is a victim of an unjust society that prides itself on rigid interpretations of its own moralistic and legal codes, to the detriment of the downtrodden, placing Sisko in the role of the unyielding, relentless policeman Inspector Javert, a man whose own interpretation of right and wrong—like his greater society—leaves little room for contemplation and empathy. This is perhaps the most significant critique of the Federation as an entity in the entire series. When Eddington uses biogenic weapons to render Cardassian colonies incapable of sustaining Cardassian life, Sisko appropriates the same tactic, rendering Maquis colonies untenable for human existence. At this, Eddington finally surrenders, telling Sisko, "All right, Javert, I'll give you what you want: me!" ("For the Uniform").

The moral confusion of the Maquis storyline is perhaps one of the most interesting in all of *Star Trek*. Sisko's vociferous pursuit of Eddington is eminently understandable—it is incredibly *human*—but it is twentieth-century human, and not human by twenty-third-century standards. His actions are morally problematic at best, and his determination to capture Eddington becomes deeply personal. And yet exploring this type of moral morass is when *Deep Space Nine* is at its best. This is not to suggest that *Deep Space Nine* exists solely to critique Starfleet, the Federation, and/or humanity. It is not an inverted *Next Generation*. As with its predecessor series, humanity's value/s are largely lauded, and we see its/their influence on non-human, non–Federation characters (including Kira, Odo, Garak, Quark, Rom, and Nog), who all change—presumably, for the better—because of their interaction with Federation types. Yet the converse is likewise true—working alongside, coming to understand, and interacting with non–Federation individuals clearly transforms even the very construct of humanity as depicted in the series, whether on broader levels (the Maquis were inspired by the Bajoran fight to overthrow the Cardassians) or on individual bases (such as Sisko's gradual and eventually enthusiastic acceptance of his role as the Bajoran Emissary, their most important spiritual leader). And all of this is possible because of this prolonged double exposure, where (for the first time, at least as far as being depicted on screen) roughly equivalent numbers of Federation and non–Federation peoples alike come together for a common cause and are afforded the time to stay in one place, build relationships, and come to a broader understanding not just of each other, but also of themselves.

This is perhaps where the other contradiction—referenced several pages back—comes into play, the one in the title of the series itself. It may seem obvious to suggest that a narrative called *Deep Space Nine* allows for a sustained exploration into single subjects—allows the characters to go "deep" as they explore both the immediate world(s) around them and within them—but unlike *The Original Series* or *The Next Generation*, it does exactly that. José Sanders and Kobie van Krieken, in contemplating the construct of narrative time, write that "several time spaces may be built into one viewpoint space such that time progresses within individual embedded viewpoint spaces" (283–284). This is what *Deep Space Nine* does so well compared to its progenitor series; it creates within its narrative, and within each character, opportunities for both interstellar and interpersonal exploration. Existing as they do on a static station, though with plenty of opportunities for mobility both on board Deep Space 9 as well as in space, the characters each exist within several temporal and spatial structures at once—their own time/space; Federation time/space; Bajoran time/space—constructs of temporality and spatiality that grow ever more complicated as the narrative becomes ever more complex, both broadly speaking (the discovery of the wormhole, the Dominion War) and specifically, for each individual character (whether through Sisko's journey into faith, Julian's confrontation with his genetically-modified identity, Dax's explorations into her complex pasts, Worf's identity-crisis as both a Klingon and Federation officer, etc.). Personal identity—not national ideology—is at the heart of every journey in *Deep Space Nine*. It is this type of exploration—boldly going where no one had gone before in the *Trek* universe, deep into the heart of the *self*—that creates optimal conditions for broader, more expansive exploration into difficult subjects that *Star Trek* had previously only cursorily deigned to examine: explorations of race, gender, and faith, all wrapped up in and made possible by a narrative that re-examined its own relationship to time by altering its relationship to space.

Exploring Deep Space Nine

The long tenure of the *Star Trek* franchise in the pantheon of American popular culture (thirteen films, nine television series—including three currently on the air in 2020, with up to three more on the way—plus books, theme park attractions, and more) demonstrates a deep-seated, global fascination with the narrative world(s) created in and for the *Star Trek* universe. In their book *The Voyages of Star Trek: A Mirror on American Society through Time*, K.M. Heath and A.S. Carlisle explore what it is about the various *Trek* series that captured the imaginations of multiple generations of fans and keeps them clamoring for more. Specifically, Heath and Carlisle compare and contrast each particular *Trek* within the timeframe in which the series aired, analyzing topics such as "cultural aspects of race/ethnicity, women's rights, contemporary issues such as LGBTQ rights, the rise of computer/digital technology, and group interaction, as well as pop-culture phenomenon" (xviii).[5] In doing so, Heath and Carlisle attempt to locate the nexus of *Trek*'s success within a sense of both timeliness (reflecting the cultural and social mores of the time in which the various shows are being created) and timelessness (reflecting and anticipating themes and constructs that, for good and for ill, will stand the test of time and maintain relevancy far beyond the initial airings of each episode or film). This, they argue, is the way *Star Trek* tells stories; unlike a franchise like Star Wars, which relies more on universal, mythic themes that have been interpreted and reinterpreted by world culture since the earliest oral traditions, *Star Trek* endeavors to address the issues of the day through the lens of futurism, connoting today and tomorrow, sometimes offering hope for a better world, and sometimes strongly critiquing the one we have.

In regards specifically to *Deep Space Nine*, Heath and Carlisle observe that the series aired during "the Good Decade" of the 1990s, a period of prosperity for most people living in the United States. America's economy was strong, with increases in income and decreases in poverty for most people. Violent crime rates fell to all-time lows; the majority of people felt safe in their communities and comfortable with their lives. Reflecting this, strongly capitalist/anti-capitalist themes made their way into the series, usually explored in episodes focusing on the Ferengi—first introduced in *The Next Generation*—and often highlighting corporate greed and inconsideration.

The optimism expressed by people in 1990s America with respect to financial and personal security was likewise reflected in the average American's views on religion. The percentage of Americans who agreed or strongly agreed with statements such as "Prayer is an important part of my daily life" and "I have never doubted the existence of God" hovered between fifty-two and seventy-eight percent for the first statement and seventy-two to eighty-eight percent for the second across the 1990s (Rosentiel). Most Americans declared themselves to be religious during that time, a trend that has slowly declined since then. Perhaps reflective of those feelings,

Deep Space Nine explored religion and spirituality moreso than any other series in the franchise. Although it can be considered the most "religious" *Star Trek*, *Deep Space Nine* was quite adept at not explicitly defining the religious beliefs and practices of the Bajorans or any other species depicted on the series, preferring instead to illustrate individual spirituality—the search for a sense of peace and purpose—over theology.

Interestingly, however, given their stated religious views, the 1990s American populace also expressed more liberal social values, particularly with respect to gender equality (Rosentiel). Gender identity on *Deep Space Nine* was frequently examined via the character of Jadzia Dax, a female of the species Trill who was joined with a genderless symbiont. Jadzia was the eighth host of the Dax symbiont, and Dax had been hosted by both male and female Trill who had married and borne or sired children. And yet, as Heath and Carlisle point out, although the series boasted several strong and capable female characters—Jadzia Dax, Kira Nerys, and Kasidy Yates—its representation of women was dismal compared to the strides toward equality that women were making in the 1990s.

However, *Deep Space Nine* shines in terms of its depiction of species diversity and the complexities of alliances between disparate groups of beings (reflecting a larger metaphor for broadening social diversity). Heath and Carlisle's snapshot analysis of the series indicated that thirty-two percent of the individuals depicted were human, with the remaining sixty-eight percent representing non-human species. In spite of this, though, their analysis found that most characters, including the aliens, were portrayed by white actors.

No series is perfect, and that includes any (and all) *Star Trek* series; and yet, despite valid criticisms with respect to gender equity and the ethnic diversity of its players, *Deep Space Nine* has become a much-respected member of the *Star Trek* franchise in the twenty-five plus years since it first aired, in part because of the way it endeavored to reflect the social issues and conversations of its day. This collection seeks to celebrate the series and the many ways in which it engaged its audience, then and now. To that end, we selected essays for this collection that would tell the story of *Deep Space Nine*'s writers' and producers' attempts to serialize a narrative within a franchise not known for that particular type of endeavor, and to tell deeply meaningful stories, especially in relation to the manner(s) in which race, faith, and gender were and are depicted in *Star Trek*, in science fiction of the era, and continue to be depicted to this day.

Our first section, "Narrative: Creating and Crafting the Story of *Deep Space Nine*," contains five essays that all explore the manner in which *Deep Space Nine* crafts and tells its stories. In his piece "'Every choice we make has a consequence': Serialized Storytelling in *Star Trek*'s Episodic Universe,"

Val Nolan considers *Deep Space Nine* to be illustrative of what Darko Suvin termed the "strange newness" that lies at the heart of science fiction: its narrative shape (16). Over the course of seven seasons *Deep Space Nine* increasingly serialized its episodes, a strategy that became more and more widespread in other television series as time passed. If one posits that *Deep Space Nine* is about Sisko's journey from Starfleet to Emissary, then only a serialized format could have presented this journey in its entirety. Nolan also postulates that *Deep Space Nine* raised Trekkie/Trekker consciousness, from their trancelike devotion to the franchise to an awareness that it could be changed and changed in such a way as to propel it into the twenty-first century with the likes of *Discovery* (2017–present) and *Picard* (2020–present).

In "The Static Space Opera: Dispersed and Sedimental Saturation of the *Star Trek* Storyworld," Florent Favard argues that by placing the series on a set point in space—Starbase Deep Space 9—the series was able to explore its narrative in ways not seen previously on *Star Trek*. In his narratological analysis, Favard focuses on how *Deep Space Nine* approaches worldbuilding differently than other narrative frames in the franchise, drawing on the possible-worlds theory to push *Star Trek*—and televisual science fiction in general—into new dimensions of static storytelling.

The final three essays in this section seek to understand the intersectionality between the manner in which *Deep Space Nine* interrogates and understands character in its storytelling. Long noted as eschewing frantic action in favor of character development, more than any other *Star Trek* series to that point, *Deep Space Nine* relies on character to make action and to tell stories. In "Thinking Space: Identity and Cognition in *Deep Space Nine*," Franklin R. Halprin explores the construct of thought communities as defined by cognitive sociologists. In his work, Halprin observes that people do not just have an individual identity. Instead, they are affiliates of various social communities that affect their fundamental beliefs about how they should interact with members of their own group and those outside their group. Halprin applies this concept to the Bajoran Major Kira and the Cardassian Legate Damar (Casey Biggs) to illustrate how these thought communities can repel and attract interaction between oppositional parties, navigating the means through which both identity and identification progress (and regress) in both narratives and people.

In "Trauma, Psychological Development, and the Triumph of Kira Nerys," Sherry Ginn studies Major Kira Nerys' life prior to her tenure on the station and analyzes how Kira changes over time. She uses psychological theories about attachment, identity formation, cognitive development, and transition points in life to illustrate Kira's development from her early childhood at the Singha Refugee Center to her time on Deep Space 9 and beyond. Ginn demonstrates that despite the trauma of her upbringing, Kira's early family life provided her with a firm foundation upon which to build an identity and pursue her ultimate goal of freedom for Bajor. *Deep Space Nine*'s extensive interest in its characters allows Ginn to complete such a study, from the earlier formative years of a character's development to the series' end, demonstrating that, for *Deep Space Nine*, in many ways, character is narrative.

Lastly, Erin Bell analyzes Odo using Deleuze and Guattari's rhizomatic study about how connections between beings develop in a network of knowledge and power. Her essay, "'A very unformed being': Odo's Rhizomatic Journey Toward Selfhood," argues that Odo is an enigmatic character, one searching for a sense of community, particularly as he is the only one of his species (at least to his knowledge) when the series begins. His journey over the seven seasons finds him forging relationships with members of multiple species that result in his becoming more than just a Changeling, but one who ultimately saves his species from extermination even as they try to exterminate others. Bell's analysis demonstrates that Deleuze and Guattari's rhizome, with its many tendrils reaching everywhere, is an apt metaphor for Odo if not for other members of his species, since Odo seems all the more willing to explore his universe with an open mind and a yearning, if reluctant, heart. It is also an apt metaphor for the nature of narrative on *Deep Space Nine* and the kinds of interconnected, intersected stories the series sought to tell.

Part Two of this study, "Race, Gender, Religion: Examining Themes and Tropes Illustrated on *Deep Space Nine*," also has five essays. As in Part One, each essay here considers the narrative and storyworld of *Star Trek* and how *Deep Space Nine* deviates from the franchise's vision of the Federation and Starfleet, though in this section each essay focuses specifically on issues of race, gender, or faith, examining how the series re-imagines these important concepts in the *Trek* universe. In his contribution, Douglas Rasmussen considers the episode "Past Tense" from the perspective of Michel Foucault's notion of biopolitics. This episode finds Sisko, Bashir, and Dax transported into an Earth past that existed prior to the establishment of the Federation. Bleak conditions existed for the poor, who were confined to so-called Sanctuary Districts in a misguided effort by the government to provide social and economic help to those needing it. The reality of the districts is sharply evident in the treatment received by Bashir and Sisko—both men of color—and the white Jadzia Dax. In "Class Divisions and Biopolitics in 'Past Tense,'" Rasmussen reminds us that *Star Trek* may present a utopian future to which humankind can aspire, but that this utopian future conceals a much darker past that, in the ethos of *Deep Space Nine*, must still be reckoned with.

Another detailed episode study is completed by Dylan Reid Miller, who, in "The Unkillable Idea of Benny Russell: Afrofuturist Temporalities and 'Far Beyond the Stars,'" evaluates the eponymous episode within an Afrofuturist framework. Miller reminds viewers that, although *Star Trek* is predicated upon a future where all Terrans are equal, it presupposes that culture based upon white hegemonic power structures, denying the lived experiences of people of color. Benny's "dream" of writing a science-fiction adventure about the black male commander of a space station is so far beyond the reality of 1950s America that Benny is confined to a psychiatric hospital. However, as both Miller and the episode point out, the dream does not and will not die; the future as imagined by Benny exists in the reality of Sisko, a man of color who actually does command a space station and who eventually exists outside of time.

Rowan Bell, in turn, scrutinizes *Deep Space Nine*'s depiction of females and wonders, in a future where all "-isms"—racism, sexism, classism, ageism—supposedly have been eliminated, why the series' writers were unable to imagine a future beyond the gender binaries of male and female, even in the nonhuman species encountered in the various quadrants of space. In "(Un)Radical Feminism: Gender and the Limits of Imagination," Bell ponders why even in those societies that are clearly matriarchal in structure, such as the Skrreean ("Sanctuary"), the women were presented as stereotypically feminine: wearing makeup and flowing pastel clothing (usually dresses), with longer hair and an interest in fashion. They further note that even the Changelings, who exist in liquid shapeshifting lifeforms, assume male or female forms when in a "solid" state. While Bell lauds *Star Trek* and *Deep Space Nine* for endeavoring to present itself in a feminist vein, they posit that its insufficient imagination with respect to gender indicates that (on some level) the future may be lacking feminist equality as well.

In "Sisko's Conversion Experience and the Secularism of William James: Exploring Faith, Religion, and the Visions of the Prophets," Drew Chastain analyzes Sisko's conversion experience within a framework proposed by psychologist and philosopher William James. Sisko comes to Deep Space 9 under orders from Starfleet and is almost immediately confronted with the indication that he is the Emissary of the Prophets. As a man of science and one who is not particularly religious (like most humans depicted in *Star Trek*), Sisko begins a journey that, over time, eventually culminates in his acceptance of the role and commitment to it. *Deep Space Nine*'s depiction of Sisko's conversion illustrates that spirituality is not the same as religion, though both play a vital role in Sisko's development.

Concluding this section, Michael G. Cornelius evaluates the spatial importance of the wormhole in "Traversing/able Sacred Space: The Bajoran

Wormhole as Spiritual Journey." Though Cornelius begins by exploring the various reactions to the discovery of the wormhole linking the Alpha and Gamma Quadrants amongst many of the primary species that *Deep Space Nine* depicts—Terrans, Bajorans, Ferengi, Cardassians, and Changelings—he focuses mostly on the Bajoran belief of the wormhole as the Celestial Temple, inquiring why it is the Bajorans are so open to much of the galaxy traipsing through one of the most sacred sites in their faith. Positing an almost evangelical framework for debate, Cornelius concludes that, for the Bajorans, their willingness to share their sacred space with others indicates their willingness—indeed, their eagerness—to share their faith with those who travel through the wormhole.

Conclusion

In an article on the narrative structure of the subject, Želimir Vukaši-novi writes,

> Hermeneutics teaches the subject a method of *existing in the circle* or in the problem that cannot be solved. For this reason, the subject is thrown into story-telling as an activity of never-completed interpretation. History is a story, inclusively a self-interpretation of the subject, which is welling out from the historicity of misunderstanding as its basic axiological quality. This is why the subject should persist in its misunderstanding by allowing itself a hermeneutical rest from identity [34, italics original].

It is perhaps apt that space station Deep Space 9 is circular in shape, because—unlike the two *Star Trek* series that preceded it—*Deep Space Nine* presents humanity still in need of solving. It does not suggest that humanity is insoluble—indeed, like all *Star Trek* properties, its ethos is far more utopian than not—but *Deep Space Nine* sees a universe free from conflict not as the ultimate result of humanity's continuing progress, but only as the result of a concerted desire to shut out the rest of the universe, both the one without and the one within. Whereas *The Original Series* and *The Next Generation* exist in a state of perpetual motion, never slowing to ponder the meaning of their explorations, *Deep Space Nine* exists in a state of perpetual rest, with its characters occasionally speeding away from their inner and outer journeys only to end up, fittingly and circularly, back where they started. In a state of rest, the series achieves a measure of contemplation—one could say a *depth* of contemplation—that prior *Star Trek* properties had not endeavored to explore.

In some ways, it may seem that *Deep Space Nine* rejects Roddenberry's vision of a utopian future with its emphasis on moral obfuscation, interpersonal conflict, and geopolitical warfare. Yet perhaps, like the essays in this collection, the series only strives to show us all a way beyond the dark portents of our presents by pointing out that, in the future, running—whether to or from—one's problems will not actually solve them. Perpetual motion may suggest utopia, but *Deep Space Nine* intimates that it is through narrative rest that we may finally be able to achieve some things even greater than utopia: self-reflection; true connection; and contentment.

Notes

1. Siddig El Fadil changed his name to Alexander Siddig between seasons three and four. He stated that no one could pronounce El Fadil correctly. He chose Alexander "out of a hat" (Erdmann and Block 237). Interestingly though, he directed an episode using the name Siddig El Fadil ("Business as Usual").

2. While *The Next Generation* also featured a few minor recurring characters—such as Q (John de Lancie), Ensign Ro (Michelle Forbes), Guinan (Whoopi Goldberg), Worf's son Alexander (played by four different actors)—even Chief O'Brien got his start on *The Next Generation*—these characters did not drive sustained narratives but rather served as either background figures or as a source of particular narrative conflict for a single episode which, once resolved, caused the character to revert once more to background status.

3. Holmes actually narrates two of his adventures: "The Adventure of the Blanched Soldier" and "The Adventure of the Lion's Mane." In the latter, Holmes, speaking of Watson, notes, "Ah! had he but been with me, how much he might have made of so wonderful a happening and of my eventual triumph against every difficulty! As it is, however, I must needs tell my tale in my own plain way, showing by my words each step upon the difficult road which lay before me as I searched for the mystery of the Lion's Mane" (Conan Doyle 1083). In neither story does the narrative structure work to enhance either the story or Holmes' mystique as a consulting detective.

4. The newest entry into the franchise, *Lower Decks* (2020–present), follows the crew of the starship USS *Cerritos* on its mission of "second contact." The *Cerritos* visits planets previously visited by Federation starships and sometimes discovers that things are not going well at all. For example, in the episode "No Small Parts," the *Cerritos* returns to Beta III and discovers that the citizens are again worshipping Landru, the godlike figure first encountered in *The Original Series* episode "The Return of the Archons."

5. The authors randomly selected fifteen percent of the thirty seasons of television available for all *Trek* series, with the exception of *The Animated Series*, for a total of 110 episodes. They also analyzed every *Star Trek* film produced to date, a total of thirteen. Snapshots of each selected episode were made at five-minute intervals (ten for films), during which all behaviors occurring in a five-second time frame were recorded. Results for each series as well as the time intervals between series were inspected for themes occurring within and across the timeframe examined.

Works Cited and Consulted

Conan Doyle, Arthur. *The Complete Sherlock Holmes*. Doubleday, 1930.

Drushel, Bruce. *Fan Phenomena:* Star Trek. Intellect Books, 2013.

Erdmann, Terry J., and Paula M. Block. Star Trek Deep Space Nine: *Companion*. Pocket Books, 2000.

Hassler-Forest, Dan. "*Star Trek*, Global Capitalism, and Immaterial Labor." *Science Fiction Film and Television*, vol. 9, no. 3, 2016, pp. 371–391.

Heath, K.M., and A.S. Carlisle. *The Voyages of* Star Trek: *A Mirror on American Society Through Time*. Rowman and Littlefield, 2020.

Hillard, Molly Clark. "'A Perfect Form in Perfect Rest': Spellbinding Narratives and Tennyson's 'Day Dream.'" *Narrative*, vol. 17, no. 3, 2009, pp. 312–333.

Jenkins, Henry, and John Tulloch. *Science Fiction Audiences: Watching* Star Trek *and* Doctor Who. Routledge, 1995.

Landy, Joshua. "Still Life in a Narrative Age: Charlie Kaufman's *Adaptation.*" *Critical Inquiry*, vol. 37, no. 3, 2011, pp. 497–514.

Pearson, Anne M. "From Thwarted Gods to Reclaimed Mystery? An Overview of the Depiction of Religion in *Star Trek.*" Star Trek *and Sacred Ground: Explorations of* Star Trek, *Religion, and American Culture*, edited by Jennifer E. Porter and Darcee L. McLaren. SUNY P, 1999, pp. 13–32.

Rosentiel, Tom. "Trends in Attitudes Toward Religion and Social Issues: 1987–2007." Pew Research Center, 15 Oct. 2007. https://www.pewresearch.org/2007/10/15/trends-in-attitudes-toward-religion-and-social-issues-19872007/. Accessed 9 Oct. 2020.

Sanders, José, and Kobie van Krieken. "Traveling Through Narrative Time: How Tense and Temporal Deixis Guide the Representation of Time and Viewpoint in News Narratives." *Cognitive Linguistics*, vol. 30, no. 2, 2019, pp. 281–304.

Suvin, Darko. *The Metamorphosis of Science Fiction: On the Poetics and History of a Literary Genre*. Peter Lang/Ralahine Classics Edition, 2016.

Vukašinovi, Želimir. "A Narrative Structure of the Subject and the Hermeneutical Rest from Identity." *Image_Identity_Reality*, edited by Biljana Đorić-Francuski. Cambridge Scholars, 2011, pp. 29–36.

Filmography

Babylon 5. Created by J. Michael Straczynski. Warner Bros. 1993-1998.

PART ONE

Narrative
Creating and Crafting the Story of Deep Space Nine

"Every choice we make has a consequence"

Serialized Storytelling in Star Trek's *Episodic Universe*

Val Nolan

As the "first Trek show to be aggressively serialized," *Deep Space Nine* (1993–1999) represented an important break with the expectations of the *Star Trek: The Original Series* (1966–1969) and *Star Trek: The Next Generation* (1987–1994) viewer (DeCandido). Set aboard a space station rather than a starship, the characters of *Deep Space Nine* could rarely just warp away to their next adventure as the crews of the Enterprise (and, later, *Voyager* [1995–2001]) could. This rejection of Roddenberry's *Wagon-Train-to-the-stars* model in favor of a static location, a decision initially held by some fans to be a weakness of the show's premise, would in fact deliver the most involved character development and richest, most challenging long-form storytelling in the franchise. Whereas *The Original Series* and *The Next Generation* had previously offered viewers two-part episodes (such as "The Menagerie" or "Descent") or loose arcs (such as the conflict between Worf [Michael Dorn] and the ruling elite of the Klingon Empire), the serialized storytelling of *Deep Space Nine* distinguished itself on the ground of ambition and intentionality. To take the most obvious examples, *The Original Series* two-parter "The Menagerie" was devised as a cost-saving strategy to re-use already filmed material from the aborted pilot "The Cage," whereas the majority of *The Next Generation* two-parters served as season-ending cliff-hangers designed for—as Denis Broe puts it—"luring the spectator" back upon the return of the series (2). Even *The Next Generation*'s Klingon episodes only constitute an arc retroactively, as they were written gradually in response to individual story ideas, and so constitute serialization at an order of magnitude below that of the planned arcs in *Deep Space Nine*'s later seasons, which capitalize upon the artistic potential of seriality through "a blend of multicharacter narratives, overlapping time periods, and most prominently a circumvention of the contained episode in favor of a sustained story arc lasting an entire season" or longer (Broe 1). Indeed, by the conclusion of the series, serialization had become *Deep Space Nine*'s defining structural trait, one which—as a close examination of several key episodes and arcs will demonstrate—allowed the show to deliver stories both broader in galactic-political scope and deeper in terms of the relationship between character and consequence than what was elsewhere available in the franchise at the time.

The series thus presents a distinctly different viewing experience from previous iterations of *Star Trek* and, in the process, doubles down on the "strange newness" which Darko Suvin positions as central to the science fiction genre (16). In the case of *Deep Space Nine*, Suvin's new thing or *novum* is not the franchise's now familiar transporters or holograms or interstellar travel; instead, it is, in metafictional fashion, the narrative shape of the series itself. The genre's essential sense of "cognitive estrangement" manifests here on an intra-franchise level for the viewers of pre-existing *Star Trek* material and is most apparent when that audience encounters *Deep Space Nine*'s significant opposition to neat, done-in-one storytelling (Suvin 15). Where a series like *The Next Generation* generated estrangement through a single episode's focus on, say, examining the consequences of occupation and refugee crises through a science fictional lens ("Ensign Ro"), *Deep Space Nine* forces the viewer to become immersed in that estranged state of mind in a more authentic fashion, maintaining a similar focus through seven years of serialization. An aesthetic corollary of this is found in the skepticism that serialization allows *Deep Space Nine* to display towards the stereotype of *Star Trek* as utopian idea. For example, the show's sustained interest in the Bajoran recovery—and, for that matter, its interrogation of the Federation in episodes such as "Homefront" and "Paradise Lost"—allow for what Tom Moylan labels "fuller exploration of the activism required to move towards the better society," social developments which prior iterations of *Star Trek* accepted as a *fait accompli* (201). The practical result of this departure from prior *Star Trek* conventions permits *Deep Space Nine* to, as Chris Gregory says, "concentrate more on the growth the characters experience as a result of the unfolding narratives of the series itself" (69), a structural choice which led both Karin Blair and Marion Gymnich to examine this outer space show's interest in "inner spaces" (Gymnich 62). Thus, serialization here is a novum which, as Istvan Csicsery-Ronay, Jr., puts it, produces "effects in the diegetic material world that can be reasonably derived from the novum's causes," in this case a narrative evolution which complements rather than contradicts the established storyworld (47).

This, arguably, results in the most significant and challenging aspect of *Deep Space Nine*'s reputation: how the series deliberately undermines viewers' pre-existing conceptional frames of reference with regard to *Star Trek*. The true narrative texture of the series, the tendency by which it utilizes "structure as a carrier of meaning," is only apparent—is only *appreciable*— when viewed in its serialized entirety (Allrath *et al* 38). *The Original Series*, *The Next Generation*, and *Voyager* all lend themselves to casual viewing, but *Deep Space Nine*'s multitude of story arcs and ongoing narratives tells us that we need to deport ourselves differently towards the series from the outset. The occasionally off-putting truth is that it comprises not 176 separate episodes but rather a single story where the intensity of serialization phases in and out on a week-by-week basis, trending upwards across seven years of television. To put this another way, an uninitiated viewer could easily watch a second season *Next Generation* episode followed by a sixth season episode without noticing anything more than cosmetic differences in costuming and set design (though outliers exist in terms of, say, the aesthetically blander first season, or the Worf/Troi character dynamics of season seven). The same is not true of *Deep Space Nine*, where fundamental aspects of the storyworld and, for that matter, the central premise such as the Dominion War, the introduction of the *Defiant*, the lessened emphasis on exploration of the Gamma Quadrant, and so on, change substantially over time. One can imagine a confused viewer asking, "Why is O'Brien (Colm Meaney) taking orders from that Ferengi kid Nog (Aron Eisenberg)?" or "What's up with the lounge singer (James Darren)?" So, too, the formal narrative properties of the series transition across the course of *Deep Space Nine* from an initial season of fairly traditional done-in-one episodes through increasing use of loosely-linked developments in storyworld mythology and character arcs in season two to, as Jason Mittell says in his book *Complex TV*, a "forward-moving accumulation of narrative statements that create triggers for future events" (25). Seasons three to five of the series capitalize on this kind of anticipatory "narrative totality" that Frank Kelleter sees as key to serialization by presenting increasingly pointed use of waymarker episodes and delivering large-scale challenges to the stability of the franchise storyworld by integrating seemingly discrete storylines into larger thematic mosaics, the importance of which are often apparent only in retrospect (17). Such shorter arcs are announced as formal breaks to the expected forty-five-minute running time of the show, with prominent examples delivered in the form of a television movie such as "The Way of the Warrior," two-parters such as "Improbable Cause" and "The Die is Cast," or loosely-linked season finales/premieres like "Broken Link" and "Apocalypse Rising." A complete disruption of what David Bordwell calls the franchise's established "norms of narrational construction and comprehension" eventually occurs in seasons six and seven, with extended stretches of true serialization interspersed with episodes-of-the-week advancing a plethora of ongoing storylines (155).

Progressing in this fashion, *Deep Space Nine* increasingly rejected what Mittell calls "the centrality of genre formulas, repetitive situations, redundant exposition suited for surfing viewers, and structural constraints based around commercial breaks and rigid schedules" (4). Mittell's contention is that the main elements of serial narratives comprise "storyworld, characters, events, and temporality," all of which are collectively intrinsic to the narrative identity and legacy of *Deep Space Nine* (22). By contrast, whereas a series such as *The Next Generation* exhibits a coherent storyworld (which it shares with *Deep Space Nine*), its characters change merely in the broadest possible sense; it displays only conditional references to past events (episodes involving Worf and the Klingon Empire again being the most prominent example); and only a loose element of temporality (and, as such, the occasional narrative importance of past events such as Picard's abduction by the Borg or the alternate Tasha Yar [Denise Crosby] traveling back in time in "Yesterday's Enterprise" are conspicuous). *The Original Series* obviously originates both the franchise storyworld as a whole and *The Next Generation*'s approach to characterization, though it requires little knowledge of episodic history or sequence to complete its viewing experience. It is only *Deep Space Nine*, at least until the third season of *Star Trek: Enterprise* (2001–2005), or the storytelling modes adopted more recently by *Star Trek: Discovery* (2017–present) or *Star Trek: Picard* (2020–present), that offers viewers a narrative greatly enhanced by the accumulative quality of full serialization. In fact, the series repeatedly demonstrates Sean O'Sullivan's six elements of seriality: "iteration," such as the "Last time on *Star Trek: Deep Space Nine*" summaries which are increasingly important for keeping track of the show's narrative threads as it progresses; "multiplicity," particularly in terms of the series' many interlocking storylines and character arcs; narrative "momentum," discernible on both an episode-to-episode scale as well as from season-to-season; "world-building," especially in how *Deep Space Nine* expands and shades its diegetic universe over seven seasons; "personnel," that being the impressive organization and distribution of characters, both primary and supporting, utilized throughout the series as a way of manipulating narrative balance; and finally "design," the question of authorship and the degree to which *Deep Space Nine*, as discussed many times by the show's writers, was increasingly conceived of as a serialized story (51). In the process, the conclusive certainty offered by the majority of prior *Star Trek* is regularly denied to the *Deep Space Nine* viewer by ambiguous endings and the kinds of "polysemic and multiple plot structures" that Jane Feuer identifies as intrinsic to the serial form (15).

Such practices breach the franchise's previously established demarcations of "episode" and "season" in a manner which, in concert with the series' emphasis on war, politics, religion, and interpersonal conflict, frequently rearticulates established notions of what constitutes *Star Trek*.

Three arcs in particular stand out in this regard for their increasing narrative ambition and their importance in reframing *Deep Space Nine* as a "hybrid" form combining features of episodic done-in-one series and ongoing open-ended serials (Allrath *et al* 5). These stories are herein referred to as The Circle Trilogy in season two (a "combination of political intrigue, Machiavellian schemes, Broadway-style farce, and even a hint of sex" according to Terry Erdmann and Paula Block [79], comprising "The Homecoming," "The Circle," and "The Siege"); The Occupation Sextet ("A Time to Stand," "Rocks and Shoals," "Sons and Daughters," "Behind the Lines," "Favor the Bold," and "The Sacrifice of Angels"), which removed many of the series protagonists from the Deep Space 9 setting and shifted the series' focus to the war between the Federation and the Dominion; and the nine part/ten hour Final Chapter in season seven ("Penumbra" through to the series finale "What You Leave Behind"), which concluded the Dominion War along with a variety of character arcs. Together, these serialized stories challenge not just the closure and "dramatic tradition" of hour-long television but also, in The Occupation Sextet in particular, "the very nature of the traditional *DS9* writing process" (Erdmann and Block 486). The arcs function as a series of striking miniseries within *Deep Space Nine*'s wider practice of series-serial hybridity, a formal interruption to the weekly episodic structure which allowed the show, as Glen Creeber says, to "break free of the narrative limitations of single drama and exploit some of the more seductive elements of serialization" by repositioning characters and plotlines in innovative fashion (9). Thus, for the production staff as much as for the viewer, the story of *Deep Space Nine* would "become much more than the sum of its individual parts," and towards the end of the show's run "there was no way to escape the demands of continuity," with disruptions of the franchise's established norms and associated expectations becoming as identifiable with the series as the episode-of-the week was with *The Original Series* (Erdmann and Block 592).

Unlike prior and, for that matter, subsequent *Star Trek*, *Deep Space Nine* is less about boldly going than it is about boldly *staying*, doubling down on television's practice of providing "a certain amount of closure, but no *definitive* closure, which would forestall a continuation of the series" through the accumulative use of ambiguous and open-ended individual episodes (consider, for example, the lack of character and plot resolution respectively in "Necessary Evil" or "The Quickening") (Butler 29). Ironically, shunning the definitive episodic closure previously favored by the franchise in this fashion permitted a deeper exploration of the *Gulliver's Travels*-style social, political, and philosophical commentary proffered by *The Original Series* and *The Next Generation*. The series accomplished this through its commitment to the accumulation of events and their consequences, with the narrative strategies adopted by the writing staff evolving over the course of seven years to reflect this approach. For example, *Deep Space Nine* asserts an intention to focus on the long-term ramifications of past events from its earliest textual beginning. The pilot episode, "Emissary," conveys the importance of previous events to the viewer in a manner very different from the pilot of *The Next Generation*. Within the episode's opening minutes, viewers are taught that, though *Deep Space Nine* takes place firmly within the established franchise storyworld (something reinforced by the opening text crawl), they should expect an emphasis on repercussions, in the initial case those resulting from the involvement of Benjamin Sisko (Avery Brooks) in the Battle of Wolf 359 several years earlier (which occurred off-screen in the second part of *The Next Generation* episode "The Best of Both Worlds"). "Emissary" thus relies on established narrative events within the franchise in a more active fashion than the pilot of *The Next Generation* (or even *Voyager*, which also begins with an expository text crawl, though one which is focused on enhancing plot rather than character; in fact, it would not be until the debut of *Star Trek: Picard* in 2020 that an opening entry in the franchise would so pointedly refer to prior events within the storyworld). Threaded through otherwise typical pilot material, "Emissary" makes good on this thematic departure from its largely discontinuous predecessor through Sisko's encounter with the extra-dimensional species the Bajorans call the Prophets, aliens who exist within the ostensible in-universe novum of *Deep Space Nine*: a wormhole to the distant Gamma Quadrant. The wormhole manifests as a rupture in spacetime, one which telescopes the remote galactic backdrop into narrative foreground (more on that later), as well as symbolizing how *Deep Space Nine*'s use of serialized storytelling in an episodic universe itself manifests as a rupture in storytime. From within the wormhole, the Prophets are capable of seeing all events as a continuous whole rather than a series of discrete episodes. They teach the audience, through the surrogate of Sisko, that everything matters—that everything is "part of your existence" ("Emissary"). These aliens exist in a non-linear spacetime or, as a member of their race puts it, "what comes before now is no different than what is now, or what is to come. It is one's existence" ("Emissary"). Their free movement across Sisko's life, from his first meeting with his wife to her death and back again, reflects less science fiction than it does "myth in its timeless suffering or bliss," and does so in a way that foreshadows Sisko's own eventually mythic role (Suvin 34). Yet, from the perspective of Sisko in "Emissary," what these beings are describing is the exponential accumulation of narrative events and how, together, they offer meaning to one's story in a manner which reflects Brian McHale's assertion that "segmentivity" (his term for seriality) must always "contribute meaningfully" to overall narrative structure (18).

Moreover, the narrative choices of "Emissary" anticipate *Deep Space Nine*'s later use of serialization within arcs such as The Circle Trilogy, The Occupation Sextet, and The Final Chapter. In those sequences, which take up the accumulative narrative promise of Sisko's disjointed visions in "Emissary," the typical A/B storyline division of *Star Trek* episodes collapses into a collection of ongoing serial narratives which share and trade prominence across multiple weeks. A representative episode from The Final Chapter, "'Til Death Do Us Part," offers a good example, balancing as it does developments in Sisko's relationship with Kasidy Yates (Penny Johnson Jerald); Gul Dukat's (Marc Alaimo) manipulation of Kai Winn (Louise Fletcher); Ezri Dax's (Nicole de Boer) struggle to move past Jadzia's feelings for Worf; Damar's (Casey Biggs) growing dissatisfaction with Weyoun's (Jeffrey Combs) treatment of the Cardassians; and the inking of the Breen's alliance with the Dominion, all in a single forty-five minute installment. The sheer amount of fragmented narrative material presented at once makes integrating these vignettes into the overall structure of The Final Chapter a more demanding challenge to audience attention and commitment than either *The Next Generation* or the directly contemporaneous *Voyager*. It requires the viewer to, as O'Sullivan says, "perform intellectual and imaginative labor," an aspect of *Deep Space Nine*'s consumption which makes the production of meaning a more involved experience than elsewhere in the franchise and which becomes one of the show's "distinguishing narrative characteristics" (51).

As the pinnacle of *Deep Space Nine* serialization, the structure of The Final Chapter in particular satisfies Suvin's cognitive estrangement by how it engenders "not only a reflecting *of* but also *on* reality," in this case both the diegetic reality of the *Star Trek* franchise and the actual reality of the viewer (22). It "implies a creative approach tending toward a dynamic transformation"—more ambitious forms of television narrative—"rather than toward a static mirroring of the author's environment"—a repetition of past narrative forms that, arguably, *Voyager* and the first two seasons of *Enterprise* reproduce (22). Viewed separately, the vignettes of "'Til Death Do Us Part" offer disjointed glimpses at a surfeit of events within the storyworld; however, when the episode is viewed within the larger sequence, their accumulative narrative weight actively propels significant developments in character and plot in a similar way to Sisko's original visions from the Prophets. "Emissary" thus indicates how accumulative serialization was a distinctive aspect of the series waiting to be unlocked from the outset. Nonetheless, the first season of the series exhibits a tension between the traditional episodic *Star Trek* format and a willingness to take advantage of the possibilities for serialization offered by the *in-situ* setting. Early in its run, *Deep Space Nine* experimented with follow-ups to previous *Star Trek* narratives, such as the stories of archaeologist Vash and omnipotent Q ("Q-Less") or the romantic travails of Lwaxana Troi ("The Forsaken"). However, rather than mere sequels, even these ostensibly standalone episodes—particularly "Q-Less"—are stealth continuations of storylines established on *The Next Generation*. The debut season is thus composed primarily of original standalone storylines, a handful of episodes connected to established *Next Generation* plots, and a series of installments planting the seeds of ongoing arcs. The most successful of these involved a continuing—and non–*Trek* typical—emphasis on the political and religious machinations of post–Occupation Bajor (among them "Progress" and "In the Hands of the Prophets"), with these leading to the first elaborate use of direct serialization on the show at the beginning of season two, The Circle Trilogy.

Adapted from an initial *Next Generation* story pitch by Jeri Taylor, and with teleplays by Ira Stephen Behr, Peter Allan Fields, and Michael Piller, "The Homecoming," "The Circle," and "The Siege" demonstrate the attributes that made *Deep Space Nine* different from any *Star Trek* that had come before. The trilogy represents the first sustained use of true episode-to-episode serialized storytelling in a *Star Trek* context and is the first series storyline to accept the challenge of accumulative narrative metafictionally laid down by the Prophets in "Emissary." For though *The Next Generation* gestured towards meaningful longer forms in some respects with, say, the two halves of "The Best of Both Worlds" combined with "Family" comprising a notional three-parter in how the latter served as a thematic and character-based coda to the former, such episodes were never designed to be consumed as a complete story in the manner that "The Homecoming," "The Circle," and "The Siege" were. The Circle Trilogy— from authorial intention to audience consumption—distinguishes itself as both a serialized narrative in its own right and, simultaneously, one unit in the larger narrative arc of the series, building upon and enhancing prior developments in the *Deep Space Nine* storyworld. Though this first "leap into ever more complicated and less commercial forms of seriality" eventually brought critical acclaim, it also began to earn the series a reputation as the "difficult" *Trek* (Broe 127). Such obstacles extended to the writers' room, where the trilogy required a radical change in the show's creative practices, one which would echo through later seasons of the series and foreshadow the wider necessity for "new ways of managing plotlines" demanded by contemporary television's tendency "to rely increasingly on continuity instead of striving for closure at the end of an episode" (Allrath *et al* 25).

Yet The Circle Trilogy serves not just as an expression of *Deep Space Nine*'s accumulative model, it also functions as an early self-reflective critique—and then round dismissal—of resistance to the innovations in seriality and tone proffered by the series. In "The Homecoming," Major Kira discovers that legendary Bajoran Resistance leader Li Nalas (Richard Beymer) is still alive and imprisoned in a Cardassian labor camp. Her rescue of Li coincides with an attempted coup against the Bajoran provisional government by a xenophobic movement known as the Circle, extremists who are secretly backed by the Cardassians in an effort to expel the Federation from Bajoran space. Though the coup is defeated with Li's assistance, the reputation of this revered figure is revealed to be based upon what people wanted to believe about him rather than on actual occurrences. The character's own recollection of his greatest victory is somewhat less epic that his reputation as a brilliant fighter and strategist suggests. In his version of how he killed the notorious war criminal Gul Zarale, he remembers tumbling down a slope to a lakeshore just as the massive Cardassian emerged from the water. Gul Zarale, standing in his underwear after bathing, could only stare at the unexpected interruption. Li, too, remembers being frozen in shock, coming to his senses only when Zarale reached for a rifle. He shot the Cardassian, whose body fell on top of him. When Li's companions discovered them moments later, they refused to believe that it had been anything other than a savage struggle for the freedom of Bajor. Despite Li's protestations, his companions insisted on spreading the story far and wide so that, before too long, any victory won by the resistance was attributed to his valor and audacity. The Bajoran people, in search of a hero, were only too willing to believe.

In a sense, Li Nalas is an allegory for *Deep Space Nine*'s reception and a personification of audience expectation itself. He represents the potential return of an idealized, even idolized, version of the franchise's "repertory of functions, conventions, and devices" propagated by those fans—and, for that matter, by some on the studio and production side of things—wary of the seriality and moral ambiguity which *Deep Space Nine* had promised since "Emissary" (Suvin 23). Killing off the character at the conclusion of "The Siege" is therefore an object lesson in not giving people—in this case the longstanding *Star Trek* viewer—exactly what they want or, for that matter, expect. That Behr and company chose to make this break with expectation in a serialized story is further significant in that it gives notice of not just a tonal or thematic departure from *Star Trek*'s past, but a structural one. It served as a declaration of "look what we can do" delivered on not just the focal, but on the formal level (Erdmann and Block 76) and speaks to the manner by which composition and reception are "intertwined in a feedback loop," something which is more appropriate to the philosophy of *Deep Space Nine* than to the other *Star Trek* series (Kelleter 13).

Nevertheless, it would be several years before *Deep Space Nine* again attempted a multi-episode arc that exceeded the ambition of The Circle Trilogy. Seasons three, four, and five in particular display a mix of standalone episodes; a scattering of stories like "Blood Oath," "Crossover," and "Trials and Tribble-ations" that offered continuations and new perspective on *Original Series* episodes beyond the usual "intertextual family resemblance between events and settings" that had previously defined the franchise; as well as short sequences consciously signaled as continuous narratives in the form of two-parters distinguished by the words "to be continued" (Pearson 118). Thus, in its middle years, *Deep Space Nine* offered softly continuous storytelling closer to the contemporaneous models of *Buffy the Vampire Slayer* (1997–2003) or the original *The X-Files* (1993–2002), the individual installments of which typically advanced "the season's arc while still offering episodic coherence and resolutions" (Mittell 19) along with—and corresponding to—Sean O'Sullivan's definition of seriality: "continuing narrative distributed in installments over time" (50). Combined with this, the show honed the "capacity for multiple characterizations" that Kelleter ascribes to contemporary seriality: Sisko as both Starfleet captain and religious icon; Kira as both resistance fighter and military officer; Dukat as fascist, father, and fanatic (Kelleter 22). Such episodes include the Michael Eddington (Kenneth Marshall) storyline spread across "For the Cause," "For the Uniform," and "Blaze of Glory," or the ongoing developments in the Mirror Universe episodes, as "each supposedly stand-alone element cumulatively built the serial content" in hybrid fashion (Broe 131). Many of these story arcs—Gul Dukat's fall from power; the Changeling infiltration of the Alpha Quadrant; and so on—eventually dovetailed in *Deep Space Nine*'s next extended experiment with serialized episode-to-episode storytelling: The Occupation Sextet at the beginning of season six.

These episodes are prefigured by the season five finale "A Call to Arms," which in turn follows up on the trigger event during the episodes "In Purgatory's Shadow" and "By Inferno's Light," the arrival of hostile Dominion forces in the Alpha Quadrant. On the surface, "A Call to Arms" is a cliffhanger of a type which might not be out of place on either *The Next Generation* or *Voyager*, one which establishes significant stakes for the protagonists and, in its final scene, promises a dramatic confrontation to come with Sisko and Starfleet forced to abandon Deep Space 9 when it comes under combined Dominion/Cardassian assault. Yet observant viewers will note how the construction of the episode suggests something more elaborate than a single forty-five-minute resolution. For one thing,

Captain Sisko's "I will not rest until I stand with you again" speech on the Promenade explicitly evokes General Douglas MacArthur's "I shall return" comments after leaving The Philippines in 1942 ahead of the Japanese invasion, and so suggests a prolonged wartime absence ("A Call to Arms"). For another, "A Call to Arms" makes a series of unambiguous declarations of narrative change: Sisko mines the entrance to the Bajoran Wormhole, heretofore one of the central plot devices of the entire series; the Federation abandons Deep Space 9, the primary setting of the show; Jake (Cirroc Lofton) chooses to stay behind; and antagonists such as Dukat and Weyoun are essentially elevated to contingent regulars—something viewers will encounter again in The Final Chapter. The significance, and for that matter the success, of The Occupation Sextet thus rests on how it reconfigured the series' "scenario in a way that was diegetically consistent" with *Deep Space Nine*'s norms and mythology, as well as being "narratively engaging, and emotionally honest to the characters and relationships" (Mittell 47).

Moreso than in The Circle Trilogy, it is here that *Deep Space Nine* begins its firm challenge to "the old commercial constraints of having to tell a story in one episode so that the series can be syndicated as a stand-alone entity" (Broe 4). In the process it reverses the established *Star Trek* relationship between what we might call narrative foreground and narrative backdrop. Episodes of *The Original Series*, *The Next Generation*, and *Voyager* are largely concerned with narrative foreground—that is, the events introduced in/occurring in the immediate episode itself, and where the audience does not require extensive knowledge of past material. In those cases, it is enough to know only the barest of the narrative backdrop—for instance, that the Enterprise is the flagship of an interstellar Federation, or that Voyager is lost on the other side of the galaxy. Like the velvet star fields beyond the real world set windows, this backdrop completes the fictional illusion without being necessary to the narrative. Full enjoyment of the material is not contingent on paying significant attention to events from three episodes or three seasons ago, and although the occasional two-parter or the return of a significant guest character—think Vulcan ambassador Sarek (Mark Lenard)—might refocus audience attention, these are not frequent occurrences. By contrast, the serialized aesthetic experience of *Deep Space Nine*'s The Occupation Sextet and the episodes which follow is at the very least greatly enhanced by—and at times utterly dependent on—detailed knowledge of the show's narrative backdrop, that is the specifics of prior events and character arcs not just within the *Star Trek* franchise more generally but the interlaced serial narrative of *Deep Space Nine* itself. Whereas the series demonstrated elements of this approach in The Circle Trilogy, it is in The Occupation Sextet that the narrative backdrop becomes an essential aspect of how the series adopts the complex "narrational patterns of contemporary television seriality" (Broe 2). In some respects, the novum here is not a new thing but instead an old thing, the pre-existing story material once again made new or strange for the viewer via its integration into a narrative tapestry of intimidating size and complexity. Consequently, with the series' cast enhanced by a sprawling array of secondary and tertiary characters accrued over the previous five years, and the density of its already rich storyworld increased, The Occupation Sextet marks *Deep Space Nine's* true break with what Christopher Anderson calls the "safe bet" episodic model defined by "a high degree of redundancy and repetition" and "plots that are resolved by the end of the episode" (79). With it, whole seasons of narrative backdrop are lensed into the foreground, not just as "conditional seriality" but as a culmination of *Deep Space Nine's* cumulative plot and character development across years of story material (Mittell 21). Here, too, Suvin's estrangement is fully activated, as The Occupation Sextet inverts the longstanding narrative expectations of the *Star Trek* viewer; the collapse of easily digestible episodic storytelling suggested as far back as season one finally occurs as the narrative backdrop of *Deep Space Nine* is entirely integrated into the foreground with the viewer's *ex post facto* realization that this has been the project of the series all along.

Of further significance is how serialization allows The Occupation Sextet to dispense with tidy *Original Series* or *Next Generation* style pseudo-calendrical demarcations, delivering only one stardated log entry—in "Behind the Lines"—throughout the whole six episodes. Indicators such as these are useful for episodic narratives with clearly defined beginnings and endings, but the more ambitious storytelling of *Deep Space Nine* recognizes their artificiality and limitations. Instead, the use of serialization in The Occupation Sextet allows for O'Sullivan's "distributed, structural gaps that define serials—the time gaps between the publication of instalments, the diegetic gaps (and overlaps) that often occur between one episode and another" (51) or, in Broe's words, creates "a parallel world of real or pure time that itself synchronizes with the viewer's time" (23). Such "real" time is already evident in the months-long time jump from "A Call to Arms" to the first Sextet installment, "A Time to Stand," a jump which mirrors the real-life hiatus between seasons five and six. Yet where that episode was a "sequel, of sorts, to the previous season's finale," the remainder of the arc was constructed as a cumulative and experiential rendering of war and occupation in the *Star Trek* storyworld, as well as a conscious foregrounding of elements which previously constituted narrative backdrop (Erdmann and Block 488). "Rocks and Shoals," which continues directly from "A Time to Stand," provided a "ground war episode" riffing on the 1965 Frank Sinatra movie *None But the Brave*; "Behind the Lines" further manipulated viewer focus with "a show about being on the occupied station"; "Sons and Daughters," with its strong A-story, became the "closest thing to a stand-alone episode" in the sequence as well as a foregrounding of character elements from not just previous seasons of *Deep Space Nine* but also, with the appearance of Worf's son Alexander (Marc Worden), from *The Next Generation*; and, finally, "Favor the Bold" and "The Sacrifice of Angels" served as "the big broad-canvas shows" which depended for their conclusion on plot material from as far back as "Emissary" (Erdmann and Block 488). However, where "A Call to Arms" was always envisioned as setting up a multi-episode Dominion War arc, the initial thinking was to conclude the conflict at the end of the arc. It was, according to Ronald D. Moore, only later "decided that we'd get the station back by the end of the last episode of the arc, and then we'd see how long the war ran after that" (Erdmann and Block 486).

This commitment to the sustained use of serialization was, Moore has said, "a learning experience for everyone" (Erdmann and Block 476). Yet the knowledge gained by the production staff during The Occupation Sextet, as well as its reception—*The Hollywood Reporter* collectively ranks the Sextet as among the best *Star Trek* episodes—is largely responsible for the distinctive flavor of the final seasons of *Deep Space Nine* (Couch and McMillan). Whereas earlier years of the series negotiated a firm and traditional line between instances of narrative backdrop and foreground, seasons six and seven blurred these delineations to creative effect. Even superficially standalone episodes in these years added textually significant departures from established tone and style to the overarching series narratives. Many of these installments—such as Sisko's into-the-camera confession regarding deceiving the Romulans into joining the war effort during "In the Pale Moonlight"—further enabled, to paraphrase Tom Moylan, *Deep Space Nine*'s self-critical articulations of deep tensions within the unconscious of the *Star Trek* franchise; in this way, "the imposed totality of the single utopian text gives way to the contradictory and diverse multiplicity" of the ongoing Dominion War storylines, something only possible to execute authentically across multiple hours and, for that matter, seasons (201). In other words, seriality enabled *Deep Space Nine* to take artistic and philosophical risks with the *Star Trek* franchise which, in turn, enabled—one might even say *demanded*—that the show perform further experiments with seriality. This process of feedback culminates in The Final Chapter, a farewell to *Deep Space Nine* that, unlike the finales of other *Star Trek* series, stretches over ten interconnected hours. The circularity of risks begetting seriality begetting risks is readily evoked by the arc's fulfillment of the cumulative narrative potential originally presented by "Emissary." Sisko's vision in the arc-originating episode "Penumbra" does not just link back to his first encounter with the Prophets but, in this instance, takes place against multiple images of the wormhole—symbolic of seriality's rupture in *Star Trek* storytime—flickering ominously on the screens in Ops. These displays, which typically all show different information, now all exhibit the same image; however, it is one of intricate complexity and countless moving parts, as the show's narrative backdrop is made real in set design and detailing, with the concentric circles of this wormhole depiction here signifying the completion of not just Sisko's journey but that of *Deep Space Nine* as a whole.

The Final Chapter therefore serves not just to conclude the serialized storytelling of *Deep Space Nine* but to conduct a self-examination of the series from within that storyworld. The arc represents a maximalized deployment of O'Sullivan's six elements of seriality, "structural choices or preferences" which the series has rehearsed throughout its run (51). This is further acknowledged in how The Final Chapter is the only story arc given official paratextual titling on-screen, presumably because these episodes not only ended the Dominion War but brought the entire series to its much-hyped conclusion. Though the titling appeared only in commercial previews for the final nine episodes, it underlines, as Terry Erdmann and Paula Block note, how the serialization of this last group of episodes was "inevitable" and how "by this point, it would have been difficult to reverse course and try to put the series on a more episodic footing" (591–592). While much of the viewers' attention during The Final Chapter is obviously absorbed by the endgame of the Dominion conflict, the manner in which Sisko's relationship to the nonlinear wormhole aliens reaches its culmination provides a narrative backbone of no less importance. The return to the Prophets and their interest in the story of Sisko's life as a story from which he cannot deviate serves as the kind of "inward turn toward metafiction" which often demarks a television finale (consider, for example, the use of a *Next Generation–era* holodeck story as the finale of *Enterprise*) (Mittell 324). It is, in fact, only at the end of "What You Leave Behind" that the viewer truly experiences the weight of Sisko's remark, when initially confronted with the nonlinearity of the Prophets, that "a human is ultimately the sum of [their] experiences" ("Emissary"). Although an argument could be made that the same is true for any iteration of *Star Trek*, the case of *Deep Space Nine* is exceptional in how it pushed the franchise "toward new aesthetic directions and slowly grew to match or surpass the earlier series in critical reputation" (Mittell 218). Where *The Original Series* and *The Next Generation* unexpectedly align more closely with Suvin's notion of naturalistic fiction—"the basic rule" of which is "that man's destiny is man"—the serialized format of *Deep Space Nine* allows the series to afford Sisko a mythic status in the literal sense, one buffeted by the whims of God-like beings (23). His eventual ascension to the non-linear ranks of the

Prophets is at once a more conclusive and more open-ended ending than, for instance, that of Captain Picard in "All Good Things…." By "postulating a metaphysical world beyond the empirical one in which the narrative finds its true, compensatory ending" in this way, the finale of *Deep Space Nine* performs one final rejection of traditional *Star Trek* narrative form (Suvin 32). Whereas *The Next Generation* concluded with the implication of continuing episodic missions beyond the horizon of ceased production, and *Voyager* offered a definitive ending to that show's story by depicting the crew arriving home, *Deep Space Nine* instead furthered its central protagonist's journey with a capstone gesture of mythomorphic "supertemporality" (Suvin 38). Asked when he will return from the Celestial Temple, Sisko replies, "Maybe a year, maybe yesterday" ("What You Leave Behind"). For him, the serial narrative never ends; the circle remains unbroken.

As such, Sisko's story transcends episodes or seasons or even the demarcations of a television series in a manner which recasts what Lincoln Geraghty considers a "failure to bring adequate closure to many of its ongoing stories" as a final evocation of the show's established narrative style and philosophy (137). Yes, it evokes a traditional pattern of trial, death, and resurrection, but it is not reducible to any single one of those. Characters like Kirk, Picard, or Janeway might be defined by significant moments—episodes—such as Kirk's conflict with Khan, Picard's assimilation by the Borg, or Janeway's decision to destroy the Caretaker's Array, but Sisko's story spans the entirety of *Deep Space Nine*. Serialization allows the character a different kind of dimensionality than that of his predecessors and contemporaries. The result is a refreshing of *Star Trek* fans' consciousness, awakening them, to quote Csicsery-Ronay, from the trancelike sense of the franchise "as fated and empty, into awareness that it can be changed" (47). This allows us to place *Deep Space Nine* more firmly within the evolution of the *Star Trek* franchise overall, no longer merely the difficult *Trek* or "The One on the Space Station," but constructed in a manner which parallels Suvin's "historical movement of [science fiction]" as an "enrichment of and shift from a basic direct model to an indirect model" of storytelling (24). *Deep Space Nine*'s introduction of serialization to the *Star Trek* franchise in the late 1990s further satisfies Csicsery-Ronay's definition of Suvin's novum as being both "historically immanent and situationally transcendent" (47). It anticipated the by-now widespread use of serialization in television science fiction and simultaneously transformed storytelling within *Star Trek* in ways that continue to have structural and narrative repercussions today. The expansive narrative of *Deep Space Nine* asks both casual and committed viewers of the series to reflect on their own interaction with the franchise. By displacing the standalone episode as the primary narrative unit of *Star Trek*, *Deep Space Nine* offered a platform for problematizing viewers' understanding of what the franchise is and can accomplish—aspects of which come to later fruition in *Discovery* and *Picard*. For throughout its evolution, and especially in later seasons, *Deep Space Nine* serves as a reminder of both *Star Trek*'s ambition and of the fact that some stories about the human condition cannot be told in discrete forty-five-minute segments. Two decades after the series finale, the willingness of *Deep Space Nine*'s writers to simultaneously destabilize the established franchise storyworld and to participate in genre television's contemporaneous transition to long-form storytelling (perhaps equally epitomized by *Babylon 5*, 1993–1998) remains what defines the series in the most resonant fashion. *Deep Space Nine* placed *Star Trek* firmly at the forefront of the seriality revolution, revitalized the franchise with exercises in narrative invention, and modeled later developments in television production and consumption. It may have boldly stayed, but it did so as no *Star Trek* had done before.

WORKS CITED AND CONSULTED

Allrath, Gaby, Marion Gymnich, and Carola Surkamp. "Introduction: Towards a Narratology of TV Series." *Narrative Strategies in Television Series*, edited by Gaby Allrath and Marion Gymnich. Palgrave, 2005, pp. 1–43.

Anderson, Christopher. "Television Networks and the Uses of Drama." *Thinking Outside the Box: Television Genres in Transition*, edited by Gary Edgerton and Brian Rose. UP of Kentucky, 2005, pp. 65–87.

Blair, Karin. "*Star Trek* Old and New: From the Alien Embodied to the Alien Imagined." *Yankee Go Home (And Take Me With You): Americanization and Popular Culture*, edited by George McKay. Sheffield Academic Press, 1997, pp. 78–88.

Bordwell, David. *Narration in the Fiction Film*. U of Wisconsin P, 1985.

Broe, Dennis. *Birth of the Binge: Serial TV and the End of Leisure*. Wayne State UP, 2019.

Butler, Jeremy G. *Television: Critical Methods and Applications*. Wadsworth, 1994.

Couch, Aaron, and Graeme McMillan. "*Star Trek*: 100 Greatest Episodes." *The Hollywood Reporter*, 8 September 2016. www.hollywoodreporter.com/lists/star-trek-episodes-best-100-924455. Accessed 9 June 2020.

Creeber, Glen. *Serial Television: Big Drama on the Small Screen*. British Film Institute, 2004.

Csicsery-Ronay, Jr., Istvan. *The Seven Beauties of Science Fiction*. Wesleyan UP, 2008.

DeCandido, Keith R.A. "*Star Trek: Deep Space Nine* Rewatch: First Season Overview." *Tor.com*, 2 July 2013. www.tor.com/2013/07/02/star-trek-deep-space-nine-rewatch-first-season-overview/. Accessed 1 May 2021.

Erdmann, Terry J., and Paula M. Block. Star Trek: Deep Space Nine *Companion*. Pocket Books, 2000.

Feuer, Jane. "Melodrama, Serial Form, and Television Today." *Screen*, vol. 25, no. 1, 1982, pp. 4–17.

Geraghty, Lincoln. *Living with* Star Trek: *American Culture and the* Star Trek *Universe*. Bloomsbury, 2007.

Gregory, Chris. Star Trek *Parallel Narratives*. Macmillan, 2000.

Gymnich, Marion. "Exploring Inner Spaces: Authoritative Narratives and Subjective Worlds in *Star Trek: Deep Space Nine*, *Voyager* and *Enterprise*." *Narrative Strategies in Television Series*, edited by Gaby Allrath and Marion Gymnich. Palgrave, 2005, pp. 62–79.

Kelleter, Frank. "Five Ways of Looking at Popular Seriality." *Media of Serial Narrative*, edited by Frank Kelleter. Ohio State UP, 2017, pp. 7–36.

McHale, Brian. "Beginning to Think about Narrative in Poetry." *Narrative*, vol. 17, no. 1, 2009, pp. 11–30.

Mittell, Jason. *Complex TV: The Poetics of Contemporary Television Storytelling.* NYU Press, 2015.

Moylan, Tom. *Demand the Impossible: Science Fiction and the Utopian Imagination.* Peter Lang/Ralahine Classics Edition, 2014.

O'Sullivan, Sean. "Six Elements of Serial Narrative." *Narrative*, vol. 27, no. 1, 2019, pp. 49–64.

Pearson, Roberta. "Additionality and Cohesion in Transfictional Worlds." *The Velvet Light Trap*, no. 79, 2017, pp. 113–119.

Suvin, Darko. *The Metamorphosis of Science Fiction: On the Poetics and History of a Literary Genre.* Peter Lang/Ralahine Classics Edition, 2016.

FILMOGRAPHY

Babylon 5. Created by J. Michael Straczynski. Warner Bros. 1993–1998.
Buffy the Vampire Slayer. Created by Joss Whedon. 20th Century Fox. 1997–2003.
None But the Brave. Directed by Frank Sinatra. Warner Bros. 1965.
The X-Files. Created by Chris Carter. 20th Century Fox. 1993–2002.

The Static Space Opera

Dispersed and Sedimental Saturation
of the Star Trek *Storyworld*

Florent Favard

"To boldly go where no one has gone before" is both the final sentence of *The Next Generation* (1987–1994) title sequence *and* a narrative pledge between the program and its audience: every week, a new adventure, a new corner of the galaxy, a new wonder. Most of the series within the franchise focus spatially on a spaceship, usually designed for exploration—like the various Enterprises and *Discovery* (2017–present)—or forced to navigate through an unknown quadrant of the galaxy, such as *Voyager* (1995–2001). *Picard* (2020–present) slightly alters this formula, but the protagonists aboard La Sirena still warp from planet to planet in order to investigate a Romulan plot. The animated series *Lower Decks* (2020–present) returns to the classic exploration formula with a twist, as the protagonists have to handle "second contact" and boldly go where others *have* gone before.

Only one entry in the franchise distinguishes itself from this premise: *Deep Space Nine* boldly *stays* where no one has stayed before. It features a space station, a fixed point, near the planet Bajor. The Federation—represented aboard the eponymous station by its commander, Benjamin Sisko (Avery Brooks)—intends to remain in this remote region of the galaxy, hoping to both help the Bajorans recover from the Cardassian occupation and facilitate Bajor's entrance into the Federation. Over its seven broadcasted years, the discussion around *Deep Space Nine* centered mainly on the bending of *Star Trek* creator Gene Roddenberry's cardinal rule: that there should be no heavy interpersonal conflicts between protagonists belonging to the utopian Federation. Nevertheless, the choice of a fixed point as a setting added fuel to the raging debate about its legitimacy. Twenty years after its series finale, this was indeed the first main point addressed in Executive

Producer Ira Steven Behr's documentary, *What We Left Behind* (2019), as members of the cast read comments of unclear origin:

> [Nana Visitor, then Colm Meaney, reading]: The whole idea of *Star Trek* is the idea that they would be exploring new worlds and going where no man has gone before, not blabbing around a space station talking about their feelings.

Yet, *Deep Space Nine* is now fondly remembered by fans and critics alike as the darkest, most political, most serialized, and perhaps the most mature of all the entries in the franchise. The series offered new ways to explore its storyworld: rather than adding dispersed information and narrative threads as the characters explored the galaxy, it accumulated them in one central location. It could then be argued that the static aspect of its setting is not only what makes *Deep Space Nine* stand apart within the *Star Trek* franchise and the generic history of space opera on television, but also what allowed it to defy the narrative constraints of its era, embodying a leap forward in terms of narrative complexity, blending episodic and serialized narration (Mittell 18). As such, there may be a correlation between the dispersion or sedimentation of narrative data within the space of the storyworld and the balance of episodic, independent episodes and long-term, overarching serialized structures. Such a claim can be discussed through a detailed narratological analysis of the structure of storyworlds and the plots they allow their narratives to thread, drawing from possible-worlds theory as applied to fiction. The aim is to better understand how worldbuilding, a key aspect of science fiction and fantasy franchises, helped *Deep Space Nine* reshape the franchise and televised space opera towards more complex and serialized plot threads.

Worldbuilding Within Narrative Complexity

To best understand how *Deep Space Nine* narratively transformed the franchise, Thomas Pavel's "internal approach" must be used, diving deep into the fictional world while not forgetting that these narratives are designed with specific economic, aesthetic, and cultural goals in mind (25). The series was broadcast during a critical period in television series history, notes Jason Mittell, as "narrative complexity redefine[d] episodic forms under the influence of serial narration" (18). During the 1990s, television series started to increasingly blend episodic, weekly plots with long-term character development and storylines; these series also used more complex "narrative special effects" and character networks (Mittell 46–48; Booth). These evolutions gave rise to what writers, fans, and critics alike call "mythologies," which, in the context of television series, could be seen as a way to describe the overarching, serialized, complex narrative structure of these programs, making them more than the sum of their parts, or episodes (Favard, *Écrire une série TV* 133). Mythologies are not restricted to what is canon, already established in the narrative; they also account for the thematic and symbolic dimensions of the series, and for its unfolding narrative possibilities. As both a narrational mode and a way to read and interpret television series, mythologies primarily originated within science fiction and fantasy programs in the late 1980s (Favard, *Écrire une série TV* 115). One of their particularities lies in the way these series saturate their storyworlds to make them as coherent and complex as possible (Favard, *Le Récit dans les series* 59).

According to David Herman, "interpreters attempt to reconstruct not just what happened … but also the surrounding context or environment embedding existents, their attributes, and the actions and events in which they are more or less centrally involved" (13–14). This task is hampered by the fact that storyworlds are fundamentally incomplete; no text can be wholly exhaustive about them. Nevertheless, through any narrative, a storyworld slowly accumulates explicit and implicit information that defines the evolving texture of the text and its fictional encyclopedia (Doležel 169). Texture is the product of both reference and sense (extension and intension)[1]: the former can be described as the relation between signified and signifier, while the latter focuses on the aesthetics of sense-making, the various ways the signified can be referenced to in order to create a distinctive text (Doležel 35–36; 135).

Lubomír Doležel focuses on wording and paraphrasing in literary texts. With an audiovisual text such as a television series, texture lies in the *mise-en-scène*, in actors' performances, in pre- and post-production work, and also in the specific ways a text divided into weekly episodes will blend episodic and serialized subplots. Both Doležel and Pavel usually describe saturation as explicit, "clear" data aggregating around a core, surrounded by implicit information and then the absence of data. Pavel talks about a circle of light surrounded by darkness (120–123), while Doležel refers to determinate and indeterminate domains surrounded by gaps (182). It can be argued, however, that certain texts, and their respective textures, can use different modes of saturation, especially as space is becoming a central question of both narratology as a whole, and narratological analysis of television in particular (Ryan; Mittell 274). The difference between *Deep Space Nine* and the rest of the *Star Trek* franchise may lie precisely in the way the storyworld space, the texture and the balance between episodic and serialized modes of narration, emerge(d) from a sedimental mode of saturation which, as different as it may seem from the requirements of space opera as a genre, is not incompatible with the dispersed mode of other *Star Trek* entries.

Star Trek's *Dispersed Saturation Model*

Star Trek could be described as using the same narrative structure as most American space opera programs, drawing upon a genre full of galaxy-wide adventures and old clichés, abandoned or made fun of by the New Wave in science fiction literature (Westphal 203). Science fiction television series of the 1950s showed great efforts to entertain the audience with interplanetary settings despite budget limitations, from *Space Patrol* (1950–1955) to *Buck Rogers* (1950–1951) to *Flash Gordon* (1954–1955). *Star Trek: The Original Series* (1966–1969) was broadcast ten years later, amid a production landscape more equipped to handle the representation of many different planets. Although it predates *The Original Series*, *Lost in Space* (1965–1968) eventually shifted from a "planet of the season" to a "planet of the week" format during season three in order to follow the trend and provide the audience with brand-new worlds each episode. The "lost in space" format would then influence other major productions focused on a crew adrift in the galaxy, from *Space: 1999* (1975–1977) to *Battlestar Galactica* (1978–1979); even the protagonists of *Blake's 7* (1978–1981) wander around multiple stellar systems.

By the time *Star Trek* came back through a new live-action television series, *The Next Generation* crew was able to create and maintain both an artistic autonomy and a "craft-workshop mode of production" capable of producing twenty-six episodes per season, an impressive number given the amount of visual effects and set building the format required (Pearson and Messenger Davies). On average, thirteen episodes per season featured a planet the crew either beamed on or orbited, discounting a few more episodes dedicated to space anomalies, nebulae, and deep space encounters with other ships (season two being the most below average, with only seven planets). The rest of the episodes usually followed a "ship in a bottle" format, with events occurring exclusively aboard the Enterprise-D. Whereas its narrative structure remains close to *The Original Series*, *The Next Generation* succeeded in creating engaging episodic shows while slowly developing its characters, and entire civilizations such as the Klingons, over the years. It showed some signs of what Writer and Executive Producer Damon Lindelof would call early "stealth serialization," such as with the character development of the android crewmember Data (Brent Spiner) (qtd. in Bennett 79).

The *Star Trek* franchise, however, is not only about spaceships exploring the galaxy, but also about spaceships *warping* from place to place: the map of the galaxy does not slowly expand with Earth as its center but reveals itself through dispersed glimpses of stellar systems whose structure and relation to others are not always made clear—they may remain indeterminate, implicit. Even if maps are shown onscreen, within canon material, or designed by fans, there is, quite literally, always space between the stars for a new system, a new planet: the map may never be complete. From a spatial perspective, the *Star Trek* storyworld is not saturated outward, but rather through discrete additions, not unlike pointillist brushstrokes.

What could be defined as a dispersed saturation is not limited to science fiction, as even stories taking place in storyworlds similar to our real world and including frequent travels will dispatch discrete information in time and space. However, for stories set on Earth, the audience can use their real-world encyclopedia to try and fill in the blanks (at least from a spatial perspective). One of the main attractions of fantasy and science fiction storyworlds lies precisely in the endeavor that is making sense of it all with no point of reference, since these worlds are "salient" (Pavel 76), a reading strategy favored by geek culture (Peyron 68).

Furthermore, the episodic format of *The Next Generation* allowed for very brief, superficial encounters, leaving plenty for the imagination after each new civilization was revealed during a "planet of the week" episode. This meant that many of the secondary characters and civilizations encountered would not return and thus would not be further detailed. Most of the explicit data presented by the series concern the Enterprise-D and its crew. The audience is given slightly more information about a few recurring planets and civilizations, such as Qo'noS, Risa, or Earth. The text density, dictated by the episodic plots and the influence of the "planet of the week" format, in turn dictates the dispersed saturation of the storyworld, with the Alpha Quadrant the equivalent of Swiss cheese, full of gaps, indeterminate zones (the planets of the week), and a few determinate places here and there.

The Enterprise-D is the most familiar setting of the series but does not constitute a "place" *per se*, as it is constantly moving. It is a structured space, a micro-society, and one could argue that, from a semio-pragmatic standpoint, there is no difference between the Enterprise-D and Deep Space 9: both are, on the level of production, familiar settings built to last, with recurring shots allowing the audience to master its architecture and its cultural codes. Within the storyworld, spaceship and station are the equivalent of spacefaring cities. They may both invite the same process of "diegetisation" when interpreted by the audience: they are fictional, professional, and domestic spaces somewhere in interstellar space (Odin 19; Delaporte). The difference lies first and foremost in the storyworld that, even if it *can* move, the station remains largely in the same place.

Switching to a Sedimental Saturation Model

Rather than a dispersed saturation, *Deep Space Nine* fosters what could be defined as a sedimental saturation, used by any narrative focusing on a specific place and time: it aims at accumulating layers and layers of conflict, experiences, and history in a narrative nexus that stays in place so as to not wash down too many of these layers in the currents of warp travel.

As Executive Producer Rick Berman explained in a *Deep Space Nine* season one special feature, "It just seemed ridiculous to have two shows and two casts of characters that were off going where no man has gone before" ("A Bold Beginning"). This marketing argument, however, is only part of the reason why *Deep Space Nine* is different from *The Next Generation* and *The Original Series*. *Deep Space Nine* is also the manifestation of a shifting creative direction for the franchise, as creator Gene Roddenberry was slowly handing over the reins to Rick Berman, the latter ready to bend (but not break) the rules established by Roddenberry with *The Original Series* (Pearson and Messenger Davies). *Deep Space Nine* was a renegotiation of Roddenberry's vision and influence, and seemingly halted the forward movement (within the storyworld) of the franchise a year after Roddenberry's death—a symbolic coincidence that the fans disappointed with *Deep Space Nine* and quoted in *What We Left Behind* may have picked up at the time.

Since Deep Space 9 is not a ship, there is no captain to steer it across the galaxy, to performatively instruct the crew to "engage" or to "go to half-impulse." It could be argued that Sisko, without those repetitive demonstrations of performative authority—barring the classic "battle stations" whenever the station is attacked—has to actually lead and manage a crew. From a structuralist point of view, the time devoted to space maneuvers and planetary scans in most of the other series can be used to increase moments of negotiation, confrontation, and mutual understanding. Moreover, the setting itself is not thrown into constant battle, and, contrary to *The Next Generation* and *Voyager*, is not confronted by a mysterious nebula or space anomaly seemingly every other episode. Hence the threats to the station itself are generally treated as an exception rather than a rule, and make for episodes with increased narrative tension, especially the opening of season four, when Klingon Chancellor Gowron's fleet attacks the station, and the ending of season five, during which Cardassia and the Dominion take back Deep Space 9 and control it up until its liberation in "Sacrifice of Angels." If *The Next Generation* highlights a ship that is constantly repaired and appears brand-new after each episode, thereby focusing on a *homeostatic* narrative that always reverts to the *status quo* (Beylot 11), *Deep Space Nine*, with its long-term plot involving an escalating war, features a more *unbalanced* version of the storyworld, where the situation is slowly degrading season after season, culminating in the disappearance of the wormhole at the end of season six (Favard, *Écrire* 215).

The setting then influences the characters populating it. The protagonists' goal is not to explore the galaxy; hence their focus is not directed outward, but inward, or as actor Jeffrey Combs puts it in *What We Left Behind*, the series "pursued the journey inside, not the journey out." The main protagonists (as well as secondary characters) are indeed faced with ethical dilemmas and political decisions set ablaze by their very different origins: far from the Enterprise and its multi-species crew under the sole command of Captain Jean-Luc Picard, the Federation has to share leadership on the station with the Bajorans, while various parties defend their own interests—especially the Ferengi—and a few lone wolves struggle to find their place, among them Odo (René Auberjonois), the only shapeshifter, and Garak (Andrew Robinson), the mysterious Cardassian tailor. The protagonists are indeed "blabbing around the space station talking about their feelings," as they must learn to live together in difficult times. Interestingly, the characters mostly "babble" in the same kind of setting viewers can find in other series within the franchise: the station commander's office serves as a ready room, and Deep Space 9 features a wardroom, the equivalent of the Enterprise D's observation lounge, where Sisko can gather the crew or engage in political negotiations with members of the military and elected officials. Long corridors are used for walk-and-talk beats, just as they are in *The Next Generation* or *Voyager*. What really distinguishes Deep Space 9 from the Federation starships is the addition of a promenade, a vast commercial area that further underlines the station's status as a spacefaring city and a port of call—thus, a static place witnessing the coming and going of numerous spaceships. Most characters arriving on the station will make an appearance there; it is also where the powers that be deal with the general public, whether it is through acts of terror (the Cardassians executing prisoners during the occupation, or the mob that demands Odo be judged for the alleged murder of a Bajoran in "A Man Alone"), or political appearances and speeches, such as Bajoran First Minister Shakaar (Duncan Regehr) causing a commotion when Bajorans welcome him on the station in "Crossfire." The promenade is used to feature the general public of the Federation more frequently than in other series within the franchise, and present them not simply as tertiary characters, but as a mass, a synecdoche for the larger, implicit population of the storyworld, that has to deal with the consequences of the protagonists' actions and can hold them responsible by directly challenging them (which happens, for example, in "In the Hands of the Prophets," with fundamentalists demonstrating in front of the school). Confronting the Federation with the realities of a day-to-day life on the farthest outpost, to the Maquis defectors, the Bajoran people, and the political games with Cardassia, was for Berman, Piller, Behr, and their writers the only way to bend the rules set by Roddenberry and infuse a healthy dose of cabin fever into the franchise. It could be argued, however, that the differences between the spaceship and space station are subtle at times. *Deep Space Nine's* unique spin on the franchise may not only lie in the space station itself, but also in its close ties with many civilizations, most notably Bajor.

Bajor as the Other Fixed Point of the Series

Whereas Picard and his crew can forever change the course of history for an entire civilization and then warp away, never to be seen again, *Deep Space Nine* is "stuck" with the Bajorans, and Bajor itself, one of the rare planets in the *Star Trek* canon to have been so thoroughly mapped on television. The Bajorans represent an especially challenging civilization narrative-wise, since their history with the Cardassians and ties with the Maquis frequently underline the limits of the Federation's utopian model of society. *Deep Space Nine* closely examines the deontic and axiological modalities of the *Star Trek* storyworld, that is, what is permitted, prohibited, or obligatory and what is perceived as good, bad, or neutral (Doležel 120). Whereas "planet of the week" series like *The Next Generation* and *Voyager* can come up with a new ethical dilemma each episode, *Deep Space Nine* focuses on recurring complex problems generally tied to either its characters or its long-term subplots. This is not to say that *Deep Space Nine* is more thorough, but rather that the structure of the storyworld allows it to avoid the constant *tabula rasa* of other 1990s *Star Trek* series and stretch the examination of the same political or religious matters upon several episodes. It is useful to borrow the concept of a television series "matrix" (*matrice*) from Guillaume Soulez, who distinguishes it from the formula of a given series and defines it as the "semantic and symbolic core that drives the narrative and its moral or philosophical horizon," as a creative and productive way of exploiting the repetitive nature of all series by constantly reformulating the main philosophical and political stakes of the narrative (par. 8). Although *The Next Generation* and *Voyager's* matrices lean heavily on perpetual discovery, and the various settings are a means to an end, in *Deep Space Nine* the structure of the fictional world is designed to ignite this productive repetition, allowing for a deeper and constant re-examination of issues such as terrorism, war crimes, and, of course, religion.

Although *Deep Space Nine* explains away the divinity of the Prophets by presenting them as "wormhole aliens," the Federation has to deal with a semi-secular government deeply influenced by religious leaders, a theme that resonates with the plots dedicated to the main villain of *Deep Space Nine*, the Dominion, with the Founders being considered as gods. Previous and subsequent series did not serialize and re-examine religiosity, although Klingon culture and frequent adventures with the Q continuum "sedimented" those questions around specific, detailed, determinate characters and civilizations. *Deep Space Nine* goes further, however, by re-injecting religion and spirituality as key defining traits of a few protagonists—most notably Major Kira (Nana Visitor)—and two major civilizations, one that technically owns the station (the Bajorans) and the other threatening the entire quadrant (the Dominion). Narrative tension thus stems from the conflict between alethic modalities and epistemic modalities, namely what is possible (the laws of nature) and what is known, unknown, or believed (Doležel 115).

For example, *Deep Space Nine* ends its first season with a political conflict opposing secular and fundamentalist views on society and especially pedagogy. Vedek Winn (Louise Fletcher) criticizes Keiko O'Brien (Rosalind Chao) for teaching schoolchildren about the Prophets by describing them as alien entities. In the same episode, Winn is covertly conspiring to have Vedek Bareil (Philip Anglim) assassinated, as she considers him to be too moderate, wanting to secure her place as Kai ("In the Hands of the Prophets"). Such an episode could have been a one-time plot in *The Next Generation*, but *Deep Space Nine* is able to use it to slowly develop the character of Winn and portray her as a major secondary character in the long-term plot. Her thirst for power makes her a tragic antagonist, allowing the writers to reformulate questions about religion and fundamentalism, especially by repetitively opposing her to Kira, who is torn between her faith in the Prophets, the authority of her Kai, and the influence of the Federation. "In the Hands of Prophets" is especially representative of this long-term dynamic as it also resonates with Kira's portrayal as a freedom fighter, or terrorist, depending on who is describing her. In the episode, Winn is also about to coordinate a terrorist attack against what she considers to be a new invasion of Bajor, this time by the Federation and its atheist philosophy: where should the line be drawn, and what motives can justify such desperate measures?

With Bajor and Deep Space 9 as the two sides of the same coin, the series is able to slowly connect to other civilizations, each represented by a protagonist onboard: as the enemy of Bajor and belligerent neighbor to the Federation, Cardassia quickly becomes another star system of interest. The wormhole paves the way for the Dominion, against which Bajor and the Federation are literally on the front lines. Season after season, *Deep Space Nine* can build upon existing civilizations, including the Klingons, whose society is already detailed throughout *The Next Generation*. While they remain mostly neutral in the conflict, the Ferengi are also given a larger role. It may seem paradoxical, yet *Deep Space Nine* is able to use its fixed focal point to create a network of civilizations atop its network of characters, allowing it to extend the overarching narrative far beyond Bajor.

Finding the Balance Between Dispersed and Sedimental Saturation Models: Deep Space Nine *and* Babylon 5

It would be inexact to claim that *Deep Space Nine* worked actively *against* the trend of dispersed saturation in space opera, as the Bajoran wormhole, opening the way to a brand-new quadrant of the galaxy, allowed for discrete travels to brave new worlds, while the introduction of the *Defiant* let the characters move more freely. Season one is, in fact, the only season to resist the "planet of the week" format, with only two new planets and three episodes set in part on Bajor. On average, *Deep Space Nine* seasons contain nine episodes featuring a planet, again, discounting interstellar encounters and space anomalies. That being said, many of these planets are recurring: Bajor and Cardassia both appear on average two times per season, especially during the heavily serialized last tier of the final season, and Earth, Ferenginar, and the Founders' homeworld make almost one appearance by season. These numbers sustain the idea that the station is not the only fixed point the series is focused on, instead creating a greater network of detailed, complex places belonging for the most part to the main belligerents of the galactic war *Deep Space Nine* intends to depict; whether the station is under Cardassian, Federation, or Dominion control, it is always a major narrative hub. The series could thus be seen as combining sedimental *and* dispersed modes of saturation, each in service to the other: instead of the pointillist brushstrokes of *The Next Generation*, *Deep Space Nine* needs constant coming and going, with the station as the nexus of a figure closer to a spiral or a flower (akin to what a Spirograph would produce). The major protagonists and antagonists, and their respective civilizations, are then inextricably linked across the galaxy to Deep Space 9. This is especially important in later seasons, as the narrative focuses first on Dominion alliances and conquests, and then on hard-won battles materialized by maps in seasons six and seven. The strategic importance of, say, the battles of Chin'Toka or Cardassia can only generate narrative tension if the audience is able to understand what is at stake and how these places are connected spatially and politically: indeed, *Deep Space Nine* spent entire seasons slowly building this galactic network while tying it to major characters (most of them living on the station) so that the audience might better understand what motivates each belligerent.

It is interesting to underline the fact that, during a decade in which the *Star Trek* franchise was still focused on a dispersed mode of saturation, *Deep Space Nine* was not the only series trying to build a galactic network in service of serialized, mature space opera; *Babylon 5* (1993–1998) did the same thing. Both series used a multi-layered approach combining a causal link of events and themes across a dense network of characters and planets. J. Michael Straczynski's series featured characters forced to live with the consequences of their actions and the ripples they leave in space and time, as "any word or action has an impact upon surrounding events" (Johnson-Smith 192). *Deep Space Nine* and *Babylon 5* thus count among the earliest "narratives of interconnectedness" on television, prefiguring the late 1990s' and 2000s' modes of narration used by *Lost* (2004–2010), for example (Mousoutzanis 44).

It is even more interesting that the two space station series are themselves tightly connected, despite their respective fandoms sometimes being unable to find common ground. The long list of troubling similarities between *Deep Space Nine* and *Babylon 5* has been the subject of intense debate since the inception of both series. Even when setting aside the issue of possible plagiarism, and a narrative arms race to present similar plotlines weeks before the *other* "space station show," it is striking how similar the structure of both storyworlds turned out to be.

Both stations are located near a wormhole (in *Babylon 5*, it is a network of "jumpgates"), and if Babylon 5 is orbiting a (mostly) barren planet, it compensates with its status as a galactic diplomatic hub, while Deep Space 9 becomes a mandatory port of call on the way to the wormhole. Thus, aboard both stations, drama comes from inside as well as outside: their settings may be static, but their storyworlds were designed in such a way that the stations became "plot magnets." Both series featured stations that made the entire galaxy of their storyworlds come to them, and yet both were still unable to resist the call to outer space.

In another troubling echo, their main long-term plot—focused on galactic war—justifies the introduction of a warship: the *Defiant* in *Deep Space Nine*, and the fleet of White Stars in *Babylon 5*. Thus, both Commander Sisko and Captain Sheridan (Bruce Boxleitner) can participate in distant conflicts and explore the galaxy, even if *Babylon 5* is less interested in marooning the crew on a barren planet every now and then. A fundamental difference must be pointed out: *Babylon 5*'s five-year storyline was planned years in advance by creator Straczynski. As a result, beyond a first season dedicated to exposition, the series focuses on heavily serialized plots involving government conspiracy, a detailed fall into fascism and civil war on Earth, and a galactic chess game led by two powerful and very advanced civilizations. *Deep Space Nine*, the most serialized *Star Trek* series of the 1990s—so much, in fact, that it made Rick Berman "allergic to serialized storytelling," according to Bryan Fuller—still had to satisfy *Star Trek* fans and the economic imperative of episodic storytelling in order to maintain its audience (qtd. in Altman and Dochterman).

Straczynski frequently declared he was trying to do for science fiction what *Hill Street Blues* (1981–1987) had done for police procedurals: create a setting where serialized plots, albeit focused essentially on character development, could rise from a sedimental saturation. *Hill Street Blues* is frequently identified by television scholars as one the first narratively complex television series, mobilizing deep political themes, innovative *mise-en-scène*, and a balance between episodic (one day in the life of a police station) and serialized (character arcs) modes of narration. As a police drama, it featured a narrative nexus (the police station), but one revolutionary aspect of the series' narrative at the time was the dense network of protagonists working within this nexus, calling for richer interactions and character development. *Deep Space Nine's* models were closer to the western genre, with the station a space equivalent to the cities of North Fork (*The Rifleman*, 1958–1963) or Dodge City (*Gunsmoke*, 1955–1975), but the core narrative remains the same: characters working and living in the same place, forced to deal with each other and the consequences of their actions ("New Frontier: The Story of Deep Space Nine"). It could be argued that, while sedimental saturation is not *de facto* linked with serialized storylines, it may have facilitated serialization at a time when the economic and technological context allowed for it: reruns, the syndication market, and the home video system worked along with diegetic retelling—characters talking about what happened in previous episodes—to help the audience follow the increasingly immersive and complex series an expanding and competitive market called for, even if serialization itself would continue to be treated as a problem by studio executives up to the 2000s (Mittell 181).

An Increasingly Serialized Landscape

Looking at the space operas of the late 1990s and the 2000s, one can observe variations in the balance between episodic and serialized television and its association with a more dispersed or more sedimental mode of saturation. The Stargate franchise especially tried to blend the two modes of saturation while focusing more on the episodic/dispersed side, with the missions requiring the teams to frequently explore other planets. That being said, Earth and Atlantis offered fixed settings able to enrich the series' mythology through political intrigue. *Stargate SG-1* (1997–2007) featured an enduring political intrigue through the NID conspiracy and the cooperation with Russia, while long-term "stealth" plots slowly established key planets and civilizations throughout the Milky Way, allowing the series to return to specific worlds such as Dakara, home of the Jaffa, antagonists who became a liberated people attempting to create a republic. *Stargate Atlantis* (2004–2009) went further by isolating its protagonists in the remote Pegasus galaxy, aboard the fabled city of Atlantis, a space station that, without the appropriate source of energy, remains still on the surface of planet Lantea's ocean. Unable to contact Earth and dealing with refugees they saved on their first exploration, the protagonists also have to make sense of the mysteries hidden within the abandoned Manhattan-sized city. Atlantis, through loose, semi-serialized plots, thus becomes a hub for all the civilizations of the Pegasus galaxy hunted down by the Wraith, precisely because it is an isolated, discrete point, a beacon of hope, and not a military base belonging to the army of one of countless nations on Earth: a melting pot of different nationalities, and soon, planetary civilizations, Atlantis is, not unlike Deep Space 9, a small world of its own, around which the rest of the storyworld orbits. By contrast, *Stargate Universe* (2009–2011), while more serialized, used a dispersed model of saturation, with the Destiny, an old spaceship, jumping almost randomly to any star system it deemed fit along its mysterious quest. It could be argued that, storyworld-wise, *Stargate SG-1* is to *The Next Generation* what *Atlantis* is to *Deep Space Nine* and *Universe* is to *Voyager*. Each series was built with a new storyworld dynamic to distinguish it from previous iterations, from "exploration" to "space station" and eventually a return to the classic "lost in space" format, though the correlation between episodic/serialized and dispersed/sedimented saturation is less remarkable: *Atlantis* remained mainly episodic in nature, with a focus on exploration and a new galaxy to discover; *Universe* follows in the serialized, hard science fiction steps of *Battlestar Galactica* and, despite its dispersed mode of saturation and multiple galaxies as its setting, does not, on average, feature as many planets as the other two series.

Beyond the Stargate franchise, *Farscape* (1999–2003) followed a format closer to *The Next Generation* with the sentient ship, Moya, traveling around the galaxy, and some serialized subplots within a rather episodic format. The re-imagined version of *Battlestar Galactica* (2003–2009) featured a whole fleet wandering through space and can be located somewhere between *Deep Space Nine* and *Babylon 5* when it comes to the balance between the "crisis of the week" and the slow, long-term decay of the fleet. Generally avoiding barren planets, the series featured moving ships and yet appears to stand still, with the fleet a singular point usually stranded in the indeterminate darkness of space. *Battlestar Galactica* also tried to re-create a spacefaring city, with distinct ships serving as specialized districts harboring the political and judicial system (mainly the Colonial One), industries, a leisure complex (the Cloud 9), and even a prison (the Astral Queen), before slowly collapsing the entire fleet within the eponymous battleship as other vessels are destroyed episode after episode. Designed as a military ship already ripe with drama (part of the protagonists belong or are connected to the Adama family), the Galactica welcomes, in later seasons, civilian refugees that take over part of the ship to install a market and a bar, turning it into a city of its own (Ambal, Favard). The presence of civilians only increases the tension with the military, already embedded within the series' matrix, in a configuration that is reminiscent of *Deep Space Nine*. Looking back, it thus seems evident that both *Deep Space Nine* and *Babylon 5* opened a broad new horizon for televised space opera during what could be deemed its golden age.

Writer Ira Steven Behr reflects on the heritage of *Deep Space Nine* in *What We Left Behind*: "The studio was very clear. 'You are killing the series by serializing it.' I knew what they were saying made sense to them, but I did not think it made sense for *Deep Space Nine*. *Deep Space Nine* seemed to call out for serialization." Perhaps Behr understood that the static setting of his storyworld allowed for a sedimental saturation and called out for layers and layers of meaning and themes and plots to echo with each other. A look at the subsequent *Star Trek* series underlines the hypothesis that episodic does not equate dispersed saturation, and serialized does not equate sedimental saturation, but that there may be a correlation between these two axes. In the late 1990s, *Voyager*, using a dispersed saturation model as the eponymous ship sailed through the Delta Quadrant, focused on episodic plots. Heavily serialized storylines were avoided: an entire season devoted to a planned "year of hell" was shut down by Rick Berman, and converted into a fan-favorite two-parter, "Year of Hell." A few years later, *Enterprise* (2001–2005) featured a heavily serialized season three focused on the Xindi War. During the 2010s, *Discovery* was able to weave complex season-long plots while warping around the galaxy, as did *Picard*. After the blending of episodic and serialized modes of narration, it could be argued that televised space operas—and planet operas such as *The Expanse* (2015–2022)—are yet again a fertile ground of experimentation, balancing dispersed and sedimental saturation within their storyworlds, on a scale that *The Next Generation* and *Deep Space Nine* could not have reached in their time. It seems fair to say, however, that *Deep Space Nine* was indeed one of the numerous television series that paved the way to serialization and more complex storyworlds in televised science fiction.

Conclusion

Deep Space Nine was the first *Star Trek* series to break the formula established by the original series, its animated continuation, and *The Original Series*. The creators and writers of *Deep Space Nine* had to generate an unusual setting while respecting continuity and opted to focus the series on a space station, thereby fundamentally changing the way this narrative would expand on the *Star Trek* storyworld; the previous model of dispersed saturation, fostering a discrete, pointillist mapping of the galaxy through constant discovery, was counterbalanced by a sedimental saturation that turned the centrifugal narrative forces of previous series into centripetal forces, allowing for a deeper and more nuanced characterization and more complex storylines along a dense network of characters and their respective civilizations. Whereas subsequent series reverted to more episodic and dispersed narratives, *Deep Space Nine* provided the franchise with an opportunity to reinvent itself. Reignited in the 2010s, more recent *Star Trek* series carried on this trend and tackled new challenges, especially when it comes to themes. *Discovery* bent Roddenberry's cardinal rule further, and *Picard* proved to be overtly critical of the Federation utopia. If narrative conventions continue to evolve, and the storyworld structure of *Discovery* and *Picard* continues to grow even more complex than *Deep Space Nine*'s, then the franchise will continue to open its matrix to discussion by an ever-faithful fandom—and beyond.

NOTE

1. To be more specific, Doležel links texture with the intentional function when he studies narrative motifs: "Texture is the exact form of expression, the original wording in which the motif appears in the literary text" (35–36). His chapter on saturation, however, could be interpreted as linking texture with both the intentional and extentional functions, as he defines implicitness—that is, unclear, incomplete or vague references to specific elements of the storyworld—as "a factor of [literary texts] aesthetic effectiveness" (172–173).

WORKS CITED AND CONSULTED

Altman, Mark A. and Daren Dochterman, hosts. "*Voyager* 25th Anniversary Party w/ Bryan Fuller." *Inglorious Treksperts*. Apple Podcasts, 23 May 2020, https://podcasts.apple.com/us/podcast/voyager-25th-anniversary-party-w-bryan-fuller/id1439126593?i=1000475481608. Accessed 19 Aug. 2020.

Ambal, Julie, and Florent Favard. "Une ville dans les étoiles: Lieux de vie en mouvement(s) dans la série *Battlestar Galactica*." *Lieux de vie en science-fiction*, edited by Danièle André, BoD, 2021, pp. 193–207.

Bennett, Tara. *Showrunners: The Art of Running a TV Show*. Titan Books, 2014.

Beylot, Pierre. *Le Récit audiovisuel*. Armand Colin, 2005.

Booth, Paul. "The Television Social Network: Exploring TV Characters." *Television and New Media*, vol. 12, no. 4, 2011, pp. 370–388.

Delaporte, Chloé. "Aux marges de la fiction sérielle télévisuelle: sémio-pragmatique de la shortcom familiale." *TV/Series*, no. 15, 2019. https://journals.openedition.org/tvseries/3661. Accessed 08 June 2021.

Doležel, Lubomír. *Heterocosmica: Fiction and Possible Worlds*. John Hopkins UP, 1998.

Favard, Florent. *Écrire une série TV : La promesse d'un dénouement*. PUFR, 2019.

_____. *Le Récit dans les séries de science-fiction.* Armand Colin, 2018.
Herman, David. *Story Logic: Problems and Possibilities of Narrative.* U of Nebraska P, 2002.
Johnson-Smith, Jan. *American Science Fiction TV: Star Trek, Stargate and Beyond.* I.B. Tauris, 2004.
Mittell, Jason. *Complex TV: The Poetics of Contemporary Television Storytelling.* New York UP, 2015.
Mousoutzanis, Aris. "Determinism, Traumatic Temporality, and Global Interconnectedness." *Looking for* Lost: *Critical Essays on the Enigmatic Series,* edited by Randy Laist. McFarland, 2011, pp. 43–58.
Odin, Roger. *De la fiction.* De Boeck, 2000.
Pavel, Thomas. *Univers de la fiction.* Seuil, 1988.
Pearson, Roberta, and Máire Messenger Davies. Star Trek *and American Television.* U of California P, 2014.
Peyron, David. *Culture Geek.* FYP, 2013.
Ryan, Marie-Laure. "Diagramming Narrative." *Semiotica,* vol. 2007, no. 165, 2007, pp. 11–40.
Soulez, Guillaume. "La Double répétition." *Mise au point,* no. 3, 2011. https://journals.openedition.org/map/979. Accessed 08 June 2021.
Westphal, Gary. "Space Opera." *The Cambridge Companion to Science Fiction,* edited by Edward James and Farah Mendlesohn. Cambridge UP, 2003, pp. 197–208.

Filmography

Babylon 5, created by J. Michael Straczynski, PTEN, TNT, 1993–1998.
Battlestar Galactica, created by Glen A. Larson, ABC, 1978–1979.
Battlestar Galactica, created by Ronald D. Moore, Sci-Fi, Sky1, 2003–2009.
Blake's 7, created by Terry Nation, BBC1, 1978–1981.
"A Bold Beginning." *Star Trek: Deep Space Nine,* season 1 DVD special feature, 2003.
Buck Rogers, written by Gene Wyckoff, ABC, 1950–1951.
The Expanse, created by Mark Fergus and Hawk Ostby, Syfy and Amazon, 2015–present.
Farscape, created by Rockne S. O'Bannon, Sci-Fi, Nine Network, 1999–2003.
Flash Gordon, produced by Edward Gruskin and Matty Fox, DuMont, 1954–1955.
Gunsmoke, developed by Charles Marquis Warren, CBS, 1955–1975.
Hill Street Blues, created by Steven Bochco and Michael Kozoll, NBC, 1981–1987.
Lost, created by Jeffrey Lieber, J.J. Abrams, and Damon Lindelof, ABC, 2004–2010.
Lost in Space, created by Irwin Allen, CBS, 1965–1968.
"New Frontier: The Story of Deep Space Nine." *Star Trek: Deep Space Nine,* season 2 DVD special feature, 2003.
The Rifleman, created by Arnold Laven, ABC, 1958–1963.
Space: 1999, created by Gerry and Sylvia Anderson, ITV, 1975–1977.
Space Patrol, created by Mike Moser, ABC, 1950–1955.
Stargate Atlantis, created by Brad Wright and Robert C. Cooper, Sci-Fi, 2004–2009.
Stargate SG-1, created by Brad Wright and Jonathan Glassner, Showtime, Sci-Fi, 1997–2007.
Stargate Universe, created by Brad Wright and Robert C. Cooper, Syfy, 2009–2011.
What We Left Behind: Looking Back at Star Trek: Deep Space Nine, directed by Ira Steven Behr and David Zappone. 455 Films, 2019.

Thinking Space

Identity and Cognition in Deep Space Nine

Franklin R. Halprin

Star Trek: Deep Space Nine (1993–1999) depicts a troubled galaxy in which socially proscribed meanings for identities drive stereotyping, produce intercultural violence, and manifest in large-scale political tensions. This pertains in particular to Cardassia's occupation of Bajor at the series' outset and subsequent shift into ally of the Dominion by the end. Yet, given the socially-constructed nature of identity, who is classified into what group and what features mark them out shifts given certain contexts and power dynamics. Cognitive sociology is the study of how cognition contains, in addition to individual mental elements, wide-ranging *social* dimensions. It enables for a deeper understanding of thoughts, words, and actions, particularly as they pertain to Major (later Colonel) Kira (Nana Visitor) and Legate Damar (Casey Biggs) as representatives of the Bajoran and Cardassian positions, respectively. A formulation of cognitive sociology's concept of "thought communities" as fluid—made possible by the fact that power asymmetries drive the classification process at *both* the community and individual level in an interrelated manner—serves as a means of explaining the role of racialized identity in Cardassia's execution of their position of superior oppressor of Bajor, transition to subservient pawn of the Dominion, and backlash to the latter as not being contradictory but in fact perfectly sensible.

The concept that multiplicities are at play in *Deep Space Nine* is not in and of itself new. Kathy E. Ferguson wrote that major characters "…are all 'in-betweens,' their liminality enabled by the station's heterotopic ability to be both linked to other spaces … and to contradict them, to loosen their demands for membership" (182). Ferguson focused on identity and subjective states as defined by being, including physical attributes, visible behaviors, and social roles, honing in on the character Dax (Terry Farrell) and the multiple roles they literally and figuratively embodied. This study departs in that it centers on identity as defined by thinking, namely as it pertains to membership, classification, and perceptions. There are thus different *kinds* of—and *categories* for—identity, which further reveals the multifaceted, dynamic, and non-essentialist nature of it. *Deep Space Nine's* portrayal of those and the political/power-infused conflicts which both produce and result from them are the foci here.

Cognitive sociologists explain "thought communities" by arguing that "we experience the world not only personally, through our senses, but impersonally, through membership in various social communities... [There are] unmistakably social ideas [which] do not originate in one's own mind" (Zerubavel, *Social Mindscapes* 7–8). Our perceptions of ourselves, others, ideas, and reality itself are mediated through the social values into which we are born and in which we are raised. This argues against a singular conceptualization of reality; as the sociologist Karl Mannheim pointed out, "there are modes of thought which cannot be adequately understood as long as their social origins are obscured" (2). That is to say, the way one thinks is not simply a product of their individuality and specific thinking, but is influenced by the styles of thought, expectations, and boundaries of possibility bestowed upon them by their upbringing. Upon the arrival of the Federation in Bajoran space, Major Kira Nerys is skeptical, viewing them as yet another untrustworthy occupying force. "I have been fighting for Bajoran independence since I was old enough to pick up a phaser," she explains. "We finally drive the Cardassians out, and what do our new leaders do? They call up the Federation and invite them right in!" ("Emissary"). The newly appointed head of the space station, Commander Benjamin Sisko (Avery Brooks), attempts to reassure her they are there to help, but she points out the Cardassians delivered the same line sixty years prior ("Emissary"). Any empirical differences between the Federation and Cardassia are subsumed by the filters imposed on them by Kira's thought community, based on its values and ways of thinking.

If one's individual cognition operates as a member of a certain group, what follows is the predilection to classify other individuals and additional aspects of life into groups and categories as well. Yet these boundaries stem from cultural values and group-specific cognitive processes, rather than reflecting an objective reality, as Eviatar Zerubavel observes: "The way we draw lines varies from one society to another and across historical periods within the same society" (*Fine Line* 2). The era unfolds rapidly and changes dramatically throughout the course of *Deep Space Nine*, and by "Rapture" (season five), Kira explicitly states to Worf (Michael Dorn) and Dax that she now feels otherwise about the Federation: "I didn't think Federation membership was right for Bajor. It hadn't been that long since the occupation…." In response to Worf's query about what changed her mind, she replied "My time on the station, my dealings with Starfleet, but mostly the Captain" ("Rapture"). As such, given the relationship between thinking at the three scales of individuals, social beings, and human beings, a shift in context—partly driven by changing power dynamics—contributes to Kira's reclassification of the Federation in her mindscape, since her membership in the earlier thought community was a fluid one (Zerubavel, *Social*).

Fluidity among thought communities also occurs because individuals "belong to several thought collectives at once" (Fleck 45). Consequently, one may struggle with their identity, as "individuality is a product of our many intersecting social group affiliations" (Brekhus, "The Rutgers School" 451). When Kohn-Ma Bajoran terrorists wreak havoc in the sector, Kira is sympathetic to them ("Past Prologue"). She identifies as a member of the same thought community, as she herself grew up as an insurgent on Bajor resisting the Cardassians. When she is torn as to whether to help them or turn against her own people, Odo (René Auberjonois) asks her, "Are they [your own people]?" Odo means to suggest that Kira is "one of them": a member of the Deep Space 9 crew and, as such, not affiliated with or similar to the terrorists. Yet it is entirely conceivable that her identity at this time exists in both thought communities at once, yielding tension and indecision. Zerubavel defines "optical pluralism" as the "many different mental lenses through which one can 'see' … [tying the] validity of those different views of that reality to particular standpoints rather than some absolute Truth" (*Social* 30). Furthermore, the constructedness of identity is laid bare here, as "mindscapes are neither naturally nor logically inevitable" (*Social* 9). Indeed, in a chapter on narrative storytelling techniques in *Star Trek* writ large, Marion Gymnich pointed out that "many episodes undermine the idea that there can be a single, authoritative view of the world, suggesting instead a highly subjective approach to reality…. *Star Trek* repeatedly confronts viewers with ontological questions about the nature and reliability of experience" (78).

Thus far, reclassification and multiple simultaneous classifications have been under discussion. Both of these processes may occur because of a shift in power, as Mary Douglas notes: "Ideas about separating, purifying, demarcating, and punishing transgressions [of boundaries of classifications] have as their main function to impose system onto an inherently untidy experience" (4). These norms are "cultural manifestations of power and control" (Zerubavel, *Plain Sight* 61). During the period of heightened Kohn-Ma activity, the Cardassians still hold a residual power over the Bajoran experience, having only recently withdrawn their occupation. Consequently, Bajoran society is reeling, and as such Cardassia indirectly influences the definition of the Kohn-Ma as being "terrorists." Yet by the next season the dynamics have shifted somewhat, as characters refer to a nativist movement called the Circle as an "extremist group," which is perhaps slightly different in that it suggests membership, albeit at the fringe. This group seeks to impose their own definitions, categorizations, and purifications of thought communities and physical communities by declaring "Bajor for the Bajorans; every other species is inferior" and must be compelled to leave ("The Homecoming"). In "Past Prologue," the Kohn-Ma terrorist Tahna (Jeffrey Nordling) also levies that phrase, but it and its implications are not received with the same gravity. Sisko observes that Bajor lacks strong leadership; by this time, the Bajoran people had become impatient with the government's inability to get things done, turning instead to the Circle in the expectation of achieving outcomes. A vacuum of centralized power contributes to the rise of a thought community with a very narrow, nationalistically-informed mental lens.

Fluidity and simultaneous thought community membership remain relevant here, as people may consciously maneuver thought community positionality in the service of their agendas. The commander of the Bajoran capital forces declares that the fight against the Circle would be Bajoran against Bajoran ("The Siege"). Odo's earlier description implied that the Circle had nativist objectives where all Bajorans are "in" and all non–Bajorans are "out," but the commander's rendition suggests different ideas as to who counts as Bajoran, and therefore who is in and who gets to be included. There could be multiple thought communities generally labeled as Bajoran, each one having slightly different culturally-mediated optical lenses, leading to different classifications of themselves and others' identities. Indeed, Kira remains in limbo regarding what viewpoint she holds, seeking instead to unite the communities against a common enemy. She spends the episode working to reveal how the Circle was unwittingly receiving its weapons from the Cardassians, who were plotting to make a return to Bajor. This strategy goes beyond the conventional aphorism "the enemy of my enemy is my friend." Rather, "things assume a distinctive identity only through being differentiated from other things" (Zerubavel, *Fine Line* 3). Kira seeks to levy Cardassian-ness and redefine power dynamics in order to reorient the optical lenses through which different Bajorans view themselves, others, *and* Cardassians, trying to create a singular, unified vision and thus consequently shift their senses of identity. Indeed, this had been a concern from the very start. In "Emissary," Captain Picard (Patrick Stewart) and Sisko discuss how Bajor is fractured by factionalism because it is no longer united against the Cardassians. At the time, the only unifying force which could stave off a looming civil war was religion; however, in "The Siege," Kira reintroduces Cardassia as a unifying force.

One of the advantages of focusing on cognitive differences, Zerubavel argues, is that it makes one less likely to be ethnocentric, because one will not assume identity characteristics are logical, rational, inevitable, objective, or essentialist (*Social*). Peter L. Berger and Thomas Luckmann establish some of the manners in which this social constructionism otherwise operates: reality of everyday life is taken for granted *as* reality and, linguistically, self-evidence means that "a thing *is* what it is called, and cannot be called anything else" (59, italics original). The episode "Cardassians" details a young Cardassian boy, Rugal (Vidal Peterson), who was raised by Bajoran parents and consequently came to hate his own race. There is nothing inherent in his genes or anatomy that dictates these patterns of thought. Rather, the cultural values at the scale of a particular society—the primary focus of cognitive sociology's thought communities—influence Rugal's cognition in this manner. While staying with the O'Briens, Keiko (Rosalind Chao) makes him a Cardassian stew, thinking he would enjoy food from his homeland. He pushes the bowl away, though, because he does not *identify* as a Cardassian, regardless of his phenotype.

According to Zerubavel, "The ability to ignore the uniqueness of items and regard them as typical members of categories is a prerequisite for classifying any group or phenomena" (*Fine Line* 17). This tends to be referred to in sociology as "typification," where one thinks in terms of types, rather than the concrete. As such, one expects interaction through typified acts, as typified persons, having typified expectations of others. Perhaps one might call this stereotyping. As Rugal is positioned in a non-intuitive thought community, Miles O'Brien (Colm Meaney) moves from one thought community to another based on a shift in context which reveals to him the nonessentialism of cognition and identity. Miles, having previously exhibited some racism/specism towards groups with whom the Federation had had turbulent relations, declares that "'gentleness' was bred out of Cardassians long ago" ("Cardassians"). Keiko reprimands Miles, and indeed Miles learns not to be so judgmental, assessing the individual instead. He subsequently tells Rugal, "You can't judge an entire race; I've met some Cardassians I haven't liked, and some that I have. Like you" ("Cardassians"). Framing is "the act of surrounding situations, acts, or objects with mental brackets that basically transform their meaning" (Zerubavel, *Fine Line* 11). Miles' prior thought community was one wherein the frames ascribed certain generalized, negative meaning to the Cardassian identity. Yet, given the position that cognition is more than mental but simultaneously depends on socialization, he moves fluidly—though perhaps not seamlessly—from one to another with a different framing and, as such, he perceives Cardassian-ness in a more nuanced and not inevitable, typified, nor essentialist manner.

Building on typifying and stereotyping, a manner in which thought communities tend to engage with identity is via "lumping and splitting." To do so, Zerubavel explains, is to "deliberately ignore differences within mental clusters, but pay special attention to differences between clusters…[we] inflate distances across mental divides" (*Fine Line* 27). Kira and key Cardassians struggle mightily with these dynamics. When a wanted war criminal named Maritza (Harris Yulin) comes into possession of the Deep Space 9 crew in the episode "Duet," he describes with unsettling pride the horrifying details of their treatment of Bajoran "scum" imprisoned in a concentration camp. He does not distinguish between any Bajoran individuals or have a nuanced perspective of them, instead lumping them all together into the same category by playing down differences. He tells Kira "What you call genocide, I call a day's work" ("Duet"). His membership in this particular thought community and its cognitive framing processes, fed by Cardassia's power over Bajor, contributes to his assessing Bajoran identity as well as the moral obligations of his own identity group in this particular way. Identities blur later, though, when it is revealed that this man is a clerk impersonating the camp commandant. He is motivated to do so because he feels that *all* Cardassians are guilty, lumping his own species, and expects his ensuing trial and execution to bring justice. It is Kira, ultimately, who learns not to discriminate based on species and to better recognize the complicated nature of individuality: "What you're asking for is another murder. Enough good people have already died" ("Duet"). Learning that he is a good man, even if he is Cardassian, she conveys to him, "What you did was very honorable. If Cardassia is going to change, it's going to need people like you" ("Duet"). In this instance, she performs the opposite of lumping. By splitting, she expands the differences between Maritza and other Cardassians, or at least what she assumes to be the traits of Cardassian-ness as indicated by their overall treatment of Bajorans. Her movement into a new thought community dynamic and its conclusions are reinforced when a disgruntled Bajoran stabs Maritza to death. Distraught, Kira asks why, since he is not the dreaded commandant. The assassin lumps all Cardassians together, responding, "He is Cardassian; that's reason enough" ("Duet"). Defeated, Kira weakly replies that it is not.

Fluid movement among thought communities can be interrelated with the process of lumping and splitting when power shifts are in question. Kira moves fluidly into a different thought community sometime later, albeit under distress. When a bitter Cardassian leader—scarred in an attack Kira's terror cell carried out during the occupation—targets former members and kidnaps her, he suggests he was innocent, along with the women and children ("The Darkness and the Light"). He therefore attempts to split. This looks like an act by an individual, but Zerubavel argues that "we do this organizing as members of particular thought communities, not individuals" ("Lumping" 427). Perhaps, then, the Cardassian is inviting Kira, given the shift in power dynamics between Bajor and Cardassia since the occupation, to join an already extant thought community who classified identities in this manner. This is an example of power influencing the cognitive process at *both* individual and communal levels. Yet Kira is defiant, qualifying her anger by detailing how Cardassia's fifty-year occupation resulted in fifteen million Bajoran deaths while Cardassia profited. She concludes, "you were all legitimate targets" ("The Darkness and the Light"). Her cognition therefore returns to an older Bajoran thought community whose values stem in part from the power asymmetries between themselves and the Cardassian occupants of the planet. She lumps all Cardassians together as being the same, a regression from what she learned from her encounter with Maritza.

Zerubavel argues that lumping and splitting compel "a mental item to belong to no more than one category... [a result of] fear and anxiety over twilight zones... [and] aversion to ambiguity" (*Fine Line* 34–36). Ultimately, fluidity and simultaneous occupation of multiple thought communities returns as a relevant factor in "The Darkness and the Light," as innate aversions to those twilight zones in theory contradict the messiness of reality, leading to inter- and intrapersonal conflict. One might see connections here to the relationship between Rugal and Miles: there can be good and bad people within any race/identity/thought community, and furthermore, Cardassian women and children could potentially be just as innocent, guilty, or complicit as Maritza.

The multiplicity of thought communities, lack of homogeneity, and nonessentialism can be navigated via the power-infused and context-defining process of marking, made evident in *Deep Space Nine* by the tensions manifesting in the theme of undergrounds versus collaborators. According to Joan Emerson, "A reality can hardly seem self-evident if a person is simultaneously aware of a counter-reality" (76). First, subjectivity and power are rampant in the acknowledgment that Cardassians might label a group "terrorists," whereas Bajorans label that same group as "the underground" or something reminiscent of "the resistance" or "freedom fighters." This is because, as Wayne Brekhus observes, "Identity is more than self-definition; it includes individual behavior, cultural attribution from others, and structural location" ("Social Marking" 499). The process of "marking," Brekhus defines, pertains to "the way the 'social mind' actively perceives one side of a contrast while ignoring the other side as epistemologically unproblematic" (500). From the perspective of Cardassia, Bajorans are viewed generally normatively (albeit negatively) with the exception of the underground, who are socially marked and attended to as such. The latter stand out because, as Brekhus explains elsewhere, there is "tremendous normative power of the unmarked; the key element in marking is that which is disattended and normalized without direct acknowledgement" (*Culture and Cognition* 26). They are not "regular Bajorans," but are defined against regularity.

This approach comports with Ashley Doane, who argues that attention to dominant groups has looked at attitudes towards subordinate groups, especially pertaining to exploitation and control, but one must look at the characteristics of dominant groups themselves, especially their identities (375). The self, Ruth Frankenburg clarifies, where it is part of a dominant group, does not have to name itself (196). As such, "collaborators" are only labeled so by Bajorans who disapproved of Cardassia's overlordship; they are marked in this manner and attract additional attention. To Cardassians, whereas collaborators could be identified as a specific group of individuals, they are still adhering to the normative cognitive framework, which is a function of Cardassia's power at the time of the occupation.

Power not only produces and assigns marks—in this case "underground" and "collaborator"—but yields differences in how thought communities process and understand each mark. "Collaborator" is a less distinctive mark than "the underground" and, once again, this can operate at the individual level in addition to that of the community. A flashback episode explains how Gul Dukat (Marc Alaimo) brought Odo to Terok Nor (the Cardassian designation for Deep Space 9 before the Federation took possession of it) in order to solve a murder ("Necessary Evil"). Odo is hesitant, countering that back on Bajor he solved petty disputes because he was viewed as a "neutral observer." This is because Bajorans do not see him as one of them or as a member of their community or identity in any way. This may have been advantageous in that he served as an effective adjudicator. Dukat reinforces this sentiment of separateness, stating that Odo indeed is "is one of them" ("Necessary Evil"). Dukat further justifies his choice of Odo because his shapeshifting ability could enable him to investigate and move about effectively and stealthily. Yet it is later revealed that his true motive for choosing Odo is that he himself has to remain distant from the case because it is related to an issue of collaborators, with whom he is affiliated, versus the underground. Collaborators do have a specific label, or mark, but are categorized within the wider Cardassian vision. On the other hand, the underground exists markedly outside of it. The boundaries of the thought communities which follow therefore shift depending on the historical moment and extent of each group's power, especially when considered in conjunction with the earlier discussion of the Kohn-Ma.

Power can explicitly weaponize the ambiguity of identity and fluidity of membership in thought communities, predicating it on certain assumptions about markedness. In "Second Skin," the issue of undergrounds and collaborators manifests within the ranks of Cardassia as well. Kira is expected to believe that she was in actuality a Cardassian named Iliana who had been disguised so as to infiltrate the Bajoran resistance. Kira wakes up from being kidnapped to find her features "restored." Yet it is later revealed that the Cardassian intelligence agency, the Obsidian Order, is trying to entrap Iliana's father (Lawrence Pressman), a high-ranking politician who is a dissident against the established Cardassian hierarchy. The Obsidian Order expects Kira's cognition and optical lenses to adjust according to their plan, based on the frames they impart. Not only do they fail, but Kira comes to sympathize with the politician and wishes him luck in finding his missing daughter. Perhaps Kira is predisposed to identify with him as they are both members of undergrounds resisting the Cardassian government. Yet the political dissenters on Cardassia hold different grievances and cannot be seamlessly equated with the Bajoran resistance. Perhaps there are multiple renditions of the same *kind* of thought community, depending on context, location, and history. Ultimately, the homogeneity of undergrounds and collaborators, both on Bajor and Cardassia, is called into question.

Tumultuous external circumstances, especially recalibration of power dynamics, can presage dramatic shifts in cognition, patterns of identity, and construction of thought communities. Doane is helpful here as well: "Dominant group members are less likely to be reminded of social and cultural differences on a daily basis" (377). Throughout the course of *Deep Space Nine*, Cardassia's political-military influence and esteem in the Alpha Quadrant decline dramatically. They move from being a dominant group to, if not a subordinate group, at least a less influential group. Consequently, they become more cognizant of their standing, self-identification, and perceptions of how others identify and classify them. Indeed, reclaiming status and respect—in addition to killing Klingons who remain from a previous war and eliminating Maquis colonies—are the primary motives, according to Gul Dukat, for Cardassia joining the Dominion ("By Inferno's Light"). Doane continues that "social discourse … is shifted from barriers erected by the dominant group to the cultural characteristics of subordinate groups" (385). Cardassians have moved from being the barrier builders who are unmarked due to their power to a weaker, marked group increasingly self-conscious of their characteristics, which they construct as being flawed and fallen. Their sense of identity is shattered as they enter an existential crisis, and as such a conscious effort to shift power once more ostensibly promises an outward restructuring of the galactic order and inward recalibration of thought community processes. Yet given the challenges of navigating identity, along with cognitive sociology's positioning of memory in the structure of a thought community, one can begin to understand why their alliance collapses.

The early sociologist Émile Durkheim declares that "society has its own nature, whose requirements are different from those of our nature as individuals" ("Dualism" 44). As such, Worf is prescient in declaring that Cardassians are a proud people but that the Dominion is treating them like second class citizens, which might bode ill ("The Changing Face of Evil"). Damar assumes the mantle of leadership and cooperation with the Dominion but, following a questionable tactical decision by the Dominion's primary field commander, the Vorta Weyoun (Jeffrey Combs), Damar's previously weakened but now subsequently resurgent identity as a Cardassian drives him to spearhead a political shift in the sector. When a half million Cardassians die in battle for a strategically-worthless planet, Damar asks Weyoun how many more of his people would be condemned to such a fate. Weyoun scoffs, responding, "*Your* people?" If they were loyal to the Dominion, he continues, they would die willingly as they are all one people ("Strange Bedfellows"). Weyoun attempts to subsume individuality and a variety of identities in the name of cohesiveness and harmony, advocating for a single identity for the purposes of politics and power. Alfred Schutz and Thomas Luckmann explain that, "Different 'versions' of general knowledge can, given certain socio-historical presuppositions, become special property of social groups, classes, etc. in the form of 'ideologies'" (318). Yet Weyoun's ideology-constructing rhetoric ultimately backfires, as he is not able to cognitively align the present and past in Damar's mind by making his own presuppositions palatable. However, by way of memory, Damar maintains differentiation and loyalties stemming from ascription to an identity and thought community that predates and overpowers the new one based on new motives, announcing that Cardassian armies will attack Dominion posts and urging all Cardassians to resist.

Berger and Luckmann describe "re-socialization," as where "the past is reinterpreted to conform with the present reality" (163). Damar's call to resistance seems ironic, given these are the same sentiments and experiences they imposed on Bajor, who had responded in the same way. Indeed, in "When it Rains…," Sisko assigns Kira to train Damar's troops for a guerrilla insurgency. Damar admits to a subordinate that he hated Kira in the past, but things have changed, and they need her now. In the following episode ("Tracking into the Wind"), a Cardassian lieutenant named Rusot (John Vickery), who disagrees with this plan and wants to "restore Cardassia to its former glory" attempts to have Kira killed. Instead, Damar kills him, explaining, "He was my friend, but the Cardassia he knew is gone" ("Tacking into the Wind").

As Zerubavel explains, "the content of our memories and how we mentally 'place' the past is affected by the social environment" (*Social* 100). Sure enough, since Damar and Rusot share the same memory but act in vastly different manners, something more must be happening here. The two characters share the same current social environment, but how they resultantly "place" the past operates differently. Zerubavel stipulates that it is "not only what we come to remember as members of a particular thought community, but *how* we remember it … much of what we remember is filtered through subsequent interpretation and the particular 'light' in which we recall them" (*Social* 87). Rusot remembers the Cardassian past in a motivating light, which contributes to his decision making in the present: one that encourages restoration aspirations. Damar, on the other hand, remembers the past as a nostalgic time, but one to which they cannot return and, as such, acts differently in the present. One possible conclusion is that the two must be members of different thought communities.

On the other hand, another possible explanation is that perhaps despite the more structural motivations of cognitive sociology, there is an individual-scale process happening here in conjunction with that of the communal level. Zerubavel defines what he calls the "Rigid Mind" in the following way:

> the world is basically made up of discrete, insular entities separated from one another by wide mental gulfs. Distinctively characterized by its unyielding commitment to the mutual exclusivity of "islands of meaning" … the rigid mind allows no "contact" whatsoever between them and eschews any effort to build "bridges" across those divides ["The Rigid" 1095].

Rusot fits into this category. Mental rigidity denies him the fluidity of movement from one thought community to another, despite the shifts in power and context so prevalent at this point in the series. Zerubavel goes on to describe the "Fuzzy Mind" as not being preferable either, as it is still necessary to have some degree of order and structure ("The Rigid" 1098). Rather, he concludes, the "Flexible Mind" is ideal because it "sculpts complex, intricate identities that are based on a 'both/and' logic. In other words, it allows for the possibility, and even promotes the idea, of maintaining multiple identities simultaneously … without having to give up any one of them in order to claim another" ("The Rigid" 1100). Damar is able to remember and value the Cardassian past, yet does not let that restrict his cognitive movement. Thus, one may argue for a dialectical experience. Rather than the unidirectional process where "we perceive things not through our own unique mental lens, but the shared mental lens of those around us in our social networks," one may conclude that society-scale and individual-scale identities evolve in tandem, as different individuals may react differently to shifts in power and context and consequently move differently through thought communities (Brekhus, "The Rutgers School" 452).

Flexible Mindedness and memory patterns can specifically influence the outcomes of power shifts and identity struggles, including the ones between Cardassia and the Dominion when the issue of "collaborators" appears once again. As Kira trains Cardassian guerrillas, Rusot is apprehensive about "killing our own," instead wanting to focus on sites occupied by the Dominion's warriors the Jem'Hadar and their other allies the Breen ("When it Rains..."). Kira understands but disagrees, adding that those Cardassians are "collaborators." Rusot seems to derive his identity from thinking within the frames of a race-based thought community that includes all Cardassians, regardless of their political allegiance. Damar, on the other hand, yields to Kira on this matter. This is the moment of consequence, as Damar's decision enables Cardassian society to rise up against the Dominion. Yet the explorations of identity and memory continue as some Cardassians attempt to provoke Kira by reminding her that Odo collaborated with Cardassia during their occupation of Bajor. Angrily, Kira disagrees with that label, retorting, "I guess that depends on your definition of 'collaborator,'" and that they have a "difference of opinion" ("When it Rains..."). Such a reaction is a strong instance of resocialization. Kira conveniently reinterprets the past to conform with the present, and in so doing fluidly moves out of and contradicts the dictates of her prior underground/freedom fighter thought community. One may have come away from "Necessary Evil" conceptualizing Odo as a neutral go-between, but the fact that Dukat gave him the assignment and he acquiesced lends credence to the Cardassians labeling him as a collaborator. Here, too, there might be an instance of simultaneous occupation of several identities and communities.

The interplay between individual scale and community scale processes of cognition which pertain to identity helps explain Cardassian and Bajoran experiences as the former occupy the latter and, later on, serve as ally of the Dominion. Patterns of thought, as cognitive sociologists have explained, do not solely originate in particular persons but are shaped substantially by previous thought patterns and socially-mediated expectations. Yet individuality remains influential in *Deep Space Nine*, as characters' minds throughout the show are not confined. Rather, as power shifts and contexts change, they—Kira and Damar in particular—seem to either move from one thought community to another or exist simultaneously in multiple ones. The multifaceted character of thought communities, particularly in conjunction with the role of outside forces on the values, classification systems, and frames that inform them, enables for an explanation of Cardassian and Bajoran actions that reveals not hypocrisy, but nuance.

WORKS CITED AND CONSULTED

Barba, Michael. "Somewhere Out Beyond the Stars: Orientalism and *Star Trek Deep Space Nine*." *One World Periphery Reads the Other: Knowing the "Oriental" in the Americas and the Iberian Peninsula*, edited by Ignacio Lopez-Calvo. Cambridge Scholars Publishing, 2010, pp. 380–392.

Berger, Peter L., and Thomas Luckmann. *The Social Construction of Reality: A Treatise in the Sociology of Knowledge*. Anchor Books, 1966.

Brekhus, Wayne H. *Culture and Cognition*. Polity Press, 2015.

_____. "The Rutgers School: A Zerubavelian Culturalist Cognitive Sociology." *European Journal of Social Theory*, vol. 10, no. 3, 2007, pp. 448–464.

_____. "Social Marking and the Mental Coloring of Identity: Sexual Identity Construction and Maintenance in the United States." *Sociological Forum*, vol. 11, no. 3, 1996, pp. 497–522.

_____. "A Sociology of the Unmarked: Redirecting Our Focus." *Sociological Theory*, vol. 16, no. 1, 1998, pp. 34–51.

Doane, Ashley T., Jr. "Dominant Group Ethnic Identity in the United States: The Role of 'Hidden' Ethnicity in Intergroup Relations." *The Sociological Quarterly*, vol. 38, no. 3, 1997, pp. 375–397.

Douglas, Mary. *Purity and Danger: An Analysis of Concepts of Pollution and Taboo*. Routledge, 1966.

Durkheim, Émile. "Dualism of Human Nature and its Social Conditions." *Durkheimian Studies*, vol. 11, 2005, pp. 35–45.

_____. *The Elementary Forms of Religious Life*. Translated by Carol Cosman. Oxford UP, 2001.

Emerson, Joan P. "Behavior in Private Places: Sustaining Definitions of Reality in Gynecological Examinations." *Recent Sociology*, vol. 74, no. 2, 2008, pp. 74–97.

Ferguson, Kathy E. "This Species Which Is Not One: Identity Practices in *Star Trek: Deep Space Nine*." *Strategies*, vol. 15, no. 2, 2002, pp. 181–195.

Fleck, Ludwik. *Genesis and Development of a Scientific Fact*. Translated by Fred Bradley and Thaddeus J. Trenn. U of Chicago P, 1979.

Frankenberg, Ruth. *White Women, Race Matters: The Social Construction of Whiteness*. U of Minnesota P, 1993.

Gymnich, Marion. "Exploring Inner Spaces: Authoritative Narratives and Subjective Worlds in *Star Trek: Deep Space Nine, Voyager,* and *Enterprise*." *Narrative Strategies in Television Series*, edited by Gaby Allrath and Marion Gymnich. Palgrave Macmillan, 2005, pp. 62–79.

Mannheim, Karl. *Ideology and Utopia: An Introduction to the Sociology of Knowledge*. Translated by Louis Wirth and Edward Shils. Harcourt, 1936.

Mullaney, Jamie L. "Making it 'Count': Mental Weighing and Identity Attribution." *Symbolic Interaction*, vol. 22, no. 3, 1999, pp. 269–283.

Schutz, Alfred, and Thomas Luckmann. *The Structures of the Life-World*. Northwestern UP, 1973.

Turner, Victor. *The Forest of Symbols: Aspects of the Ndembu Ritual*. Cornell UP, 1967.

Waugh, Linda R. "Marked and Unmarked: A Choice Between Unequals in Semiotic Structure." *Seimotica*, vol. 38, no. 3/4, 1982, pp. 299–318.

Zerubavel, Eviatar. *The Fine Line: Making Distinctions in Everyday Life*. U of Chicago P, 1991.

_____. *Hidden in Plain Sight: The Social Structure of Irrelevance*. Oxford UP, 2015.

_____. "Lumping and Splitting: Note on Social Classification." *Sociological Forum*, vol. 11, no. 3, 1996, pp. 421–433.

_____. "The Rigid, the Fuzzy, and the Flexible: Notes on the Mental Sculpting of Academic Identity." *Social Research*, vol. 62, no. 4, 1995, pp. 1093–1106.

_____. *Social Mindscapes: An Invitation to Cognitive Sociology*. Harvard UP, 1997.

Trauma, Psychological Development, and the Triumph of Kira Nerys

SHERRY GINN

As noted by authors in this collection and elsewhere, *Deep Space Nine* presented a radically different *Star Trek* than *The Original Series* and *The Next Generation* (e.g., Nolan; Gregory). The most obvious difference is in its serialized storytelling, something which, although common in daytime soap operas, was not common in prime-time dramas during the 1990s. Providing viewers with an overarching story was considered anathema to studio executives who doubted the prime-time audience would be willing to stay with a developing plotline, especially one that unfolded over multiple years. One advantage, however, for the viewer watching a series that aired for multiple years was the opportunity to witness characters grow, change, and evolve over time. Viewers watching *The Original Series* or *The Next Generation* were unlikely to see much dynamism in the characters' personalities. Bones (DeForest Kelley) continued to complain that he was a "doctor, Jim," not a "fill-in-the-blank." Spock (Leonard Nimoy) continued to belie his human half, not actually reconciling the dichotomy in his hybridity until the *Star Trek* films of the 1980s. Lt. Commander Will Riker (Jonathan Frakes) was still refusing to acknowledge his feelings for Counselor Deanna Troi (Marina Sirtis) when *The Next Generation* ended in 1994, while Data (Brent Spiner) was still yearning to be human. Despite numerous episodes that explored these aspects of the characters, they never really changed in their regard toward these attributes, until (and always in the filmic versions of the characters) they make sudden leaps forward.

Deep Space Nine was different. Perhaps through the sheer power of Ira Steven Behr's vision and Rick Berman's focus on creating and producing *Voyager*, *Deep Space Nine* generated some of the most well-written and well-rounded characters in the franchise. For the ensemble of characters inhabiting space station Deep Space 9, life was anything but status quo.

Much like its contemporary interstellar way station Babylon 5, Deep Space 9 was a spatial nexus, a point where multiple races and species of beings could converge, converse, and commerce. Each particular character had his or her reason for being on the station. Commander Benjamin Sisko (Avery Brooks) assumed command under orders, but only intended to stay for a short period of time before resigning from Starfleet and returning home to Earth with his son, Jake (Cirroc Lofton). For Major Kira Nerys (Nana Visitor), it was an attempt to help her planet, Bajor, deal with the consequences of a more than fifty-year occupation by a villainous race called the Cardassians. For Miles O'Brien (Colm Meaney), it was a promotion of sorts, allowing him to assume the role of Chief of Operations and bring his extensive experience with engineering to a station fraught with damage and peril. Doctor Julian Bashir (Siddig El Fadil) jumped at the chance for the position on Deep Space 9, looking forward to practicing what he called "frontier medicine," much to the irritation of Kira ("Emissary"). Jadzia Dax (Terry Farrell) was happy to reunite with her old friend Sisko and serve as his Science Officer. The Ferengi bar owner Quark "decided" to stay on the station after the Cardassians left (and Sisko essentially blackmailed him); his primary purpose was to make money, as much as possible. Finally, the shape-shifter Odo (René Auberjonois) had nowhere else to go. Odo had been on the station for several years; he served as Head of Security during the Cardassian occupation, and he saw no reason to leave the station once Starfleet assumed command. It was his home.

When these people encounter each other and the station itself, their lives change in more ways than they could ever anticipate. For each of these beings, arriving on Deep Space 9 represents a turning or transition point in their lives. In some significant way, each of the main characters of the show arrives on Deep Space 9 in need of identity codification. The station represents, for them, spatial newness, a fresh place to not only test out a new self, but the place where that self will ultimately be discovered. Sisko arrives adrift, mourning his lost wife and questioning his Starfleet-centered quiddity. O'Brien seeks a chance to jump from the lower decks and take on a role of authority and leadership. Bashir, freshly minted from Starfleet Medical, seeks to test and prove his mettle and his masculinity (his construct of the station as the "frontier" belies his vision of how Deep Space 9 may mold him); Dax, freshly joined with her symbiont host, seeks out her former mentee Sisko as an anchor in establishing her new sense of self.

It is not only the Starfleet officers who find Deep Space 9 shaping newly formed senses of self; Odo's journey for his heritage and his people frames a significant part of the series narrative, and Quark's transformations due to his contact with the Federation likewise reflect the shaping of identity structures. Yet Odo and Quark are not new arrivals to the station; former residents, it is not the station that alters them so much as their new associations with those who now live there. Of all of the major non–Federation figures, only Kira is new to the station (in her current role), and it is her psychological journey— where space and association meet—that is perhaps the most compelling of all.

Kira Nerys is one of the most dynamic, most interesting, and perhaps the best female character in all of *Star Trek*. I state this not as hyperbole; I truly believe this, and have stated so previously (*Our Space, Our Place* 113– 116, 151–153). I agree with Frank Oglesbee, who observed that "Kira fights well with words, integrity, cunning, and adaptability honed from years of resistance.... But there's more to Kira than a good punch or a quick draw with a phaser"— much more (266). This essay examines how much more by asking questions such as *why* Kira is this way and *how* she develops into one of *Star Trek's* most enduring, most fully-formed characters. To get at these answers, I propose to examine what happens to Kira on Deep Space 9 following her first meeting with Sisko. This is a turning point in her life, one which begins her reflection upon the life she has led and the choices that she has made. To accomplish this end, I will use Kira's history from both the series and novels (e.g., J.M. Dillard's *Emissary*) written during the years in which *Deep Space Nine* aired as well as the relaunch novels which were written about the station and its characters beginning in 2000 (e.g., S.D. Perry's *Unity*). These sources allow me to explore Kira's psyche, investigating what we know about her childhood in order to understand how she became the woman she is. Although the novels may not officially be canon, the rich character development contained therein (which generally builds on what the show has already described) allows this psychological approach to understanding Kira's character in the full flower of psychosocial development.

My examination includes psychological theories about attachment, cognitive development, identity formation, and transition in order to determine how each is reflected in her story. I scrutinize the ways in which interpersonal relationships—and lack thereof—shape her character. Yet especially important to her adult development is her relationship with Commander, later Captain, Benjamin Sisko—her senior officer, Emissary to the Prophets, and eventually friend—which begins in adversity and ends with genuine respect and affection. Kira's story ultimately demonstrates the tragedy of deprivation, trauma, and loss, yet also illustrates how one can overcome adverse childhood events and create a new self.

Psychological Influences on Kira's Traumatic Childhood: Trust and Attachment

Kira spent her childhood with her parents and two brothers in the Singha refugee camp, which was, in reality, a forced-labor camp ("Kira

Nerys"). Her father told Kira that her mother died when she was three years old, and she spends the next nine years or so in the camp. Kira joins the Resistance when she is twelve; this may seem young, although she notes that children younger than her also joined ("Duet"). The Resistance is eventually successful in their efforts to win their freedom back from the brutal Cardassian occupation. After the occupation Kira joins the Bajoran Militia and is given the rank of Major. She is posted to Terok Nor, renamed Deep Space 9 by the United Federation of Planets, and reluctantly accepts the order to serve as the Bajoran liaison to the Federation and second-in-command to Commander Benjamin Sisko ("Emissary"). She resents Starfleet's interference in Bajoran affairs and is angry that she has to serve as Sisko's second, telling him bluntly, "I don't believe the Federation has any business being here" ("Emissary"). Throughout the first couple of seasons, we see her anger, and her anger is justified. Her planet had been ruthlessly invaded, and her people conquered by the Cardassians, a race that had decimated the natural resources on their own planet and thus sought them from other worlds through conquest (McCormack). The Cardassians enslaved Bajor's population, forcing men, women, and children to work in various mines with little or no food or water. The subjugation of Bajor had profound effects upon Kira's development into adulthood; several psychological theories are particularly relevant to that development and illustrate how Kira relates to people in her life as well as situations that occur around her. These theories consider childhood events to be defining features of development, with significant ramifications as one matures.

Early twentieth-century psychology was dominated by Sigmund Freud's Theory of Psychosexual Development and Jean Piaget's Cognitive-Developmental Theory.[1] Freud was particularly interested in elucidating the stages through which the individual's personality developed from birth into adolescence. Piaget, on the other hand, was concerned with the changes that occurred in the way children and adolescents think. Each theory was important for shaping the field of developmental psychology; however, neither postulated development past adolescence, proposing instead that human beings' personalities and cognitive structures were molded by childhood experiences. Neither Freud nor Piaget proposed that significant changes occurred beyond adolescence and into adulthood, unlike theories proposed by Erik Erikson and Daniel Levinson. Nevertheless, certain aspects of Piaget's theory provide some insight into Kira's psychology.

Unlike Piaget, Erikson proposed that development of the personality proceeds through a series of eight stages, with each stage occurring in response to the social demands placed upon the individual by his or her environment.[2] An individual must resolve a conflict occurring in response to these demands. Resolution of the conflict leads to growth and psychological development. That is, resolving the conflict at any particular stage compels the individual toward growth, and failure to resolve the conflict results in failure to develop. Each of Erikson's stages is a time of increased vulnerability but also a time of challenge and potential, representing a turning point in life.

Erikson labeled his first stage Trust vs. Mistrust, and it encompasses the first year of life. An infant must come to trust that his or her caregivers will fulfill his or her needs for food, warmth, comfort, and love. Feelings of physical comfort coupled with a minimal amount of fear about the future set the stage for the lifelong expectation that the world will be a good place in which to live. When children fail to have their needs met, they come to mistrust not only their caregivers, but also others in their social environment as well.

Kira is born during the Cardassian occupation of Bajor. Life is extremely difficult: there is not enough food to go around, and stronger people prey upon the weak, stealing the little food available. Kira's mother, Kira Maru (Leslie Hope), is chosen to become a "comfort woman" for Cardassian soldiers serving on Terok Nor, but Kira does not learn this until she is grown, and only finds out because Gul Dukat (Marc Alaimo) tells her. Kira's childhood memories are of a family torn apart by the Cardassians. Her father, Kira Taban (Thomas Kopache), had led her to believe that her mother died when she was three; Taban referred to Maru as the bravest women he had ever met.

Kira's world is turned upside down on what would have been her mother's sixtieth birthday when she receives a transmission from Gul Dukat (Marc Alaimo), who claims that Maru was his lover until she died ("Wrongs Darker than Death or Night"). Kira does not believe Dukat, but he knows enough about Maru to plant a seed of doubt. Unable to stop thinking about it, Kira begs Sisko, as the Emissary, to give her permission to use the Orb of Time in order to travel back to discover the truth for herself.

Kira remembers that her childhood occurred during a time of great danger; the smallest incident could lead to serious repercussions. Failure to follow an order given by a Cardassian could lead to death or enslavement in one of the many mining or ore-processing facilities on Bajor or Terok Nor. Kira's mother actually had a facial scar that she received because a Cardassian soldier deemed she had not shown him the proper respect. Following Kira's use of the Orb of Time, she arrives at Singha and for a brief moment re-experiences the brutality of her and her family's existence. However, she also observes Maru feeding her children *prior* to feeding herself. Maru obviously loves her children, and Maru knows that becoming Dukat's mistress will ensure that her children survive, at least for the time in which she lives with him. Kira's trust in the reality of her childhood is shaken; it is possible that other "truths" she has accepted about her life might also be false. However, the trust she developed with respect to her parents as a young child appears to be justified.

Another theory relevant to Kira's childhood is attachment theory.[3] Attachment is a lasting emotional bond that one person has with another person, and attachments begin to form in early infancy. These bonds influence a person's close relationships throughout life, and a failure of attachment can have lasting emotional consequences for children who fail to develop such bonds with others. Four types of attachment bonds have been observed in research with infants and their caregivers. The most common form is secure attachment, in which an infant obtains both comfort and confidence from the presence of his or her caregiver. Children who are securely attached trust their caregivers to be there for them; their caregivers respond to their needs for food, warmth, comfort, and security appropriately and as necessary. These children become more independent and confident with age. Other children unfortunately receive inadequate or haphazard care from their caregivers, and their anxiety and insecurity around those caregivers is easily seen. Such children are not as independent later in childhood and adolescence; nor are they as confident as their securely attached peers (Feldman 248–251).

Based upon her recollections of her childhood and the glimpse we get when she travels back in time, Kira exhibits behavior that indicates she was securely attached to her parents. When she meets her family at Singha, she introduces herself as Luma Rahl, and proceeds to fight off men who would steal the family's food. Almost immediately a group of Cardassian soldiers arrive at the camp and begin choosing women to become "comfort women" for those soldiers stationed on Terok Nor. Kira allows herself to be chosen at the same time as Maru so that she can not only spend time with a mother she thought she had lost when she was three, but also to learn the truth about Dukat's revelation. Much to Kira's dismay, she watches as her mother is seduced by Dukat: he heals her facial scar; he gives her beautiful clothes; the food available for her to eat is overwhelming. In addition, Dukat is charming, considerate, and attentive, behavior in stark contrast to his actions with respect to the Bajorans living on the planet and on Terok Nor. Kira calls Maru a collaborator for engaging in a relationship with Dukat, one in which she appears to be complicit, and Kira plans to kill Maru (and Dukat). She is unable to go through with her plan, however, when she watches Maru's reaction to a message from her father with respect to the children. It is in this message that Kira hears her father Taban call her mother the bravest woman he ever met. Taban understands that Maru's only responses upon being chosen as a "comfort woman" were to refuse and probably be killed along with her family or to submit. Maru chose to submit, thereby saving her family; however, Kira is appalled to see that Maru has developed a loving relationship with Dukat, one she learns lasted for seven years. All evidence within the episode suggests that Maru is besotted with Dukat. She tells Kira that she wishes she could explain her relationship with him. It is possible that Maru does love Dukat and is not just complying with his desires in order to ensure the safety of her children. It is possible that Maru is experiencing Stockholm Syndrome, or capture-bonding, a form of post-traumatic stress disorder (PTSD) in which hostages and other victims begin to identify, sympathize and empathize with, and eventually defend their captors (see Demarest for more on this topic). Yet, as Kira tells Sisko upon her return to Deep Space 9, Maru lived in luxury with Dukat while thousands of Bajorans died. Kira is devastated to learn that everything she believed about her mother was a lie. Sisko points out that it was Maru's choice to remain on Terok Nor as Dukat's mistress, but such a fact does little to assuage Kira's anger at her mother and her horror at being the daughter of a woman she considers to have been a collaborator.

Psychological Influences on Kira's Traumatic Childhood: Egocentrism and Identity Formation

The foundation upon which Kira has built her life, trust and attachment, is shaken by the events of her journey into the past, but it is not broken. Prior to that journey, Kira remembered events of her childhood fondly, such as when she talked about finger painting when she was a little girl ("The Circle"). Even in the midst of tragedy, life continues. We never learn what happened to Kira's brothers in the series; their deaths are mentioned in the novel *The Soul Key* (Woods). Kira Taban was killed by the Cardassians as he tried to defend his village, and Kira was devastated to learn that he had died while she was away on a mission for the Resistance ("Ties of Blood and Water"). According to Piaget, young children take much to heart and have a tendency to blame themselves for events that happen to those around them, especially when they are young.

Based upon observations of children's attempts to solve problems, Piaget proposed that cognitive development proceeds through a series of stages, with each stage having to be successfully mastered before the individual can advance to the next. He called the first stage the sensorimotor period, which lasts from birth to about two years. This stage provides the basis of all cognitive development; herein the child begins to interact with the world. As she or he grows older, the child seeks new and more interesting stimulation. At approximately eight months, children develop intentionality (i.e., they begin manipulating their environment). During the second half of the stage, the child begins using language and begins to develop a sense of cause and effect. The hallmark of this stage of development is object permanence, the concept that objects continue to exist even when they are out-of-sight. In Eriksonian terms we could say that the child begins to trust the reality of his/her surroundings. Hide a toy from a young child and he/she will act as if it no longer exists. Hide it from a slightly older child and he/she will attempt to find it.

The second stage is termed pre-operational thought; it lasts until the child is roughly six years old. The hallmark of this stage is egocentrism, the inability to see (literally) from another's perspective. This is not egocentrism in the egotistical sense, although young children can be quite egotistical. It is simply that the child has not learned that the world can be viewed from multiple perspectives. Children in this stage have no concept of other people's feelings because they have not learned enough about other people to understand the concept. An example of a child at this stage would be the one who chooses to buy their mother a toy because that is what they would like for their birthday. In addition, children in this stage cannot explain their actions or adapt their speech to other people. Fantasy and play are important developmental tools; these actions allow the child to explore future roles.

The third stage is called concrete operations, and it encompasses the primary school years, roughly seven to eleven. Children are able to take care of themselves in basic ways. They begin to make friends and are influenced by people other than their parents. They learn certain facts and rules about the world, such as the law of conservation (i.e., that physical properties such as mass, volume, and number do not change despite a change in form). This is the stage when children begin to question the reality of Santa Claus: how can Santa come down the chimney when the house does not have one? Finally, the fourth stage is that of formal operations and begins around age twelve. In this stage of development, the adolescent begins to transcend concrete situations and is able to think abstractly. The hallmark of this stage is hypothetico-deductive reasoning. Adolescents begin to think about the future. They can conceive of different ways to represent situations and begin to try to organize their world and deal with it in terms of the future.

In Piagetan terms, Kira loses her mother when she is preoperational. Her egocentrism leads her to make sense of her world in terms of herself. Thus the loss of Maru may have significant effects on Kira's psyche. She may blame herself for her mother's disappearance, wondering what she might have done to drive her mother away. Even Taban's attempts to protect his children by telling them that Maru has died may still be interpreted in terms of the children's cognitive abilities. A three-year-old child is probably incapable to understanding the loss of a parent, even when told that the parent has died. It is also possible that a three year old does not understand the absolute reality of living in a refugee camp. However, the child is probably capable of understanding the fear that pervades the people living there. She certainly knows that she does not have enough to eat and is fearful of the (Cardassian) soldiers who occasionally come into the camp and take people away. Kira leaves Singha and joins the Shakaar Resistance Cell when she is twelve years old. She would have been bridging the third and fourth stages of development, seeing the world in black and white (a concrete vision) but also thinking of a future different from the one in which she is living (an abstract vision). She is looking for a reason to live, a reason to survive, and for that she needs to determine exactly who she is and what that means in terms of her identity.

Developing a sense of self, a personal identity, is the focus of Erikson's fifth stage of development and occurs during adolescence (which begins at puberty). It is at this time that one confronts the questions, "Who am I and why am I here?" The heart of this stage of development, Identity vs. Role-confusion, is the identity crisis. According to Erikson,

> the word "crisis" no longer connotes impending catastrophe…. It is now being accepted as designating a necessary turning point, a crucial moment, when development must move one way or another, marshaling resources of growth, recovery, and further differentiation [*Identity: Youth and Crisis* 16].

Adolescents must confront the roles they have played in their lives to this point in time and synthesize these roles into a cohesive identity. Adolescents must be allowed to explore new and different roles or a different path in a former role; they seek to find what is unique and distinctive about them compared to their peers. In addition, they confront themselves with respect to their morals and values, political, religious and spiritual beliefs, and sexual identity. Failure to synthesize an identity leads to the inability to find direction in life and pursue a meaningful future.

In many respects we can consider Kira's pre–Federation identity to be confused. Or, to use a better term, to be in a state of foreclosure, which occurs when an adolescent's options are limited. Choices cannot be made because the adolescent does not see that choices are available. For example, a child born into a family of military veterans may not argue with such a legacy, deeming the only future he or she will have is to follow in the family's footsteps. Growing up in the Singha refugee camp with little to eat and no hope for a better future as long as the Cardassians ruled Bajor limited Kira's options. One could consider those only included dying young, remaining in the refugee camp and working as forced labor, collaborating, or joining the Resistance. The first three were not options as far as she was concerned, and so Kira joined the Resistance. Initially, she only ran errands ("The Darkness and the Light"), but quickly joined her first mission and continued her terrorist actions against the Cardassians until the liberation of Bajor, when she became a member of the Bajoran Militia. However, Kira's actions while in the Resistance cause her distress, as illustrated by several episodes occurring during seasons one and two. In the episode "Past Prologue," for example, she is stunned, angry, and perhaps doubtful when a former member of the underground named Tahna Los (Jeffrey Nordling) tells her that she is "in bed" with the Federation and no longer has Bajor's best interests at heart; he tells her she is a traitor. Talking to Odo, she acknowledges that she did things during the occupation that she was not proud of, confessing she still has nightmares about a raid on the Haru Outpost. Continuing, she says, "I was sure about what I was doing then…. It was so much easier when I knew who the enemy was" ("Past Prologue"). Kira's pain over her past activities—which she is unwilling to acknowledge even to herself—resurfaces later in the season when she, Sisko, Bashir, and Kai Opaka (Camille Saviola) visit a planet where two opposing forces have battled each other for centuries. Unfortunately for the combatants, the planet resurrects anyone who dies on its soil, and that includes Kai Opaka, the religious leader of Bajor.

Kira is deeply religious and, like most Bajorans, worships the Prophets. Although we do not learn much about the tenets of the Bajoran religion during the course of the series, *Deep Space Nine* is certainly the most religious series in the *Star Trek* franchise, which is something of a surprise given Gene Roddenberry's emphasis on secular humanism and distrust of organized religion (Pearson). Nevertheless, we see Kira regularly attend religious services on the station. When she is troubled, she seeks the wisdom of the Prophets. When she needs rest and recuperation, she travels to one of the many monasteries on Bajor in order to be closer to the Prophets ("The Circle"). According to Lexie Baron, "by presenting Kira as a complex, thoughtful, well-developed character who benefits from and relies on her religion, *Star Trek: Deep Space Nine* is showing that there can still be a place for religion in a seemingly secularized, advanced technological society, and highlights the possible advantages of religiosity." I propose that Kira's spirituality and religiosity are important factors in her ability to withstand the negative consequences of her traumatic life.

Opaka is one of the few people with whom Kira feels comfortable talking about her past. She does not want Opaka to think that she is violent, without conscience or a soul, or that she enjoys fighting. Their conversation in "Battle Lines" illustrates how Kira must confront the violent acts in which she participated when in the Resistance:

KIRA: I've … fought my entire life, but for a good cause. For our freedom, our independence…[i]t was brutal and ugly, and … that's not who I am. I have known nothing but violence since I was a child…. I am afraid the Prophets won't forgive me.

OPAKA: They're just waiting for you to forgive yourself.

This dialogue underscores that Kira is having a difficult time defining and redefining herself. Is she a freedom fighter, a terrorist, an officer in the Bajoran Militia, second-in-command of Deep Space 9? All of those are roles that she has played in her life, but what and who is she? This is the question that she faces as she talks with Opaka and cries about her fear of being judged harshly by the Prophets, who may view her as irredeemable, something that would shatter someone with her spiritual beliefs.

This scene in "Battle Lines" lets us know that Kira is affected by the traumatic events that occurred in her lifetime. As Lenore Terr writes, "psychic trauma occurs when a sudden unexpected, overwhelming intense emotional blow or series of blows assaults the person from outside" (8). The transmission Kira received from Dukat about her mother is a sudden and unexpected blow. Being transported into the past to confront the truth about her mother's relationship with Gul Dukat is traumatic. Psychiatrist Bessel Van der Kolk observes that, "Traumatization occurs when both internal and external resources are inadequate to cope with external threat" (393). If we consider that Kira was born into trauma—the Cardassians already occupied Bajor when she was born—she then lived through the occupation for about twenty-five years. Many victims of traumatic experiences have difficulty with the way they think, act, learn, remember, and feel about themselves, and we would expect Kira to be no different. One might consider that she would suffer from a Traumatic Stress Disorder (TSD), given she spent her life subjugated to the Cardassian occupation of Bajor. However, Kira does not present with the symptoms one would normally expect of someone diagnosed with a stress disorder (DSM-V). For example, she does not display startle responses or irritability in a persistent fashion, nor does she display acts of unprovoked aggression, although she is certainly hot-tempered in the beginning. In Peter David's novel *The Siege*, Quark says that "she has no love for Starfleet. She stomped around this place for the first several weeks after Sisko arrived. She's calmed down a bit since then" (109). Kira does not appear to have atypical dreams or problems with normal personality functioning. She does exhibit a fixation on the trauma—indeed her very *raison d'être* is to ensure that Bajor is never subjugated by Cardassia again—yet the fixation keeps her focused on the task at hand in order to work toward solutions to the problem of Bajoran independence and self-government. Kira's trauma at the hands of the Cardassians melded her into a formidable woman.

Nevertheless, her traumatic experiences during the occupation almost certainly affected her ability to trust other people. Interestingly, the issue of trauma is addressed infrequently on *Deep Space Nine*, even though post-traumatic stress disorder (PTSD) had become a recognized psychiatric diagnosis in 1980, when it was added to the third edition of the *Diagnostic and Statistical Manual of Mental Disorders* (DSM-III). It is also not a major plot point in other *Star Trek* series, even though several characters could be said to suffer from the disorder, such as Captain Jean-Luc Picard (Patrick Stewart) following his return from assimilation by the Borg ("The Best of Both Worlds"), and especially Chief O'Brien after his virtual twenty-year incarceration by the Argrathi ("Hard Time"), during which O'Brien "murdered" his cellmate because he believed him to be hiding food from him. O'Brien especially exhibits classic symptoms of PTSD; however, he is quickly "cured" of his most obvious symptoms through the intervention of Bashir and a prescription for drugs. A much more realistic and extended portrayal of PTSD occurs on *Discovery* (2017–present) in the character of Voq/Ash Tyler (Shazad Latif) who, like O'Brien, has memories of being incarcerated implanted into his psyche, but who eventually learns that he is Klingon by birth and has been surgically altered to appear human and infiltrate Starfleet. Voq/Tyler is especially traumatized by the memory of the pain of the surgery, and psychological ramifications include his inability to understand exactly who he is. He is both Klingon and human but knows that neither side wants him nor trusts him (other than the two women who love him, one Klingon and one human). Yet unlike these men, Kira appears to have dealt with any residual effects of the trauma she suffered in childhood at the hands of the Cardassians.

Whereas the atrocities committed against the Bajoran people by the Cardassians are sometimes compared to those committed against the Jewish people by the Nazis, Matthew Kapell believes that in its depiction of the Bajoran occupation and resistance, *Deep Space Nine* Americanized the Holocaust, saying, "it was a glorious fight for freedom, full of heroes bent on throwing the Cardassian perpetrators off their planet. And, lo and behold, they succeeded heroic to the end" (111). Kapell is particularly critical about how Kira is portrayed: as someone who is not adversely affected by the trauma experienced by Bajorans, unlike Ro Laren (Michelle Forbes) in *The Next Generation*, who is scarred emotionally by the traumatic events she experienced during the occupation.

It is my contention that Kira *is* adversely affected by the events that occurred in her childhood; however, Kira weathered these events because of strengths she acquired at the hands of her parents, such as the development of attachment bonds and trust.[4] These factors provided what psychologists refer to as a "secure base," a focal point that a developing child uses as she begins to explore the physical and social environment surrounding her. In the vernacular, we might say that "someone has our back" and, in the child's case, that would be her parents. Kira had Maru for only a short period of time, but Taban for much longer. In addition, she developed close friendships with members of her resistance cell as well as with various people on Deep Space 9, such as Dax and Sisko. In all likelihood, her own ability to control various incidents in her life—by fighting in the Resistance, for example—reduced feelings of helplessness and powerlessness that many people develop in response to trauma and stress. That is not to say that Kira is unaffected by the occupation; but it may be that fighting in the resistance along with her intense spirituality provided the buffer she needed to resist the negative effects of that trauma. Yet despite this, we do see lingering effects of her traumatic childhood throughout her time on Deep Space 9.

Episodes in the series that show Kira confronting her actions in the past include "Battlelines," "Duet," "The Circle," "Necessary Evil," and "The Darkness and the Light." She is forced to take sides against former comrades in the underground, reaffirming her earlier statement to Sisko, that "my priorities are straight, Commander. Let's not be confused here. My loyalties are to Bajor" ("Past Prologue"). She learns that not everyone on Bajor has the best interests of Bajor in mind when they engage in activity that might harm the provisional government. Keith D.A. DeCandido speculates that Kira's assignment on Deep Space 9 was the result of a decision by that government to get her out of the way as "her intemperate ways [were] too much for them to handle—at least nearby. So they sent her into orbit" (631). Bajor's provisional government is not one that she respects, but it is the one she has sworn to serve, and she refuses to let sentimentality, friendship, or past loyalties get in the way of ensuring that Bajor is free of Cardassian influence. That is not to say that Kira is unable to bend, to grow, and to change. As a matter of fact, her contentious feelings about Sisko evolve as she gradually comes to respect him as a commander and friend, as he does her.

Nevertheless, Sisko is the Emissary as well as her commanding officer, and Kira has difficulty reconciling the two at times. This comes to a head in the episode "Starship Down," when Sisko is injured following an attack by the Jem'Hadar upon the *Defiant* as it hosts trade negotiations with the Karemma. Sisko gets a concussion and Kira tends to him, attempting to keep him from falling asleep and entering a coma. She tells Sisko a story from Bajoran fables and also prays to the Prophets, begging them to save his life. Kira is not certain of how aware Sisko is of her ministrations until the danger has passed and he asks her to tell him the ending of her story. After their return to Deep Space 9, Sisko invites her to go to a holosuite baseball game with him. Baseball is very important to Sisko, and that he would share his passion for it with her delights her very much. From this point onwards their relationship is more relaxed; their friendship grows and deepens as time goes by. This is illustrated poignantly in the episode "Accession," when the poet Akorem Laan (Richard Libertini) emerges from a two-hundred-year sojourn in the wormhole. He believes that he is the Emissary and wants to return Bajor to the old ways, one in which every Bajoran is assigned to a caste in which they remain for life. Kira should be an artist according to this system, not a military officer, and she decides to resign her post at the station and return to Bajor. As Sisko and Kira say their goodbyes, he tells her that even if someone else takes her post as his Second, she can never be replaced. Both Kira and Sisko are very emotional in this moment, revealing the depth of their feelings for one another. Later in the series, following the Federation's forced departure from Deep Space 9, Sisko's baseball reinforces his presence as the true commander of the station and the Emissary of the Prophets, a point made by Barbara Silliman, who observes that the baseball is a "constant reminder of his essence and his presence… [It] allows her [Kira] to feel the presence of Benjamin in her life" (111). The baseball also is a message to the occupying forces that he would be returning to the station (DeCandido). Even after Sisko enters the Celestial Temple, Kira finds it hard to do away with it, a reminder of their friendship. In these scenes, the baseball illustrates the trust Kira has in Sisko and how much she misses his presence on the station. She has come a long way since their first contentious meeting in "Emissary," which one might refer to as a turning point or transition in both of their lives.

Turning Points and Transitions

Yet another psychological theory that provides insight into Kira's story was proposed by Daniel Levinson, who found that both men and women have several occasions in their adult lives when they experience transition points, or shifts, in their developmental trajectories. Levinson and his colleagues developed this Life-Course Theory based upon extensive and in-depth interviews with men and women at various times in their adulthood, beginning in late adolescence and continuing until late middle adulthood. Based upon the interviews with his sample of women, Levinson separated women into two categories. His homemaker sample included women who married at an early age either directly after high school, in college, or shortly after college and begin having children shortly after marriage. Like their husbands, these women believed that a woman's primary responsibility was to her children, and therefore she should not work outside of the home. Levinson's anti-homemaker sample consisted of career women who worked in corporate America or academia and who were less likely to be married and have children. They believed in what Levinson called the Successful Career Woman myth, which stated that women can have it all: career, marriage, family, leisure time, everything—if they just work hard enough. However, by middle age, during a period referred to as the Mid–Life Transition (approximately 40–46), these women were questioning this myth, realizing that instead of being a Successful Career Woman, they were actually Jugglers, "who managed to keep several spheres moving at the same time, but who had a very restricted life and little connection to her self and her inner spheres" (372). The mid-life transition marks a period of time when career women begin to question and reconsider what it means to have a career or a marriage or a family, perhaps asking the question, "Is this all there is?" In other words, many women reach a point in their lives when they face a turning point. Some might call it a "midlife crisis," although that term carries a lot of baggage with respect to the type of psychological thoughts occurring within people at this point in time.

Just as with the other theories discussed, Levinson's model provides some insight into Kira at this stage of her life. Kira is approximately twenty-six years old when we first encounter her on Deep Space 9 ("Kira Nerys"). She has spent over half of her life fighting for Bajor's freedom from the Cardassians and now she must spend time trying to protect its fragile government from enemies both foreign and domestic while navigating a path between her violent past and her hopes for her future. One thing that occurs in Kira's life during this period in time is the development of a physical and emotional relationship with Vedek Bareil Antos (Philip Anglim). She is shocked when she sees the two of them naked and sexual when she gazes into the Orb of Prophecy and Change ("The Circle"). However, she becomes more and more attracted to him, and their relationship continues until his death ("Life Support"). For Erikson, this aspect of adulthood is inevitable following identity development. As the adolescent enters young adulthood, the overwhelming social pressure is to find a mate. Increasingly intimate relationships with friends and the drive toward marriage and procreation characterize this stage. Thus, young adulthood becomes the period of childbearing and childrearing.

However, as we see in Levinson's research, not all women choose to pursue this trajectory, instead choosing another path until reaching the "turning point." Kira appears to have reached that point in her life: Bajor is free of the Cardassians and she can relax her vigilance somewhat because she is not the only person attempting to keep Bajor safe. The Federation is there as well, and although she might not always agree with the Federation's decisions and policies, she has to admit that they seem to have Bajor's best interests in mind. Such knowledge means that she can relax and begin to enjoy her life more. She and Jadzia Dax (Terry Farrell) become good friends, and she develops a close relationship with Gul Dukat's half-Bajoran daughter, Tora Ziyal.[5] She also develops a close relationship with Odo that eventually becomes romantic. She never expresses a desire for children until she is forced to carry Miles and Keiko O'Brien's (Rosalind Chao) baby to term following an accident aboard a runabout ("Body Parts"). These events also reflect the changes that have occurred in Kira's life with respect to the way she thinks about things, which can be examined using Piaget's theory of cognitive development.

One of the criticisms of Piaget's theory is its neglect of adulthood. The theory proposes that people reach the formal operational stage of thought and utilize abstract thinking and hypothetico-deductive reasoning in order to solve problems. Real life, on the other hand, does not always require such elaborate cognition. Rather, several researchers have proposed that adult cognition is more dialectical in character; the solutions to life's problems are seldom black and white. When we first meet Kira, she is adamant about the Cardassians: they need to be punished for their actions on Bajor during the occupation, and the only good Cardassian is a dead one. However, we observe her change her opinions as the series proceeds. She never forgives the Cardassians for what they did to her people, but she realizes that not all Cardassians were involved and that not all of them are evil, just as some Bajorans that she liked and respected were collaborators ("Duet"; "The Collaborator"; "Ties of Blood and Water"). She develops an almost father-daughter relationship with one Cardassian, mourning him deeply when he dies ("Second Skin"). She develops collaborative relationships with Cardassians such as Damar (Casey Biggs) during the Dominion War, and she even manages to become more tolerant of Dukat with time ("Return to Grace"), although she is repulsed by his romantic advances toward her. The thought that Kira would be attracted to him would have betrayed everything she believed in and fought for, not to mention the fact that he was her mother's lover for many years. As a matter of fact, Kira tells Ziyal that Dukat wants her forgiveness for his actions on Bajor and that he will never get it ("Return to Grace"). Still, the totality of Kira's multifaceted responses in her interactions with various Cardassians demonstrates the conflicting tensions she still has in regards to her relationships with both individual Cardassians and the Cardassian people in general; Kira is all in when trying to save Cardassia from the Dominion, risking her own life, but she never forgets the past and how her people and her own life were negatively impacted by Cardassian intervention.

Conclusion

According to Ira Steven Behr, Kira came to Deep Space 9 as "an angry woman … the toughest broad in the galaxy" ("Crew Dossier: Kira"). Nana

Visitor observed that Kira "gets to evolve because she has security on the station," a far cry from when she had to sleep under rocks and in caves as a member of the Shakaar Resistance Cell, showing that she has come to trust the people aboard the station ("Crew Dossier: Kira"). Visitor continues, in the same special feature, that Kira "came full circle" in the seven seasons of *Deep Space Nine*: she began as the Commander of the station and that is how the series left her. However, Kira is not the same angry woman we first met. Dukat once told her: "You are the embodiment of the new Bajor. A Bajoran born out of the ashes of the occupation, a Bajoran tempered with Cardassian steel" ("Return to Grace"). Dukat meant his words as both a compliment and an excuse, but this was not how Kira received them. She would have preferred, no doubt, to have lived a peaceful and uneventful life, one in which she did not watch friends and family die, one in which people had enough food to eat, and one where her planet was not decimated by the exploitation of its natural resources. Instead, we got a woman struggling to survive, to make the most of the life she fought for, and to become more than she ever thought she could be.

Kira was born into a nightmare of a world, yet she had a loving family, even if only for a few years. Losing her mother early had a profound effect on her, even though she learned later in life that the story she had been told about her mother's death was a lie. Joining the Resistance at an early age, Kira embraced the role of freedom fighter / terrorist, never losing sight of her goal: to free Bajor of Cardassian rule. She not only succeeded in that goal, but she became part of the Bajoran Militia and served as the liaison between Bajor and the United Federation of Planets, eventually becoming Commander of Deep Space 9. Even with that power, Kira never lost sight of her past; she never denied it or apologized for it. She continued to embrace her spirituality, being perhaps the most religious of all the women on the various *Star Trek* series. In addition, Kira was freely sexual, enjoying relationships with several men over the course of the series. Psychological theories about trust, attachment, cognition, identity formation, and transitional periods provide insight into Kira's development; each provides another layer for explaining how she was able to overcome the traumatic and stressful events that happened to her in childhood and adolescence. It is my opinion that Kira was the most positively portrayed of all of the *Star Trek* women: angry, powerful, sexual, spiritual, funny, devious, and loyal—a hero boldly going where few *Star Trek* women had gone before.

Notes

1. Research by and about Freud and his theory of psychosexual development is voluminous, as is research about Piaget and his theory of cognitive development. The interested

reader is directed to any introductory psychology textbook, such as Licht, Hull, and Ballantyne's *Presenting Psychology*, or developmental psychology textbook, such as the one by Robert Feldman (see note 3). In addition, one can consult Peter Gay's *The Freud Reader* or Barry Wadsworth's *Piaget's Theory of Cognitive and Affective Development: Foundations of Constructivism*.

2. All of Erikson's stages are summarized in Feldman: 12–13, 265–267, 283–285. Books by Erikson are listed in the Works Cited and Consulted below.

3. The research surrounding attachment in children is extensive. John Bowlby, a British psychologist, psychiatrist, and psychoanalyst, was one of the first to study the issue, proposing that children bonded with their parents for psychological reasons (i.e., parents provide comfort and security) rather than simply for biological reasons (i.e., parents feed the child). Mary Ainsworth and her associates developed a method to investigate attachment bonds in children. It is her research and research extending her results that led to the categories described in the text. Because this research data base is so extensive, I am referencing a developmental psychology textbook that summarizes this research. See Feldman, *Life Span Development*, 248–251.

4. In the documentary *What We Left Behind* (2019), Nana Visitor states that Kira did present with Post-Traumatic Stress when *Deep Space Nine* began but she recovered by the end of the show. Her comments can be found in the chapter "The Cost of War."

5. Tora Ziyal was played by three different actors: Cyia Batten, Tracy Middendorf, and Melanie Smith.

WORKS CITED AND CONSULTED

American Psychiatric Association. *Diagnostic and Statistical Manual of Mental Disorders,* 5th edition, 2013.

_____. *Diagnostic and Statistical Manual of Mental Disorders*, 3rd edition, 1980.

Baron, Lexie. "Religion in *Star Trek: Deep Space Nine*." *Religion in Society Sociology of Religion Blogging Noosphere*. 15 December 2017. Media Commentary Blogs. onlineacademiccommunity.uvic.ca/sociologyofreligion/author/acbaron/. Accessed 11 July 2020.

David, Peter. *The Siege*. Pocket Books, 1993.

DeCandido, Keith R.A. "Horn and Ivory," collected in *Twist of Fate*. Pocket Books, 2001.

Demarest, Rebecca A. "The Relationship Between Stockholm Syndrome and Post-Traumatic Stress Disorder in Battered Women." *Inquiries Journal/Student Pulse*, vol. 1, no. 11, 2009. www.inquiriesjournal.com/a?id=35. Accessed 28 April 2020.

Dillard, J.M. *Emissary*. Pocket Books, 1993.

Erdmann, Terry J., and Paula M. Block. Star Trek Deep Space Nine: *Companion*. Pocket Books, 2000.

Erikson, Erik H. *Dimensions of a New Identity*. W.W. Norton, 1974.

_____. *Identity and the Life Cycle, 2nd Edition*. W.W. Norton, 1980.

_____. *Identity: Youth and Crisis*. W.W. Norton, 1968.

_____. *The Life Cycle Completed: A Review*. W.W. Norton, 1982.

Feldman, Robert. *Life Span Development: A Topical Approach*. Prentice Hall, 2011.

Gay, Peter. *The Freud Reader*. W.W. Norton, 1995.

Geraghty, Lincoln, ed. *The Influence of* Star Trek *on Television, Film, and Culture*. McFarland, 2014.

_____. *Living with* Star Trek: *American Culture and the* Star Trek *Universe*. I.B. Taurus, 2007.

Ginn, Sherry. "B'Elanna Torres and The Hated Half: Negotiating Mixed-Race/Species Identity." *Exploring* Star Trek: Voyager: *Critical Essays*, edited by Robert L. Lively. McFarland, 2020, pp. 149–163.

_____. "Life Post-TARDIS? The Case for Jo Grant and Sarah Jane Smith." *WHO Travels with the Doctor?: Essays on the Companions of* DOCTOR WHO, edited by Gillian I. Leitch and Sherry Ginn. McFarland, 2016, pp. 69–78.

_____. *Our Space, Our Place: Women in the Worlds of Science Fiction Television*. University Press of America, 2005.

Gregory, Chris. Star Trek: *Parallel Narratives*. St. Martin's Press, 2000.

Kapell, Matthew. "Speakers for the Dead: *Star Trek*, the Holocaust, and the Representation of Atrocity." *Extrapolation*, vol. 41, no. 2, 2000, pp. 104–114.

"Kira Nerys." memory-alpha.fandom.com/wiki/Kira_Nerys. Accessed 3 May 2020.

Levinson, Daniel J. *The Seasons of a Woman's Life*. Ballantine Books, 1996.

Licht, Deborah M., Misty G. Hull, and Coco Ballantyne. *Scientific American: Psychology*, 3rd ed. Worth, 2020.

McCormack, Una. *Cardassia: The Lotus Flower*. Pocket Books, 2004 (Kindle Edition).

Mlawski, Shana. "Why Strong Female Characters Are Bad for Women." *Overthinking It*. Overthinking It, 18 April 2008. Accessed 27 March 2015.

O., Jack. "Creating Emotional Resonance Through Writing." *Scripted*. Scripted Inc, 21 Feb. 2014. Accessed 23 April 2015.

Oglesbee, Frank W. "Kira Nerys: A Good Woman Fighting Well." *Extrapolation*, vol. 45, no. 3, 2004, pp. 263–275.

Owen, Luke. "Why the Bechdel Test Doesn't Work." *Flickering Myth*. Flickering Myth, 24 July 2013. Accessed 16 Feb. 2015.

Pearson, Anne M. "From Thwarted Gods to Reclaimed Mystery? An Overview of the Depiction of Religion in *Star Trek*." Star Trek *and Sacred Ground: Explorations of* Star Trek, *Religion, and American Culture*, edited by Jennifer E. Porter and Darcee L. McLaren. State U of New York P, 1999, pp. 13–32.

Perry, S.D. *Unity*. Pocket Books, 2003.

Porter, Heather M. "In Search of the Complete Female Character in Marvel's Cinematic Universe." *Marvel's Black Widow from Spy to Superhero: Essays on an Avenger with a Very Specific Skill Set*, edited by Sherry Ginn. McFarland, 2017, pp. 22–37.

Silliman, Barbara A. "Batter Up! The Mythology and Psychology of Sports and Games in *Star Trek: Deep Space Nine*." The Influence of Star Trek *on Television, Film and Culture*, edited by Lincoln Geraghty. McFarland, 2008, pp. 100–111.

Silverstein, Melissa, and Inkoo Kang. "Goodbye to Strong Female Characters." *Indiewire*. Indiewire, 30 Dec 2013. Accessed 15 Oct 2015.

Smith, Stacy L., and Marc Choueiti. "Gender Disparity on Screen and Behind the Camera in Family Films: The Executive Report." *Geena Davis Institute on Gender in Media*. Geena Davis Institute on Gender in Media, 2010. Accessed 1 March 2015.

Solomon, Stefan. "What the Bechdel Test Doesn't Tell Us About Women on Film." *The Conversation*. The Conversation, 14 Nov. 2013. Accessed 16 Feb. 2015.

Terr, Lenore. *Too Scared to Cry: Psychic Trauma in Childhood*. Harper and Row, 1990.

Van der Kolk, Bessel A. "The Compulsion to Repeat Trauma: Reenactment, Revictimization, and Masochism." *Psychiatric Clinics of North America, Vol. 12. Treatment of Victims of Sexual Abuse*, vol. 12, no. 2, 1989, pp. 389–411.

Wadsworth, Barry J. *Piaget's Theory of Cognitive and Affective Development: Foundations of Constructivism, 5th Edition*. Allyn and Bacon, 2003.

Woods, Olivia. *Deep Space Nine: The Soul Key*. Pocket Books, 2009.

FILMOGRAPHY

Babylon 5. Created by J. Michael Straczynski. Warner Bros. 1993–1998.

"Crew Dossier: Kira Nerys." *Deep Space Nine* Season One DVD Special Feature. Paramount, 1993.

What We Left Behind: Looking Back at Star Trek: Deep Space Nine, directed by Ira Steven Behr and David Zappone. 455 Films, 2019.

"A very unformed being"

Odo's Rhizomatic Journey Toward Selfhood

Erin Bell

Although fans of *Star Trek* frequently debate many facets of the franchise's extended universe, one aspect that most enthusiasts appear to hold in common is their fondness for many of the non-human characters within the *Trek* canon. Citing beloved figures such as Mr. Spock (Leonard Nimoy) in *Star Trek: The Original Series* (1966–1969) and Lt. Commander Data (Brent Spiner) in *Star Trek: The Next Generation* (1987–1994), conventional criticism suggests that such characters are intriguing to fans and critics alike because they are outsiders that look in at humanity—thus serving as the basis for interrogating what it means to be human as well as to exceed the limits of humanity all together. Such extraterrestrial characters are at once extraordinary and recognizable. That is, although these characters are not human, their patterns of behavior often resonate with human experiences. The many worlds presented in the numerous iterations of *Star Trek* may be centuries ahead of us, but futuristic alien characters often grapple with issues humans confront now.

Star Trek: Deep Space Nine (1993–1999) features a number of non-human and non-humanoid characters, but within this group, Odo (René Auberjonois), the station's shape-shifting, short-tempered chief of security, is clearly positioned in the genealogy of outsider characters noted above. Similarly to Spock, Odo frequently offers astute observations about both the absurd and sublime qualities of humanity. Odo's character development is also slightly reminiscent of Data's in that Odo expresses an implicit yearning to become part of a greater and more connected community. While Odo's initial desire is to connect with a community of others that are like him, Odo ends up forming important relationships with humanoids along the way, including Lwaxana Troi (Majel Barrett), Major Kira Nerys (Nana Visitor), and arguably, even Quark (Armin Shimerman).

Indeed, Odo's quest for subjectivity, purpose, and selfhood mirror many human experiences. In a 2011 interview with writers at *Star Trek*.com, Auberjonois commented extensively on Odo's journey toward development and self-discovery, noting that Odo was a "very unformed being" ("Catching Up"). Continuing on, Auberjonois explained that, "Odo was a mass of liquid, really, and he was trying to get some kind of shape to his life and to who he was and he wanted to answer the questions he had about what his role was meant to be in that particular universe" ("Catching Up"). As the outsider looking in and searching for his purpose and place in the universe, Odo's experiences on *Deep Space Nine* serve as means for interrogating human conceptions of identity and collectivity. Indeed, many viewers are drawn to Odo as his attempts to negotiate his subjectivity and his efforts to connect with his peers reflect experiences that many humans have endured.

Previous scholarship about shape-shifters on *Deep Space Nine* has often called attention to the power structures and brutal ideologies of the Founders rather than upon Odo alone. Marc Napolitano, for example, provides an insightful reading of the Founders' pursuit of domination via Michel Foucault's theorization of biopolitics. Napolitano details and discusses a central contradiction in the Founders' system of order which is that the Dominion paradoxically seeks to foster life by adopting a politics of death. Napolitano compares the Founders' genocidal doctrines to those of the Nazi party during World War II and enumerates the Founders' violent and deadly methods for control. Even though the Founders eventually end their devastating offensive, they do so only after ordering the mass destruction of numerous planets and the murder of millions of beings across the universe. Significantly, the Founders terminate their war only because their species is at risk of extinction. Thus, notes Napolitano, "although the Dominion War is physically won by the Federation, the ideological battle is won by the Founders" (219). The Founders do not cease the war due to ethical considerations—they have not altered their belief that "solids" are lesser than Changelings—but they surrender to protect the future of their own species from annihilation due to the life-threatening morphogenic disease. At the end of the series, Odo chooses to save the Founders from this bio-engineered disease that was introduced into the community by covert operatives from Section 31.[1] Although the Founders rarely show compassion to those outside of their sphere, Odo feels called to save his species based on his own sense of ethics.

So while Napolitano and others analyze the Founders' fascist ideologies, in this essay I call particular attention to Odo as a being who is both inside and outside of the Federation and of the Dominion. I argue that Odo's journey away from the Founders' home world and his interactions with "solids" grant him the means to develop an ethical perspective that is distinct from the rest of his species. Odo's individual sense of justice is demonstrated in moments such as the one noted above (whereby Odo saves his species) and throughout the series. In what follows, I contend that Odo's development and journey as an individual can be defined as rhizomatic, and that the rhizomic quality of his trajectory grants him the means and mindset to save the Founders from mass extermination and bring an end to the Dominion's violent assault on solids. Importantly, Odo forges a unique identity directly related to his excursion away from the Founders' home planet, although ironically, it is the Founders who set him upon this path in the first place. Rhizomatic images and connections are prevalent on *Deep Space Nine*, and thinking about the series in such terms establishes some striking similarities between the ideologies of the Federation and Founders as both entities embrace and encourage a rhizomatic network of power and presence to extend their reach.

An Interstellar Rhizome

In horticultural studies, the term "rhizome" describes a subterranean stem which sends out countless roots and shoots from its nodes. French philosophers Gilles Deleuze and Félix Guattari develop an extensive discussion of rhizomic connections to construe how networks of knowledge and power develop in their seminal 1987 collaborative text *A Thousand Plateaus: Capitalism and Schizophrenia*. Deleuze and Guattari suggest that which is "rhizomatic" stands in opposition to representations of knowledge and power that are "over-simplified," linear, and reliant upon "binarities" (328). As they explain,

> unlike trees or their roots, the rhizome connects any point to any other point, and its traits are not necessarily linked to traits of the same nature; it brings into play very different regimes of signs, and even nonsign states. The rhizome is reducible neither to the One nor the multiple [21].

A rhizomatic entity can generate an infinite number of points of connection between bodies in an assemblage (loosely explained as a multiplicity of disparate elements and components drawn together and functioning as a single entity). Because rhizomatic organisms favor a rather nomadic system of movement, their trajectory for expansion and growth is often manifested in seemingly random patterns.

Whereas an arborescent or tree-like model is organized in a linear mode (represented by branches), the rhizome may appear more chaotic or disorganized in structure, allowing for networks of trans-species connections to emerge at unexpected junctures, and thus generates multiplicities rather than strictly binary modalities. In the years since the publication of *A Thousand Plateaus,* Deleuze and Guattari's conception of the rhizome as a metaphor has been appropriated and extended by scholars across multiple disciplines, including those who study political science, organizational theory, and popular culture, to name a few.

In addition to bringing understanding to Odo's personal trajectory of growth, the rhizome is a practical metaphor for understanding the many power structures that converge on *Deep Space Nine,* as depicted from the earliest scenes of the series. The station itself is often discussed in scholarship about *Deep Space Nine,* with many authors calling attention to the fact that it is the only *Star Trek* program not based on a ship (thus far). Kathy E. Ferguson, for example, explores the station's unique position through Foucault's conception of the heterotopia, defining it as a space that is "potentially disruptive" and posed against other "stable spaces from which people move to and from" (182). Ferguson goes on to suggest that the station's "heterotopic ability" renders it a liminal space or a threshold for those who are in between—the outcasts, the renegades, those who do not fit within social norms, and even those who are facing a crisis in identity (182). There are also numerous hierarchies of authority present on Deep Space 9 as the Federation, the provisional Bajoran government, and the Cardassians intersect, splicing one power structure to another, connecting at multiple intervals, only to break away from one another at later junctures. The expansion of the Federation across galaxies and its interest in maintaining a presence on station Deep Space 9 can also be understood as rhizomatic. From *The Original Series* on, each new captain and crew pushes beyond Earth, further and further into the "final frontier," establishing nodes and connections across multiple quadrants of the galaxy. Though Deep Space 9 remains in a fixed location for most of the series (with the exception of its move closer to the Bajoran wormhole in the series' premiere), its proximity to the wormhole makes it an ideal location for extending Federation presence into the Gamma Quadrant. The station is a central location from which numerous "root stalks" will extend out into the universe. If, as Deleuze and Guattari suggest, "A rhizome ceaselessly establishes connections between semiotic chains [and] organizations of power," then the Federation-controlled station is emblematic of such organizations of control and command (7). In fact, the series' premiere, "Emissary: Part I and Part II," opens with numerous allusions to shifting alliances and identities, situating Odo into a milieu of flux and change which leads to deeper philosophical, ethical, and political questions about who "belongs" where.

The opening sequence of the series premiere of *Deep Space Nine* is violent and distressing, presenting the deadly consequences of assimilation as a mode of bringing an assemblage into existence. In this sequence, audiences are reminded of the betrayal of Starfleet by Jean-Luc Picard (Patrick Stewart) as an activated member of the Borg collective (a fitting illustration of heterogeneity and rhizomic expanse, as each new member of the collective is assimilated and grafted into a larger hive consciousness). This brief allusion to collectivity, however, is overshadowed by the horror of Picard as Locutus, which is compounded by the fact that he is complicit with the Borg's destruction of the Federation vessel the USS *Saratoga*. The depiction of Picard's lost humanity in "Emissary: Part I" is tragic but not the most notable loss in this sequence. Picard's singular tragedy is eclipsed by the loss of human lives on the *Saratoga*, including that of Jennifer Sisko (Felecia M. Bell), the beloved wife of Starfleet commander Benjamin Sisko (Avery Brooks).

With a visceral sense of grief looming in the background, the program fast-forwards three years into the future, and the episode again alludes to shifting identities. A bedraggled Benjamin Sisko and his young son Jake (Cirroc Lofton) arrive at the beaten-down space station; Sisko reveals that he is only biding time until he can leave Starfleet behind for civilian life. The future of the station and the planet Bajor are also uncertain. The station is facing its own identity crisis; that which once belonged to the Cardassians now belongs to a provisional Bajoran government, with the Federation acting as administrators. This complicated system of organization is also rhizomatic in that it is, as Deleuze and Guattari explain of such structures, based upon "alliance, uniquely alliance" (25). The success of the station depends on a complicated and tenuous arrangement of alliances, many of which are fleeting and unstable.

As the series progresses, such rhizomatic qualities are also reflected in Odo and his community of Founders. Founders can literally connect to one another at any point, and the assemblage of Founders on their home world is described as the Great Link. As such, the Founders represent a seemingly unending chain of connected beings that merge and fold into a shifting assemblage of "bodies." In their respective journeys to push beyond their own known galaxies, the Founders and the Federation are not dissimilar. Whereas the Federation's rhizomatic stretch out into the universe is based upon an optimistic mission—"to meet new people and new civilizations"— the Founders' rhizomatic trajectory revealed in season three is established by their deep-seated distrust of "solids" as well as their desire to dominate and subsume new planets and peoples as resources.

The Search for Self: Fitting In and Out of Spaces

Though the station, the Federation, and the Founders can all be described as rhizomatic, Odo's character arc asks viewers to consider how one's identity can be thought of in terms of a shifting, heterogeneous collection of experiences and connections to others. This characterization is true of the development of *most* sentient beings. What is essential about Odo's rhizomatic journey, however, is that it allows him the means to move beyond the unidimensional consciousness and identity exhibited by his species (depicted later in the series). Odo's trajectory manifests in a distinct set of core values that develops over the centuries he was away from his species.

In his first scenes in "Emissary: Part I," Odo appears to be a foil for Sisko. Whereas Benjamin Sisko is out of step with the station, Odo knows its every surface. Due to his shape-shifting abilities, Odo is preternaturally conscious of each shady deal that occurs on the Promenade, at Quark's, and even behind closed doors; he is intimately connected to the landscape of the station. The contrast between how Odo and Sisko relate to Deep Space 9 is highlighted in the pair's first meeting during Sisko's initial tour of the station. In the midst of pursuing a criminal suspect, Odo shape-shifts to avoid an incoming morning star weapon and begins struggling with the alien. Sisko witnesses their fight and immediately starts firing his phaser. Odo demands that Sisko stop, acknowledging him only with the brusquely phrased, "Who the hell are you?" ("Emissary: Part I"). Major Kira Nerys clarifies that Sisko is the new Starfleet Commander of Deep Space 9, but Odo reinforces his command over the station, reiterating that *he* does not allow weapons on the Promenade. In this brief scene, Odo asserts his authority over the bodies and beings present on Deep Space 9. Whereas Sisko initially appears disconnected and aloof, Odo is confident about his professional identity.

Although Odo is adept in his duties regarding the station's security, in early episodes of the series, viewers become attuned to how Odo grapples with existential questions relating to his origins. Odo feels cut off from others, a theme which will resonate throughout many seasons. This trope echoes Deleuze and Guattari's suggestion that the rhizome "may be broken, shattered at a given spot, but it will start up again on one of its old lines, or on new lines" (9). Cut off from his roots, Odo attempts to forge a new line of life on the station, albeit with limited success. Odo's sense of feeling cut-off and "shattered" is reflected when he explains to Kira he feels drawn toward entering the recently discovered wormhole. Citing how out of place he feels on the station amongst the humanoids, Odo explains that, "I don't know where I came from. No idea if there are any others like me. All my life I have been forced to pass myself off as one of you. Always wondering who I really am" ("Emissary: Part I"). Such underlying queries about Odo's heritage and identity resound throughout subsequent episodes of the program.

In many situations, from his awkward interactions with Kira to his terse interpersonal encounters with members of Starfleet, Odo is often an outsider in the community of humanoids. There is a lingering sense that Odo is uncomfortable in his own "skin," as it were, and is uncertain about his greater potential as a shape-shifter. He functions within the confines of the station, but he is an outsider. His distance from the humanoids often provides him with an unadulterated vantage point, making him an excellent and impartial monitor of the station. Ironically, when Odo does reconnect with his community in season three, he discovers his own sense of justice greatly differs from his species, underscoring how his rhizomatic trajectory has led Odo to be both inside and outside of the communities of the Federation *and* the Founders.

Odo's confusion about his identity and subjectivity is even reflected in his namesake. As a specimen in a flask in the laboratory of Dr. Mora (James Sloyan), Odo was simply another "unknown sample" to be studied ("Chimera"). As Odo explains to Kira, his name was literally drawn from the Cardassian word for nothing—"Odo'ital"—and later shortened to Odo ("Heart of Stone"). As Odo reveals to Kira,

> for the longest time, whenever anyone would use my name, the first thing I'd think of was what it meant. Nothing. What better way to describe me? I had no family, no friends, no place where I belonged. I thought it was the most appropriate name anyone could give me ["Heart of Stone"].

Odo's initial feelings of self-worth resound with anyone who has grappled with such thoughts. Odo explains that as he became closer to Kira and the other humanoids on the station, he moved beyond this unilateral view of himself and even eventually embraced this name; he acknowledged its initial meaning but disavowed thinking of himself as an object. Instead, Odo comes to think of himself as an independent subject with agency. Such experiences away from his home world allow Odo to develop an autonomous viewpoint, and as the series moves on, it becomes clear that Odo's flight away from his community can be measured not just in spatial distance but in ethical and ideological ones as well.

The Dominion as the Villainous Assemblage

Throughout the first two seasons of *Deep Space Nine*, Odo often reflects upon the missing pieces of his identity, but his impulse to recover his roots does not reach fulfillment until season three. The season two finale, "The Jem'Hadar," lays out the series of events that will lead Odo back to his home world, where his past is revealed. There are several moments in "The Jem'Hadar" that deserve examination as they illuminate just how far-reaching the Founders' power structure extends into the galaxy, inter-twining with planets and species it deems essential for dominance.

In the episode, Sisko, Jake, Quark, and Nog (Aron Eisenberg) journey through the wormhole into the Gamma Quadrant to conduct a planetary survey for Jake and Nog's science project. Early scenes in "The Jem'Hadar" depict Quark and Sisko addressing their cultural differences. Although some of the exchange between the two is humorous, Quark provides candid criticism of Sisko's human-centric attitude, arguing that, "You Federation types are all alike. You talk about tolerance and understanding but you only practice it toward people who remind you of yourselves. Because you disapprove of Ferengi values, you scorn us, distrust us, insult us" ("The Jem'Hadar"). Quark emphasizes the perceived prejudice against the Ferengi, but Odo, of unknown origins, endures similar scrutiny from the Federation as well. A storyline in "The Search: Part I" picks up this thread and centers on how a number of Odo's security duties on Deep Space 9 are removed and re-assigned to Commander Michael Eddington (Ken Marshall). Odo suggests this personnel change is because he is not as trusted as a human in the role. The similarities between how Quark and Odo are treated by their human counterparts and colleagues led Lincoln Geraghty to suggest that Odo and Quark "feel a certain kinship because they are outcasts trying to fit into a group governed by Federation laws and human feelings" (458). Indeed, many members of the Deep Space 9 crew are often ambivalent in their tolerance and treatment of both Odo and Quark.

In addition to calling attention to prejudices against non-humans, "The Jem'Hadar" is significant because it begins to outline the Dominion's power structure. During the trip, Sisko and Quark make first contact with a representative of the Vorta as well as several Jem'Hadar soldiers. A female Vorta named Eris (Molly Hagan) is captured with Quark and Sisko by the Jem'Hadar, and the three are imprisoned in a hidden containment field. After Eris explains that the Jem'Hadar are the most feared soldiers in the Dominion, she warns Quark against trying to strike up business negotiations with the Dominion. Eris explains the tactics of the Dominion in simple terms, noting, "The Dominion decides that you have something that they want and then they come and take it by negotiation or by force" ("The Jem'Hadar"). Eris states that when the people of Kurill did not acquiesce to the Dominion's demands, "They destroyed our communications center, they executed our leaders, and before we realized it, they had seized control of the entire planet" ("The Jem'Hadar"). Eris' description of the complete absorption of her planet exemplifies the method of control that the Founders enact to bring bodies for labor into their assemblage. This conversation also demonstrates that, unlike Odo, morality and ethical concerns do not seem to factor into the Founders' strategies.

Later, Sisko and the others discover that Eris' description is likely crafted to conjure feelings of sympathy from both he and Quark. After Sisko, Jake, Nog, Quark, and Eris escape the planet, it is revealed that the circumstances of Eris' "capture" were all a ruse. Although it is unclear if the story she shares with Sisko and Quark is entirely fiction, Eris later reveals she is a Dominion spy sent to infiltrate and survey Starfleet. Based on Eris' account and Sisko's observations of the Jem'Hadar, it becomes clear that the Dominion functions as an interstellar imperialist entity, usurping natural resources as well as labor from species on planets across the quadrant, adding and reordering components into their assemblage as well as exterminating and removing those that do not fit into the plan. Terry J. Erdmann and Paula M. Block suggest that the Jem'Hadar comprise one-third of the Dominion's "villainous trinity" (154). Quoting *Deep Space Nine* writer Robert Hewitt Wolfe, who penned several episodes featuring the Jem'Hadar, Erdmann and Block clarify that the Vorta are characterized as the negotiators, and the Jem'Hadar are the "vicious warriors who would carry out the Dominion's threats" (154). Thus, a number of groups including the Founders, the Vorta, the Jem'Hadar and others function as one shifting, villainous assemblage.

Eris' account is significant because it emphasizes how the Dominion brings in multiple bodies, species, and planets to function as one assemblage. Thomas Nail's definition of the term "assemblage" is helpful to demonstrate how the Dominion functions. Nail argues that for Deleuze and Guattari, assemblages are

> more like machines, defined solely by their external relations of composition, mixture, and aggregation. In other words, an assemblage is a multiplicity, neither a part nor a whole. If the elements of an assemblage are defined only by their external relations, then it is possible that they can be added, subtracted, and recombined with one another ad infinitum [sic] without ever creating or destroying an organic unity [23].

Nail's explication illuminates my understanding of the Dominion's methodologies in a significant manner. Subsuming what it needs, the Dominion adds and subtracts species and planets into and out of its fold, grafting multiple bodies onto its greater collective, if only to expel them later. The Founders forge a shaky alliance with the Cardassians, but later betray the Cardassian people and keep their planets as a resource. The Dominion expands to splice various structures to one another in order to create its most productive mechanism of power, as a rhizome, which "operates by variation, expansion, conquest, capture [and] offshoots" (Deleuze and Guattari 21). Although the final scenes in season two bring some clarity to Starfleet's understanding of the nebulous Dominion, it is not until season three that viewers discover the Dominion is led by the Founders and the

Founders are, in fact, shape-shifting Changelings like Odo. Yet it becomes quickly clear how very different Odo is from the others in his community, and that these differences are contingent upon his line of flight away from the home world. Odo's own rhizomatic path allowed him to develop ethical and moral metrics distinct from the rest of his community.

Lines of Flight: Tethered to the Home World

There are allusions to Odo's continued search for his identity at multiple points in the season three premiere episode, "The Search: Part I." As noted, a sub-plot centers on Odo's response to being usurped by the Starfleet-appointed security officer, Lieutenant Commander Michael Eddington. After the personnel change, Sisko suggests that Odo will be in charge of all non–Starfleet security matters on the station, but Odo is not reassured. He interprets having to coordinate his efforts with Eddington as reporting to him, which Odo views as an inferior role. Odo's resentment over Eddington's appointment grows throughout the episode, revealing how much of Odo's identity is associated with his professional life and demonstrating how Odo has internalized humanoid values regarding professional hierarchies.

Later, Kira privately convenes with Odo and proposes he join the command team on an exploratory trip through the wormhole as a threat assessment advisor. As Odo's closest friend, Kira recognizes that Odo has been wounded by Eddington's appointment. Kira attempts to appease Odo, arguing, "You're still needed here, no matter what some idiot Starfleet admiral might think" ("The Search: Part I"). It is not entirely clear why Odo agrees to take on this role in what he calls a "misguided attempt" to make him feel better, but he does end up on the *Defiant* as it travels into the Gamma Quadrant. This exchange with Kira, like his earlier conversations with Sisko and with Eddington in "The Search: Part I," demonstrates the tension between Odo's abilities to bring order and control to the station and his status as non-human, as Starfleet's decision to appoint Eddington does demonstrate a human-centric attitude.

Later, and behind closed doors, Kira criticizes Eddington's appointment and presses Sisko to defend Odo's rightful place on Deep Space 9. While Kira contends that in spite of his unconventional methods, Odo "gets the job done," Sisko argues that Odo is not "a team player" ("The Search: Part I"). As Sisko explains, "He enjoys thumbing his nose at authority…. He files reports when he feels like it. His respect for the chain of command is minimal" ("The Search: Part I"). Sisko's response is ironic given that he often does not play by Starfleet's rules either, suggesting that Starfleet does grant more autonomy to humans than other species. Indeed, many of Starfleet's most renowned human captains, from Kirk to Picard to Janeway, are celebrated for employing unconventional methods to further Starfleet's agenda. Odo may not "play by the rules," but this is very human behavior.

Odo's quest for self-knowledge continues to be a main theme throughout "The Search: Part I." Later in the episode, Kira seeks Odo out on the *Defiant*, offering him a sympathetic ear, but he simply wishes for her to let him go. As he tells Kira, "Ever since we've come into the Gamma Quadrant, I've had this feeling of being drawn somewhere, pulled by some instinct to a specific place. The Omarion Nebula" ("The Search: Part I"). There is a sense of both immediacy and purpose in Odo's impulse to leave the *Defiant* for the nebula. Soon after this conversation occurs, a battle with the Jem'Hadar ensues, and the *Defiant* is badly damaged. Odo manages to move Kira onto a runabout and the two arrive at a class M planet. This planet, like Odo, is a "rogue"—an outlier with no system. As Odo and Kira disembark from their runabout and survey the strange planet, several forms emerge from the gelatinous ocean covering the surface, and Odo is greeted by a figure that resembles him. It is clear he has discovered his home world. The episode ends with the Female Changeling (Salome Jens) uttering these provocative words: "Welcome home" ("The Search: Part I").

In "The Search: Part II," Odo is provided with many answers regarding his past, including his initial journey from his home planet, but likewise distinguishes how his time away led him to develop a different perspective than the rest of his kind. The Female Changeling explains that, some centuries ago, Odo and ninety-nine other "infant" Changelings were sent out into the universe "to gain knowledge" for the Founders ("The Search: Part II"). Cut off from one another and from the greater collective, the infant Changelings set out on a different, random trajectory, which led each to forge their own way. They moved across the universe, establishing nodes through this rhizomatic path, unknowingly gathering information about other planets and species for the Founders. As such, each infant's journey can be described as a "line of flight." Deleuze and Guattari explain, "There is a rupture in the rhizome whenever segmentary lines explode into a line of flight, but the line of flight is part of the rhizome. These lines always tie back to one another" (9). In spite of his distance from it, Odo was tied to his home world, which is the "pull" he felt toward the Omarion Nebula. When Odo asks the Female Changeling how she knew he would return home, she explains, "You had no choice. The urge to return home was implanted in your genetic makeup. And now, thanks to the passageway, you're the first to return to us" ("The Search: Part II"). Odo's line of flight propelled him first to the Bajoran Institute of Science and Dr. Mora, and later to Deep Space 9, before finally returning to his home planet.

Odo's excursion and his re-immersion into his community lead to feelings of cognitive dissonance. Whereas Odo's initial connection with the Great Link conjures feelings of euphoria and joy, these emotions stand in opposition to Odo's response to the Founders' xenophobia and propensity towards violence against other species. Many of the Founders' core values, in fact, are dead-set against Odo's own sense of ethics and justice. Although Odo's discussion with the Female Changeling in "The Search: Part II" provides critical information about Odo's past, it also reveals the Founders' hatred of "solids." This revelation is reinforced by the fact that the Founders are holding Odo's colleagues captive to run simulations on them; this experimentation does not align with Odo's moral barometer or who he imagined his community would be. As noted in the *Star Trek Deep Space Nine* [sic] *Pre-Premiere Bible* and quoted by the Trek Writer's Guild, "Although he [Odo] doesn't know anything about his species, he is certain that justice is an integral part of their being, because the necessity for it runs through every fiber of his body—a racial memory." Odo may have felt his understanding of justice was connected to his past, but his rhizomatic journey *away* from his planet led to his sense of morality and ethics.

It is paradoxical, then, that after searching for his kind for so long, Odo is greatly disappointed to find that his understanding of "solids" is not proportionate to his community's. Thus, after searching for it for decades (if not longer), Odo decides to leave his home planet and free his colleagues. Before he departs, the Female Changeling tells Odo she will not hold him against his will, because "No Changeling has ever harmed another" ("The Search: Part II"). Though the Female Changeling agrees to let Odo's colleagues leave, she warns that, "The next time, I promise you, we will not be so generous" ("The Search: Part II"). In these exchanges, it becomes clear that Odo does not share many of the Founders' values.

The Female Changeling's prescient words about doing no harm to another Changeling come full circle in the season three finale, "The Adversary," when Odo is forced to choose where his loyalties lie: with the Federation or with the Founders. "The Adversary" opens with Federation Ambassador Krajensky (Lawrence Pressman) ordering Sisko and his crew to take the *Defiant* on a two-week patrol to survey the Tzenkethi border; Krajensky notes he will be joining the team to observe. From the earliest scenes of the episode, it is clear that danger is afoot. In a scene prior to the opening credits, Chief Miles O'Brien (Colm Meaney) is shown onboard the *Defiant*, performing maintenance checks before the journey. He hears some odd noises and the position of the camera angle suggests that someone or something is watching him. O'Brien brushes off his suspicions as evidence of his "old age" ("The Adversary"). As the episode progresses, O'Brien hears additional strange sounds while he is in a Jeffries tube and is startled to find Dr. Julian Bashir (Siddig el Fadil) poking around. Afterwards, the *Defiant* begins to have power fluctuations, transceiver assembly problems, and a host of other complications. When O'Brien and Lieutenant Dax (Terry Farrell) discover a worm-like, electronic parasite affecting said systems, all signs point to sabotage. Dax and O'Brien devise a test to discover who is responsible and go on to implement it—but when they approach Ambassador Krajensky to give him the test, he morphs into a Changeling form, and it becomes clear that a shape-shifter has infiltrated the ship.

Because the saboteur in "The Adversary" is a Changeling, Odo and Eddington have an extremely difficult time hunting this antagonist. During a preliminary search for the intruder, Eddington suggests that Odo take a phaser with him. Odo notes that he does not use them and adds that Changelings have never harmed members of their own species ("The Adversary"). Though Eddington argues that the Changeling would not grant anyone else aboard the *Defiant* the same courtesy, Odo remains steadfast, adding that, "I've been a security officer most of my humanoid existence, and in all that time, I've never found it necessary to fire a weapon or take a life. I don't intend to start now" ("The Adversary"). Later, Eddington suggests Odo put himself in the Changeling's mindset in order to anticipate his/her next move, but Odo explains he cannot as he does not know his people very well ("The Adversary"). In the end, and after a long pursuit, Odo finds and subsequently kills the Changeling. Here, Odo serves the needs of the many humanoids, rather than that of the one Changeling. In killing the Changeling, Odo breaks the cardinal rule of the Founders, who place their own above all others.

Odo is disciplined for this betrayal, but his punishment ironically draws him even closer to his humanoid counterparts. In "Broken Link," Odo falls ill with an undiagnosable illness. After an unsuccessful consultation with Bashir, Odo hypothesizes that the only beings who can help him are the Founders. It is later revealed that the Founders gave Odo the illness so he would be forced to return and be judged for killing the Changeling in "The Adversary." After joining the Great Link, Odo is found guilty and, as punishment, he is trapped in a humanoid body with no means of shifting. There is a Machiavellian sense of measure in this punishment: since Odo chose the humanoids over the Changeling, he is now forced to live as one of them. This strange turn of events is yet another offshoot of Odo's rhizomatic journey. Controlled by the human existential conditions of needing to eat, drink, defecate, and so on, Odo is drawn further away from his own community and closer to the "solids." Odo has not only lived with the humanoids but is forced to live *as* a humanoid. Though Odo eventually regains his abilities in "The Begotten," it is only after he inhabits this humanoid body for some time.

Many additional episodes concern Odo's conception of self and how far his rhizomatic journey has led him away from the rest of his species. "Chimera" illustrates this distance keenly, showing just how greatly Odo's line of flight differs from other Changelings. In "Chimera," Odo and O'Brien are on a runabout when they literally bump into another shape-shifter who has taken on the form of a grand, space-faring creature. The Changeling, named Laas (Garman Hertzler), explains he felt Odo's presence and was drawn to it. After Odo and O'Brien discover who and what Laas is, Odo invites Laas back to Deep Space 9. The more Odo learns about Laas, the more obvious it becomes how different they are from one another, in spite of beginning at the same point in their respective journeys. Although Odo and Laas started out as infants departing their home world, their lines of flight away from it provided each with very distinctive experiences. Whereas Odo attempts to assimilate with the humanoids' cultures and mores, even mimicking their appearance, Laas does not care much for humanoids at all.

Laas criticizes Odo for not embracing his true potential as a shape-shifter, arguing that Odo denies his true nature to fit in with those on the station. Laas asks Odo some difficult questions, including when the last time he has shifted into a non-humanoid form ("Chimera"). In Laas' estimation, Odo has been pretending to fit in for so long "it doesn't even occur to you that you can be anything else" ("Chimera"). In addition to bombarding Odo with such critiques, Laas also spurns Odo's bond with Kira. Based on his own relationship with a humanoid, Laas claims that Odo's relationship will not likely last, and even if it does, Kira will grow old and die while Odo will not ("Chimera"). Laas continues to attempt to persuade Odo to shed the confines of what Laas perceives as a rather mundane existence.

Though Laas is not considered a "Founder" (as he was one of the one hundred infants sent out into the universe), Laas echoes the same anti-humanoid rhetoric that the Female Changeling has previously endorsed. Near the end of the episode, Laas' arguments wear Odo down; it appears Odo is ready to shed the constraints of the station for a new beginning and, as Laas puts it, embark upon the adventure of a lifetime. Moments before his departure, however, Odo chooses to stay on Deep Space 9 with Kira. As he explains, "I know where I belong. Laas, humanoids are not the petty, limited creatures you perceive them to be" ("Chimera"). Though Laas determines that Odo's life on the station is just a "pale shadow, a feeble attempt to compensate for the isolation that monoforms feel," Odo has relied upon his own understanding of humanoids to make his decision ("Chimera"). The entire series of events with Laas brings Odo a clarity of self-understanding, particularly in regards to his love for Kira.

Rhizomatic Growth for the Survival of the Species

Odo's relationship with Kira demonstrates his progression toward a more autonomous identity and, as such, their bond is one that scholars have previously analyzed. Frank W. Oglesbee briefly comments upon the trajectory of Odo and Kira's connection in part of a longer conversation enumerating how Kira's character exemplifies Gene Roddenberry's vision for *Star Trek*. Oglesbee makes two salient points relevant to my own findings; first, that Odo amends his sense of justice to protect Kira ("Necessary Evil") and, second, that the two are not granted a traditional "happy ending" (269). Indeed, while Odo initially chooses to stay with Kira rather than travel with Laas, by the conclusion of the series, Odo makes an ethical decision to return to his home planet (and ostensibly stay there for the immediate future) in order to help save his species from mass extinction. His choice to return is not made lightly, and it is contingent upon the same sense of ethics and justice that Odo demonstrates throughout the series. Odo returns home because he has the ability to save all the Changelings, who have been infected with the life-threatening morphogenic virus. As noted earlier, the disease was created by Section 31 as a bio-weapon and secretly given to Odo so he would pass it on to the Founders. Much like a fungus or mold would spread throughout the rhizomatic structures of a plant, the morphogenic virus infects every member of the Founders' collective through their link. It is perhaps a sense of guilt, then, for his role in spreading the virus, as well as moral responsibility, that leads Odo back home. Even though the Founders have enslaved the Jem'Hadar, annihilated eight hundred million Cardassian civilians in an end-of-war assault and brought destruction and death to the Romulans, the Klingons, and those in the Federation (to name only a few), saving the Founders is still the most principled course of action, and so Odo must return home ("What You Leave Behind").

In the end, Odo's choice to save the Founders is the ultimate expression of his autonomy and embodiment of his principled stance. According to Odo, returning to the home world will lead to other positive outcomes for beings across the quadrants; he suggests that his efforts will likely lead to better relations between humanoids and Changelings. As Odo explains to Kira, "My people need me. They need to know what I know, to learn what I've learned from living among solids. It's the only way they'll ever learn to trust you" ("What You Leave Behind"). After ensuring that Kira will take him back to his home world, Odo wastes no time leaving Deep Space 9 behind. Still tethered to his home planet, Odo follows his line of flight back once more. This return marks the final step in finding himself and exerting agency; it also proves that Odo's rhizomatic path has afforded him the means to develop his own sense of right and wrong. As a being who is both inside and outside the communities of the Federation and the Founders, Odo stretches out into his own future while creating a just resolution for all.

The rhizome may appear disordered in structure, allowing for networks of trans-species connections to emerge at unexpected junctures. The seemingly random expansion of the rhizome, however, assures the survival of an organism, for if the destruction of one root path occurs, another may be more fruitful, leading to the continuation and further propagation of a species. Rhizomatic species shoot out tubers and nodes in countless directions so that lifeforms may live on, such as in the case of Odo and the Founders. Returning to the words of Deleuze and Guattari, "the line of flight is part of the rhizome. These lines always tie back to one another" (9). Odo's line of flight was part of his journey, but his path was likewise connected to the larger structure of the community of Founders. Though the Founders had no means of predicting where Odo and the other infant Changelings would mature, Odo's particular journey led him to establish nodes and connections with a number of other species. These connections led (in part) to Odo becoming a just, ethical being, which ultimately led to the survival of his species; thus, in the end, Odo's rhizomatic trajectory away from the Founders' home world ensures the survival of his species as well as countless others. As with the plants from which Deleuze and Guattari draw their metaphor, the rhizomatic quality of Odo's journey allows for life to flourish in new and unexpected ways across the universe.

NOTE

1. Operatives from Section 31 make appearances in several episodes of *Star Trek: Deep Space Nine* as well as other *Star Trek* programs. Although Section 31 began as an organization to protect the security interests of the United Federation of Planets, it developed into a division of Starfleet Intelligence before shifting into a rogue organization beyond the Federation's reach.

WORKS CITED AND CONSULTED

Barber, Jacob. "*Star Trek* and the Anthropological Machine: Eliding Difference to Stay Human." *Geographical Bulletin*, vol. 58, no. 1, pp. 48–50.

"Catching Up with *DS9*'s Rene Auberjonois, Part 1." *Star Trek.com*, 7 June 2011, www.startrek. com/article/catching-up-with-ds9undefineds-rene-auberjonois-part-1. Accessed 1 May 2020.

Deleuze, Gilles, and Félix Guattari. *A Thousand Plateaus: Capitalism and Schizophrenia*. 1980. Translation and Foreword by Brian Massumi. U Minnesota P, 1987.

Erdmann, Terry J., and Paula M. Block. Star Trek: Deep Space Nine *Companion*. Simon & Schuster, 2000.

Ferguson, Kathy E. "This Species Which Is Not One: Identity Practices in *Star Trek: Deep Space Nine*." *Strategies: Journal of Theory, Culture & Politics*, vol. 15, no. 2, 2002, pp. 181–195.

Geraghty, Lincoln. "Homosocial Desire on the Final Frontier: Kinship, the American

Romance, and *Deep Space Nine*'s 'Erotic Triangles.'" *The Journal of Popular Culture*, vol. 36, no. 3, 2003, pp. 441–465.

Krstić, Predrag, and Srđan Prodanović. "Smurfs, Cyborgs and Changelings: Prospects of Human Enhancement Retrospected." *European Journal of Futures Research*, vol. 1, no. 21, 2013, pp. 1–7.

Nail, Thomas. "What Is an Assemblage?" *SubStance*, vol. 46, no. 1, 2017, pp. 21–37.

Napolitano, Marc. "Reshaping the Universe in an Amorphous Image." *Science Fiction Film and Television*, vol. 5, no. 2, 2012, pp. 201–220.

Oglesbee, Frank W. "Kira Nerys: A Good Woman Fighting Well." *Extrapolation (Pre-2012)*, vol. 45, no. 3, 2004, pp. 263–275.

Pick, David. "Rethinking Organization Theory: The Fold, the Rhizome and the Seam Between Organization and the Literary." *Organization*, vol. 24, no. 6, 2017, pp. 800–818.

"*Star Trek Deep Space Nine* [sic] Pre-Premiere Bible." *Trek Writer's Guild*, www.twguild.com/resources/development1.html. Accessed 25 April 2020.

PART TWO

Race, Gender, Religion

Examining Themes and Tropes Illustrated on Deep Space Nine

Class Division and Biopolitics in "Past Tense"

Douglas Rasmussen

Fredric Jameson posits in his essay "Progress Versus Utopia: Or, Can We Imagine the Future?" that the purpose of science fiction is "not to give us 'images' of the future—whatever such images might mean for a reader who will necessarily predecease their 'materialization'—but rather to defamiliarize and restructure our *present* experience" (151). In this way science fiction uses allegory instead of prediction to comment on contemporaneous social, cultural, and political issues in a different way that will illuminate that issue. The difficulty with science fiction as a narrative of prediction is that technology advances too quickly and often becomes obsolete only a few years later. This is painfully obvious when visualized in films and television shows where depictions of obsolete technology in a future scenario removes the suspension of disbelief. In Jameson's estimation, science fiction is better as an imaginative fictional lens of futurism as a critique of contemporaneous social issues and societal ills than as a way to acclimatize society to rapid technological progress.

A prominent example of science fiction as social allegory rather than futuristic prediction is the *Star Trek* franchise. The first *Star Trek* series (1966–1969) was created during the Vietnam War and the social upheavals of the civil rights movement. Series creator Gene Roddenberry wanted to provide a liberal-humanist perspective on events viewers would see nightly on the television news through the use of a futuristic utopia where a quasi-military organization known as Starfleet worked with a united group of planets called the Federation (think an intergalactic United Nations) to better serve humanity and its alien members in a unified collective. Despite this, though, as Daniel Bernardi argues, "*Star Trek*'s liberal-humanist project is exceedingly inconsistent and disturbingly contradictory" (211). As admirable as Roddenberry's attempt at a socially progressive vision of the future through which he could comment on the strife and racism apparent in the United States at the time was, his vision unfortunately still conformed to a number of the contemporaneous social norms of the 1960s. Episodes like "The Paradise Syndrome," which presents Indigenous people in the future as still being primitive and tribal, certainly seems to affirm Bernardi's statement regarding *Star Trek*'s "inconsistency." Allen Kwan argues a similar point, contending that Roddenberry still affixed his post-racial vision of the future to a Eurocentric viewpoint: "This is a future that is absent of any influence from African, Asian, Middle Eastern, and South American members of humanity, implying that a utopian society can only be formed out of cultural and racial normality based on Western norms and ideals" (61). Despite his best effort, Roddenberry's utopia has the unfortunate effect of homogenizing cultural differences in an effort to present a post-racial future.

Star Trek: The Next Generation (1987–1994) continued this trend of using science fiction as a vehicle to explore pertinent social issues about inequality or philosophical quandaries regarding identity and consciousness. Although *The Next Generation* was more skillful in its socio-cultural explorations than *The Original Series*, it was still problematic in its detached approach to depicting liberal values and humanism. *The Next Generation* was hampered by creator Gene Roddenberry's edict of no interpersonal conflicts between members of Starfleet. Dan Hassler-Forest notes in his article "*Star Trek*, Global Capitalism and Immaterial Labour" that Roddenberry's edict created a "famous vision of a flawless human future effectively eradicating all forms of cultural difference" (376). As noble as Roddenberry's utopian vision was, it neutered a writer's ability to directly confront troubling social issues and potentially divisive politics that would normally create friction between individuals with different values and ideas within the Federation.

Perhaps somewhat ironically, Roddenberry's edict about no interpersonal conflict created an atmosphere of anger and frustration in the writer's room. In their book *Star Trek and American Television*, Roberta Pearson and Máire Messenger Davies note that Michael Piller, Executive Producer of *The Next Generation*, defended the "Roddenberry box"—as he labeled it—for inspiring creative solutions (84). The writers, however, found it difficult to accommodate Roddenberry's utopian vision in which intra-human conflicts were a thing of the past. For instance, Pearson and Davies recount an anecdote about series writer Ronald D. Moore's battle to include the scene in the episode "Family" where Captain Jean-Luc Picard (Patrick Stewart) fights with his brother and has an emotional breakdown over having been assimilated by the alien menace known as the Borg in the previous season (85). Roddenberry initially did not approve of a physical confrontation between the two brothers and Picard's subsequent emotional outburst, but Moore fought tooth and nail because he felt the struggle was integral to the scene. The driving force of a drama is conflict, and when characters are limited by the fact that the only conflict allowed is with external forces, such as aliens, it can limit the writer in a significant manner.

The third installment in the *Star Trek* franchise, *Deep Space Nine* (1993–1999), shifted gears and presented a corner of the *Star Trek* universe that was darker, more severe, and bleaker than previously depicted. *Deep Space Nine* was conceived and produced without the supervision of Roddenberry, who had passed away in 1991, and as such was not beholden to his particular utopian vision of the future. This freedom from the limiting and confining parameters of the "no-conflict" rule meant that the series could approach controversial subject matter in a manner unusual for the *Star Trek* canon. *Deep Space Nine* benefited from being able to break from the convention of Roddenberry's optimism to present a more realistic and, at times, more brutal corner of the *Star Trek* universe. The premise of having Starfleet take over an old Cardassian space station also provided a unique template for *Star Trek*, particularly with regard to Roddenberry's utopianism. The space station was harsh and severe, resembling something of a prison, as the Cardassians were not known for requiring comfort, which, in itself, could create tension. Adding to the difficulties of living in such a brutal environment were many of the individuals working on the space station who were not technically in Starfleet or who had not attended the Academy but were merely drafted into service out of necessity. Theoretically, that meant conflicts could occur between the main cast without breaking Roddenberry's edict. Characters like the Ferengi bar owner Quark (Armin Shimerman) and the Changeling constable Odo (René Auberjonois) could argue, debate, or scheme without violating the overall vision Roddenberry had for the *Star Trek* mythos.

Perhaps Kathy E. Ferguson best summarizes the tone of the series and how it differs from other iterations in the franchise's history: "It is the darkest, least pure, most ethically challenged *Star Trek* setting: the good guys are not always good and the bad guys are fascinatingly complex. It is part of this greater complexity of characters that produces the fluctuating liminality of the station" (182). By setting *Deep Space Nine* on a space station and on the frontlines of a conflict, the series can step away from the more clean-cut world of *The Next Generation* and depict a harsher and more challenging reality than had previously been seen in the *Star Trek* universe. By being on the frontlines of a Dominion War that would occupy later season storylines, *Deep Space Nine* could also present a morally ambiguous world. Deep Space 9 space station Captain Benjamin Sisko (Avery Brooks) is more pragmatic than the other captains, and as such his storylines reflect the brutal and liminal world described by Ferguson. For example, it is difficult to imagine Picard or even Kathryn Janeway (Kate Mulgrew) of *Star Trek: Voyager* (1995–2001)—who is very committed to following Starfleet protocols even when in a distant quadrant of the galaxy—engage in the same duplicitous tactics as Sisko in the episode "In the Pale Moonlight." In this episode Sisko looks the other way after discovering Cardassian tailor/ former spy Elim Garak (Andrew Robinson) bombed a Romulan ship occupied by Senator Vreenak (Stephen McHattie). The Senator had uncovered a plot to forge evidence that the Dominion was planning to attack Romulus, which would draw the Romulans into the conflict on the side of the Federation/Klingon Alliance. His elimination—and the recovery by the Romulans of said fabricated evidence—assures that the Romulans will enter the war. As Garak tells Sisko, "And if your conscience is bothering you, you should soothe it with the knowledge that you may have just saved the entire Alpha Quadrant, and all it cost was the life of one Romulan senator, one criminal … and the self-respect of one Starfleet officer" ("In the Pale Moonlight"). Sisko later notes that he "*can* live with it," and though his delivery here may read ambiguous, it does demonstrate that, more than any prior captain, Sisko is a soldier and a military leader, not a scientific explorer like Janeway or a diplomat like Picard. More used to ambiguity and difficult decisions, Sisko is more prepared to weigh his moral conscience against the needs of the greater whole.

Sisko makes an interesting addition to the *Star Trek* canon because he is an African American leader, single father to Jake Sisko (Cirroc Lofton), and a widower. What is especially intriguing about Sisko in relation to *Star Trek* is that he maintains a strong connection to his roots as an African American. In stark contrast to the homogenized monoculture of Starfleet, Sisko has a definite sense of identity formed in his racial heritage but is not solely defined by it. Lisa Doris Alexander comments on this distinct attribute of Sisko and its uniqueness when she observes, "What makes the decision to include connections to African and African American history and culture as part of Sisko's background unique is the fact that it seems wholly inconsistent with *Trek's* utopian vision of a future that conflates the demise of racism with the demise of the importance of racial identity" (152). Sisko's strong identification with African American culture better reflects the idea of *Star Trek* as social commentary. As Alexander writes, "For a franchise that originated as a series of morality plays, *Deep Space Nine* is the only *Trek* to explicitly deal with racism on earth sans allegory and the only series to integrate race into a character's identity" (157). Through Sisko, *Deep Space Nine* can more directly comment on social issues such as racism without having to use alien stand-ins as an allegory for subjugation. This is perhaps best seen in the two-part episode "Past Tense." In the narrative, Sisko and other members of his crew are hurtled into the past, where Sisko must directly confront Earth's—and *Star Trek's*—troubled racial/racist heritage. Yet as the first *Star Trek* character with roots on Earth who acknowledges and celebrates the diverse nature of Terran identities, Sisko is uniquely positioned, through his heterogeneous sense of self, to actually reckon with and even work to correct (in the storyworld of the episodes) Earth's troubled past. As such, Sisko's racial future alters Earth's racist past, suggesting, perhaps, as means of obvious allegory, possible ways for the present to do the same.

"Past Tense" and the Brutal History of Starfleet

The representation of African Americans in science fiction poses a unique challenge, especially when considering that if and when they are represented, they tend to be so from a Caucasian perspective, and at times a problematic one. Maryann Erigha observes in her discussion of African Americans in science fiction films (though the same criticism can be levied against television) that there is a significant lack of African Americans in science fiction: "Symbolically, the dearth of Black representation in the science fiction genre operates in dialogue with racialized ideological discourses that stereotype African Americans outside of intellectual cultures" (552). The absence of African Americans in science fiction, and more specifically, the underrepresentation of self-consciously African American characters in the genre, is problematic with regard to Black identity, economically devaluing their contribution to the genre and creating the distorted idea that African Americans are not interested in discussions about technology or the future of humanity. *The Original Series* at least attempted to present a post-racial future with African Americans, Asians, and Russians working together, but Sisko is the first self-consciously positive Black character in the franchise. This allows *Deep Space Nine* to engage in more direct and confrontational political episodes, such as "Past Tense."

"Past Tense" places Sisko and Dr. Julian Bashir (played by Sudanese-British actor Siddig El Fadil, who now goes by Alexander Siddig) into the heart of a racially-charged conflict in Earth's past. In these two episodes Sisko and Bashir are introduced to the reality of prejudice, classism, and social unrest in its most immediate and empirical form by becoming unwilling participants, and not just observers, engaged in a theoretical discussion about abstract principles. Through the use of Michel Foucault's concept and definition of biopolitics, I demonstrate how "Past Tense" reflects not only a darker, grittier version of Starfleet and the Federation, but that *Deep Space Nine*—unlike those series that preceded it—uses such episodes as a poignant critique of both human history and Rodden-berry's idealized but perhaps naïve utopian vision of the human future.

"Past Tense" begins with that old *Star Trek* cliché: a transporter mal-function. The senior crew are aboard the *Defiant* (the warship of the space station Deep Space 9) to meet with an admiral to discuss the Dominion when Sisko, Bashir, and Jadzia Dax (Terry Farrell) are subjected to a trans-porter malfunction that sends them to San Francisco in 2024, their past and our future. The San Francisco of *Star Trek* in 2024 is a deeply divided city, as the United States government is in political turmoil amid an economic crisis. Populations have swelled to a breaking point, and the lack of jobs has contributed to a situation of immense social strife. As a consequence, "Sanctuary Districts" have been set up in an effort to help the poor and marginalized regain their footing and find employment. Despite this lofty intent, the Sanctuary Districts have become zoning districts quarantin-ing homeless individuals into segregated areas of the city. Sisko and Bashir find themselves being mistaken for "dims" (slang for mentally disabled and unable to work) and corralled into Sanctuary District A by a guard named Vin (Dick Miller), who has a negative view of the homeless. In this world, the homeless are divided into three different types: the aforementioned "dims," plus "gimmies" and "ghosts." "Gimmies" are homeless but able to work, while "ghosts" are a collection of thieves who prey on the weaker people residing in the Sanctuary Districts. Sisko and Bashir are herded to a processing center where, in true bureaucratic fashion, they have to fill out forms and wait in an endless line.

These Sanctuary Districts are not just a far-off dystopian narrative device; they are rooted in our history. The Sanctuary Districts in *Deep Space Nine* owe their conception to a 1994 plan by Los Angeles Mayor Rich-ard Riordan to essentially fence the homeless in an assigned section of the city. As many homeless advocates pointed out, this was an excessively puni-tive measure criminalizing individuals for simply being homeless. Alice Callaghan, the director of the *Los Familias del Pueblo,* a community organi-zation helping the homeless, labeled it an "Orwellian poorhouse" intended to keep the homeless out of sight rather than provide them food and shel-ter or address any significant structural changes to Los Angeles' growing homeless problem (Duant and Nguyen). Episode writer and Executive Pro-ducer Ira Steven Behr has described the inspiration of the two-part episode thusly:

> When I look at the homeless problem that we're currently dealing with in Los Angeles and probably all over the country, yes, it's kind of weird that we did "Past Tense" and said it was five years away. I know that's a frightening thing. But that's not what it's about. The show was always about who we are, who we think we are, who we want to be and who we don't want to be.

The Sanctuary Districts can thus be read as an extrapolation of the problems with homelessness in California (and elsewhere), and the episodes' prescient nature is a commentary on flawed governmental strategies.

In fact, by commenting on the present, *Deep Space Nine* would indeed prove to be prescient—although prediction certainly was not the intention of the episodes—when looking at anti-homeless ordinances in California since the 1990s. Various vagrancy laws, such as San Francisco's Section 168, or the "Sit-lie ordinance," have effectively criminalized a section of the population based on status. Section 168 forbids the homeless from sitting on a public sidewalk or bench between the hours of 7:00 a.m. and 11:00 p.m. Other "quality of life" laws instituted by the San Francisco Police target incidents of loitering or public drunkenness by the homeless. San Francisco in particular has had some of the most stringent anti-homeless laws enacted by a number of administrations, some well-intentioned, some deliberately punitive and designed to criminalize the homeless. All of them ultimately fail to accomplish what they set out to do, including the recent creation of a "safe sleeping village" in the Tenderloin neighborhood, where homeless encampments were sanctioned and barriers put up to section off the homeless as a public health measure against the Covid-19 pandemic. There is a definite lack of imagination and care by multiple municipal and federal administrations to truly address the deep structural problems with austerity programs and how they contribute to a wealth gap and poverty. Indeed, in Roddenberry's vision, it took the Federation demolishing the entire system before equality and food would be available for everyone.

In the *Star Trek* universe, the formation of Sanctuary Districts in Earth's past performs a similar function to Riordan's homeless camp plan, and in this way *Deep Space Nine* is making perhaps its most pointed critique on American policy. As George Gonzalez notes in his book *Star Trek and the Politics of Globalism* about these two episodes, "Writing in the mid–1990s about homeless camps for the poor and the homeless being in every major American city is an explicit critique of the neoliberal project" (36). Throughout "Past Tense," Sisko and Bashir witness firsthand the devastating effects of racial and class divisions and government apathy towards suffering and inequality. The circumstances of the transporter malfunction also reveal how deep these divisions and perceptions truly are in this American society. Dax lands only a few feet away in a subway tunnel just beneath Sisko and Bashir, yet because of her white skin and attractive appearance she is presumed to be a victim of a mugging, not a "dim" who needs to be enclosed in a Sanctuary District. Her rescuer, a technology tycoon named Chris Brynner (Jim Metzler), helps her obtain new identification, thereby avoiding being placed in a Sanctuary District. Race is clearly being invoked as a mitigating factor in Dax's preferential treatment over Sisko and Bashir's less-than-fair treatment, calling attention to police profiling as a systemic problem in a political climate where poverty can, in part, be ascribed to racial factors.

"Past Tense" and Foucault's Biopolitics

The "Past Tense" episodes bring into focus what Foucault called biopolitics. Foucault identified two primary systems of control in the modern age: disciplinary and regulatory. Disciplinary control, as Foucault defines it, is the legal enforcement of laws and statutes. In this mechanism of control, the State, which as an entity was much more pervasive in the eighteenth century, governs over the individual body. Moving into the nineteenth century, new technologies were developed that allowed for the use of regulatory mechanisms of control. As Foucault observes, "Unlike discipline, which is addressed to bodies, the new nondisciplinary power is applied not to man-as-body, but to living man, to man-as-living-being; ultimately, if you like, man-as-species" (242). Because it is directed at a collective mass, these regulatory mechanisms do not have to adhere to standards inherent to disciplinary action, but rather can affect large groups of people, effectively criminalizing previously non-criminal members of society. This criminalization includes methods of population control, city planning, segregation, and, as is the case with *Deep Space Nine*, the formation of Sanctuary Districts. In effect, Riordan's homeless camps function as an exercise in biopolitics, which, as Foucault writes, "deal with the population, with the population as a political problem and as a problem that is at once scientific and political" (245).

When Sisko and Bashir are first placed in a Sanctuary District, they have a conversation which highlights the negative effects of regulatory mechanisms of control, where Bashir expresses disbelief that by early 2020s people who were without criminal records were placed in Sanctuary Districts. As Sisko explains, there was no legitimate reason to place them in Sanctuary Districts, as their only crime was a lack of employment and place to live, but otherwise the people offered no real danger or threat to society at large. Sisko even sarcastically retorts to Bashi's query, "Welcome to the twenty-first century, Doctor" ("Past Tense, Part One"). Bashir's incredulity at such excessive measures reflects how regulatory mechanisms of control can criminalize members of a society who were not previously criminals, and also how government bureaucracy acts as a *de facto* method of law enforcement by subjugating the poor and disenfranchised.

Foucault identifies the biopolitical process as being not only faceless and bureaucratic but acting as a "second seizure of power that is not individualizing, but, if you like, massifying" (242). This involves controlling how people interact with their environment and even where they live. Proposing enclosed spaces for the homeless to live and be subjected to the power and whims of armed guards is an exercise in oppressive regulatory power. The effect proves to be all-encompassing, as the guards in the Sanctuary Districts become inured to the suffering of others. This numbing effect becomes apparent in a volatile exchange between Sisko and the guard who imprisoned him:

> SISKO: You don't know what any of this is, do you? You work here! You see these people everyday, how they live, and you just don't get it.
> VIN: What do you want me to say? That I feel for them? That they got a bad break? What good would it do?
> SISKO: It would be a start! ["Past Tense, Part Two"]

Sisko's argument with Vin occurs during a hostage situation where Vin, his fellow guard Bernardo (Al Rodrigo), and a social worker named Lee (Tina Lifford) are held hostage by a Sanctuary District resident named Biddle Coleridge, a.k.a. B.C. (Frank Military), who is a "ghost." Vin, as we discover, is not a bad guy after all, just misguided. Racial profiling and a callous disregard for the personal lives of suffering individuals are endemic to the massive bureaucratic system to which Vin simply became compliant during his years working as a security officer. The overwhelming nature of the bureaucratic system is such that it eventually acclimatizes everyone to its regulatory and constrictive mode of thought. The regulatory aspects of control that Foucault discusses are not inherently disciplinary, but they do affect both those working in the system to control populations and the individuals subjected to segregationist policies where the marginalized and homeless are shunted out of view from the rest of society.

Throughout the two "Past Tense" episodes, scenes such as Vin's argument with Sisko (posing as a slain activist named Gabriel Bell) demonstrate just how dehumanizing the bureaucratic process truly is. Vin obviously feels for the people and expresses as such, yet the system will not allow him to act on his feelings of compassion for the downtrodden, and, indeed, he cannot even conceive of how to do so. Vin can only act on his established set of duties. Lee, who is also caught up in the hostage situation, expresses a similar concern when she tells Bashir a story of how she once allowed a young mother to slip through the system without being labeled and processed; it nearly cost Lee her job. In order to maintain employment, and thereby avoid becoming a resident of the Sanctuary District herself, Lee has to turn off her emotions so as not to feel too intensely. Both Vin and Lee are not villainous by any stretch of the imagination; they have just been dehumanized by the regulatory system of control that requires them to process those who are unfortunate enough to fall through the cracks of society. This is the strength of *Deep Space Nine*, where there is not as much a dependence on the binary of good versus evil, but rather a more complex and ambiguous approach to morality and ethics.

The dehumanizing effect of a faceless bureaucracy is evident in how callously the Sanctuary Districts disregard the residents. When wandering the streets, looking for a place to sleep for the night, Sisko and Bashir discuss the overcrowded conditions and the sight of an individual talking to himself in the street. As Bashir observes, there are a number of effective treatments for schizophrenia by this point in time in earth's history. All that is required is for organizations to put some effort into treatment. Bashir feels as if society simply does not care at all about these people, but Sisko responds by telling Bashir, "It's not that they don't give a damn, they've just given up. The social problems they face seem too enormous to deal with." For Bashir, this is even worse, because human suffering being caused because society has somehow forgotten to care about its disenfranchised and marginalized populations is incomprehensible to him ("Past Tense, Part One").

Sisko and Bashir are reflecting on the tragic nature of a faceless system that ignores social support systems and community efforts to deal with mental health issues, addiction, and other factors that contribute to economic disparity and poverty. The Sanctuary Districts depicted in "Past Tense" are not an outlandish science fiction narrative device but an extrapolation on the neoliberal economic policies that privileges wealth at the expense of those who occupy a disadvantaged position in society. The faceless bureaucracy of "Past Tense," not entirely dissimilar to contemporary society, is an uncaring system which requires massive social upheaval to alter the system, and, as Sisko notes, in a painful and sometimes violent process.

The hostage situation that is initiated by the "ghost" B.C. becomes central to reforming the system. B.C. is an interesting character because even though he is labeled a ghost, and indeed the first scene he is in involves him and his crew mugging a fellow resident for his food card (essentially the futuristic version of food stamps), the viewer learns he is not a clear-cut villain. In the second of the two episodes, which focuses on the hostage situation, the viewer comes to realize that even B.C. is frustrated and angry and—despite the immorality of his actions—is acting out in the only way he can conceive could make a difference. When B.C. makes his hostage demands for credits and a plane, he is doing so because he has reached the point where he believes societal change is an impossibility. The regulatory nature of the system has made it so that he is unable to conceive of any need beyond his own selfish desires. In effect, the system has crushed his hopes for a better future, and the regulatory nature of the Sanctuary Districts has forced him to become a parasite because there are simply no other options.

Conditions in the Sanctuary Districts become so horrible that only a violent revolution led by a man known as Gabriel Bell changes things for the better. Early in the episode Sisko, a student of twenty-first-century history, tells Bashir about Bell, who was involved in an event called the Bell Riots, which occurs just after the hostage situation resolves. In the first episode of "Past Tense," Sisko and Bashir were accosted by B.C., only to have Bell intervene and, as a result, get stabbed and killed, changing history. The inadvertent death of Bell results in Sisko and Bashir altering the timeline, setting off a chain of events that ultimately erases Starfleet itself. It is at this point that Sisko takes up the name and identity card of Bell and assumes his role, thereby allowing for a progression of events that would maintain the timeline as it had previously existed.

Narratively speaking, having Starfleet and its utopian vision come into existence as the ultimate result of a violent revolution stands in marked contrast with *The Next Generation*, where violence is viewed as a relic of an unevolved past. As Gonzalez writes about "Past Tense," "the overriding need to pursue social justice (i.e., topple *neoliberalism*/capitalism) is made clear" (60). Violence and aggression as the impetus for progressive change is not a message that Roddenberry would likely have allowed into the *Star Trek* canon, but *Deep Space Nine* is, of course, a more gritty interpretation of the future and less enamored with technological optimism.

In his determination of biopolitics, Foucault defines the nineteenth century as belonging to anatomo-politics, which is disciplinary and confined to the individual body, and therefore is reflective of what Bashir characterized as targeted hate. In the twentieth century, biopolitics became the new technology by which populations could be measured, surveyed, and ultimately controlled by the governing body. Foucault does not state a clear delineation between the two mechanisms of control, observing that the "technology of power does not exclude disciplinary, but it does dovetail into it, integrate it, modify it to some extent, and above all, use it by sort of infiltrating it" (242). In the integration of the two measures, disciplinary and regulatory, the mass groups of people subjected to its mechanisms of control become invisible targets of punitive measures. Groups without power, such as the homeless, become unwitting victims of a faceless bureaucratic system that embodies Bashir's concerns about forgetting to care. And, as B.C. says when watching coverage of the Bell Riots during the hostage situation, "When you treat people like animals you are going to get bit" ("Past Tense, Part Two").

Philosopher Achille Mbembe makes the connection between Foucault's notion of biopolitics and race in his conception of necropolitics, which is an extension of biopolitics, as a method of controlling the population. Mbembe characterizes necropolitics as the biopolitical control of minority populations through economic disparity, border policies, segregation, resource extraction, an unjust and disproportionate legal system, and the manipulation of social attitudes towards race, to name a few of the structural measures of control Mbembe identifies. Mbembe states that connecting race to biopolitical theory through necropolitics is self-evident, and that more than class-thinking, "race has been the ever present shadow in Western political thought and practise, especially when it comes to imagining the inhumanity of, or the rule over, foreign peoples" (166). The division of people into subgroups creates a racial hierarchy, or, as Mbembe phrases it, "the establishment of a biological caesura" (166). Biopolitics, then, functions as a series of measures used to implement an oppressive racial hierarchy. Colonialism, or directing the flow of refugees or other categories of people, such as the homeless, become methods of biopolitical control. Although the creation of Sanctuary Districts in *Deep Space Nine* is not explicitly directed at minority populations, the social strife and economic disparity would surely target the minority population more, as they are often denied access to the same strata in society. In the United States, class is often wielded as a regulatory system of biopolitical control with the intent of maintaining brutal racial divisions that harm society. Having Sisko and Bashir as visible minorities acts as a pointed criticism on the racial nature of capitalism.

Cedric J. Robinson used the term "racial capitalism" as a specific critique of how capitalism exploits people, denoting in his book *Black Marxism: The Making of a Radical Tradition* that racism and capitalism are intertwined together and that racism is, in fact, an intrinsic part of the system: "The development, organization, and expansion of capitalist society pursued racial directions, so too did social ideology. As a material force, then, it could be expected that racialism would permeate the social structures emergent from capitalism" (2). In effect, there is a vested interest by neoliberalism to maintain economic disparity and control the flow of marginalized communities through biopolitical security mechanisms. These biopolitical security controls are circulated through a diffuse network of mechanisms and *dispositifs* (various administrative, physical, or institutional systems used to control the social body) to ensure compliance, such as the creation of Sanctuary Districts in the *Star Trek* universe.

According to the National Alliance to End Homelessness, statistically, African Americans comprise the largest group of the homeless population, with 40 percent of those sheltered in facilities belonging to that demographic ("Homelessness and Racial Disparity"). There is an undeniable connection between racism and capitalism and undeniable biopolitical and necropolitical security mechanisms that are in place to navigate economic disparity and control the distribution of wealth and income. Ibram X.

Kendi notes in an interview that the two concepts are inextricably linked: "I classify racism and capitalism as these conjoined twins—right?—from the same body, but different face." Capitalism, then, is structurally built on the premise of inequity, and biopolitical security mechanisms ensure discrimination continues, even if, as in the two-part episode "Past Tense," participants are not actively engaged in discriminatory practices. The faceless bureaucracy of capitalism and how it fosters discrimination is enough, as described by Ruth Wilson Gilmore: "it develops fiscal, institutional, and ideological means to carry out these tasks. These means—or capacities— are made up of laws and lawmakers, offices and other built environments, bureaucrats, budgets, rules and regulations, rank-and-file staff, the ability to tax or borrow, and direct access to communications and education" (78). The entirety of the system is engineered for discrimination and exploitation of the lower classes, and it is no surprise that not only would Sanctuary Districts become a reality in the *Star Trek* universe, but that Sisko and Bashir would be caught up in an uncaring system where, even if the social workers wanted to, they could not escape the inherent biopolitics of control embedded into capitalism.

Worse yet, biopolitical security mechanisms are fluid, always increasing and being redefined, and center on the idea of inclusion/exclusion. Biopolitical control is adaptable to shifting socio-political contexts and, as Giorgio Agamden notes in his essay "Biopolitics and the Rights of Man," biopolitics are in "constant need to redefine what is inside from what is outside" (156). Segregation by race was a form of biopolitical control when the original series aired, and in our contemporary political situation the segregation of the homeless—who statistically are largely African American— from the wealthier members of a capitalist society is a method of using class divisions to maintain a destructive racial hierarchy, especially when used in conjunction with economic disparity. Michelle Alexander notes in her book *The New Jim Crow: Incarceration in the Age of Colorblindness*, "Any candid observer of American racial history must acknowledge that racism is highly adaptable. The rules and regulations the political system employs to enforce status relations of any kind, including racial hierarchy, evolve and change as they are challenged" (21). These forms of biopolitical control make the Sanctuary Districts in the *Star Trek* universe a very real and scary potential future.

"Past Tense" and the Right of Revolution

A callous disregard for human life is reflected in "Past Tense" and in the existence of the Sanctuary Districts. Medical Officer Bashir ponders just how moral a government (and people) must be if it can inflict such cruel disregard for the quality of human existence. In his postulation, Bashir wonders if there truly is any difference between humans and Starfleet's nemeses the Cardassians or Romulans. Startfleet posits them as warfaring races with oppressive regimes and/or an aggressive mentality, but in Bashir's mental calculus he sees humanity as equally capable of violent or harmful tactics if pushed far enough or desperate enough. Bashir wonders how humanity would react, asking "Would we stay true to our ideals or, would we just stay here, right back where we started?" ("Past Tense, Part One"). Bashir's question challenges the idea that humanity is, at its core, always a decent and compassionate species. If humans are stripped of everything and pushed to their limits by a corrupt government, how can they retain their sense of empathy and compassion? Perhaps tellingly, Quark (Armin Shimerman), the amoral bartender aboard Deep Space 9, provides a rather bleak appraisal of humanity that answers Bashir's question in the episode "The Jem'Hadar." For Quark, humanity is far worse than the hyper-capitalist alien species he belongs to, the Ferengi: "Humans used to be a lot worse than the Ferengi: slavery, concentration camps, interstellar wars. We have nothing in our past that approaches that kind of barbarism. You see, we're nothing like you.... We're better" ("The Jem'Hadar"). Quark sees Starfleet as a type of deception because humanity's past is littered with cruelty, and he is aggravated at the perceived smugness of Starfleet's superiority complex. In Quark's view, humanity's past greed for profit far exceeded the Ferengi's, because at least the Ferengi have rules of acquisition that govern commerce, whereas humanity in the past inflicted great acts of brutality in service of profit, religion, and conquest, among many myriad reasons. It is only recently, with the formation of the Federation, that humans act as diplomatic ambassadors of peace.

Under these conditions, the citizens of the Sanctuary District certainly have the right of revolution and justification for initiating the Bell Riots. Not only was everything stripped away from the people forced into the Sanctuary Districts, but according to fellow resident Webb (Bill Smitrovich), they are not even given the opportunity to look for employment ("Past Tense, Part One"). The oppressive conditions bring into focus at what point direct action, even if it includes the possibility of violence, can be considered a legitimate tactic against an unfair system. If the issue becomes a matter of survival, then any pretenses regarding civil conduct and morality become irrelevant. The inciting conflict that premises the series, that of the Bajoran overthrow of Cardassia, and that conflict's resolution at the end of the series with the Cardassian revolt against the Dominion, emphasizes war and tension as the central aspect of *Deep Space Nine*'s particular corner of the universe.

Riots—itself a racially coded word meant to inspire fear and suspicion in the news media—are an unfortunate but often inevitable last stand against the inherent problems of modern policing and systemic racism. Protests or riots, whether peaceful like Black Lives Matter or involving property damage, such as we see with the fictional Bell Riots, are not an ideal solution, but rather an inevitable result when all other options have failed. In terms of "Past Tense" and the Bell Riots, the situation is presented as an uprising by the poor against an unjust socio-economic hierarchy that has exhausted all other peaceful attempts to effect change. In the *Star Trek* universe the Sanctuary Districts were initially embraced by the poor as an opportunity for a transitional program to a better quality of life, but when the situation became untenable, direct action had to be taken. The Bell Riots might not have been an ideal solution, but they were a necessary one to make the largely ignorant public aware of just how oppressive conditions had gotten. In that regard "Past Tense" is a more realistic approach to discussing the painful growing pains to the progressive future depicted in *Star Trek*.

Roddenberry once stated that the guiding principle of *Star Trek* was that, "We must learn to live together, or most surely we will soon all die together" (qtd. in Zoglin 8). As a student of history and a resident of the Federation's purported multicultural utopia, Sisko understands this philosophy, but he also understands that the path is a slow and at times turbulent process towards racial and economic harmony. As Frantz Fanon writes in the opening sentence of his book *The Wretched of the Earth*, "decolonization is always a violent event" (1). The deeply ingrained structural problems with capitalism and its racial and class divisions almost seem to require a radical change in the biopolitical security mechanisms and economic system itself. By using the fictitious device of the Bell Riots, the genre of science fiction is here providing a window into this new world of human potential.

Deep Space Nine is a significant shift in the *Star Trek* canon because it is more consistent in how it presents liberal values to the public than either *The Original Series* or even *The Next Generation*. While there is much to admire about Roddenberry's original vision and his attempt to introduce socially-progressive politics through science fiction metaphors at a time in history when a conservative viewership would otherwise dismiss discussions of racism, sexism, or anti-war sentiments, *Deep Space Nine* benefited from being able to push the boundaries even further. Episodes like "Past Tense," which might not have resonated as much without the presence of Sisko, truly embody the idea of science fiction as social commentary.

In fact, *Deep Space Nine* would also directly address racial conflict in another notable episode, "Far Beyond the Stars." In this episode Sisko, feeling emotionally drained by being on the front lines of the Dominion War, reels upon hearing about the death of a close friend in battle. Sisko is already in a state of extreme exhaustion and stress and, as a result, begins to hallucinate visions of himself as a science fiction writer named Benny Russell living in 1953 New York City and working for a pulp magazine, with all his colleagues on the space station appearing as alternate characters. After a series of injustices regarding the publication of his work, Benny is savagely beaten by two police officers, played by Marc Alaimo (who usually plays the Cardassian Gul Dukat) and Jeffrey Combs (who plays the Dominion Vorta Weyoun). The final breaking point is when Benny returns to work, busted up as he is, and his editor Douglas Pabst (René Auberjonois, minus his usual prosthetics) refuses to publish Benny's story about a metafictional "Ben Sisko," an African American captain of a futuristic space station, on account that the public will not buy into such a narrative device ("Far Beyond the Stars"). The confluence of events, from the Dominion War to the projected world of 1953 New York City where Benny/Sisko experiences racism, causes Benny to have a mental breakdown. In the contemporary media landscape, however, at least Benny's "Ben Sisko" can be attempted, even if it is still a gradual process towards a more inclusive genre.

Conclusion

Science fiction now has the capacity to depict provocative content that more directly addresses issues of racism and sexism, how the biopolitical security mechanisms unfairly target the dispossessed and marginalized, the treatment of the homeless, representation of African Americans in popular media, and the inherently violent nature of history. In its initial configurations, *Star Trek* certainly had a progressive ideal which was complicated by the presentation of the Federation as a distinctly Westernized organization as well as having to conform to 1960s socio-cultural norms and values, which would prohibit a character like Sisko appearing on the television screen. Since it is premised on utopianism, *The Next Generation* likewise seems to lack the thematic structure to address such issues. In its testing of humanity during "Encounter at Farpoint," Picard's proposed "trial" is relatively short, simple, and somewhat perfunctory, when the Enterprise crew helps to release a sentient space creature being held captive by a non–Federation species, the Bandi. There is no opportunity to present humanity in even a nuanced light; they are exactly as Picard promised. *Deep Space Nine*, however, utilizes war and conflict as its precepting conception. Thus in *Deep Space Nine*, the struggle for survival is far more embedded into the overall narrative, tone, and philosophy of the series. Ultimately, though, in episodes like "Past Tense," *Deep Space Nine* demonstrates that Rodden-berry's utopian vision is the result of conflict. "Past Tense" does more than provide viewers with an engaging look at the issue of homelessness; it gives insight into Starfleet's troubled history. The two episodes of "Past Tense" highlight how governments use biopolitics to control large segments of the population, as well as to what extent people will allow themselves to be pushed. Revolution as a concept is rarely discussed in the *Star Trek* universe, with the notable exception of *Deep Space Nine* (which concludes with the Cardassian revolution against the Dominion), and this episode is an intriguing look at the conditions that would lead humanity to rise up against an unjust and unfair use of biopolitical repression.

"Past Tense" presents the viewer with a startling look at a dystopian future where armed guards corral the poor and disenfranchised into what are essentially internment camps known as Sanctuary Districts while the upper middle class remain in ignorance of what is truly going on (the existence of Sanctuary Districts was not revealed to the public). Emily VanDerWerff notes that "Past Tense" "reveals an extremely rigid caste system built atop race and class, a real-world problem that has taken on incredible urgency in recent years." By commenting on the social strife and issues of homelessness and the increasing militarization of the police that was occurring during the 1990s, *Deep Space Nine* did, in fact, end up predicting a potential future, but only because social conditions have not improved in the decades since the episode first aired. A writer for the episode, Robert Hewitt Wolfe, had hoped that the episodes would have ended up as just being emblematic of a gloomy period in time, and is quoted in VanDerWerff's article as saying, "It's disappointing that we're still grappling with this problem. I certainly would have hoped it would be better by now." Unfortunately, "Past Tense" is not reflective of a writer's overly cynical viewpoint, but rather is endemic of a larger systemic problem and a seeming inability to progress, at least not without some form of active resistance and rebellion against the prevailing social order. Watching "Past Tense" now, it becomes evident that *Deep Space Nine* was correct in asserting that it might, in fact, take an event like the Bell Riots to enact change in a system that otherwise seems utterly disinterested in progressive social action. The complacency of capitalist leaders to effect change reveals a harsh truth about humanity's unwillingness to address societal issues, necessitating science fiction to act as a warning in its social commentary.

Star Trek is often heralded as a franchise using science fiction as social commentary on a variety of social, political, moral, and religious issues. This is a feature of science fiction at its best, as "Past Tense" uses a dystopic framing device—unusual considering the far more common use of the utopian as the gauge against which most administrative systems and societal causes are measured by *Star Trek*—to question and interrogate an important social issue. In another episode written by Ira Steven Behr, Sisko addresses Starfleet's problems with the terrorists known as the Maquis, which helps illuminate the ethos of *Deep Space Nine*: "On Earth there is no poverty, no crime, no war. You look out the window of Starfleet headquarters and you see paradise. Out there in the demilitarized zone all the problems haven't been solved yet" ("The Maquis, Part Two"). In this episode Sisko is reacting to the disparity between Starfleet and the Maquis, who are struggling to survive in conditions far tougher than those found on Earth. When survival is at stake and the concern is for basic needs like food, shelter, and security, any notion of utopian civility is naïve at best. "Past Tense" uses history to not only illustrate humanity's litany of cruelty but connects this trauma with the progressive vision of *Star Trek*. In this regard *Deep Space Nine* not only illustrates how closely connected humanity is to its problematic past, but also presents this conflict-ordered past as essential to the construction of its utopian present. Whereas Roddenberry may have sought to keep intra-human conflict out of his series, *Deep Space Nine* ultimately suggests that his utopia would not exist without it.

Works Cited and Consulted

Agamben, Giorgio. "Biopolitics and the Rights of Man." *Biopolitics: A Reader,* edited by Timothy Campbell and Adam Sitze. Duke UP, 2013, pp. 152–160.

Alexander, Lisa Doris. "Far Beyond the Stars: The Framing of Blackness in *Star Trek: Deep Space Nine.*" *Journal of Popular Film and Television*, vol. 44, no. 3, 2016, pp. 150–158.

Alexander, Michelle. *The New Jim Crow: Incarceration in the Age of Colorblindness.* The New Press, 2010.

Behr, Ira Steven. "*DS9* Showrunner on 'What We Left Behind.'" Interview by Silas Lesnik. *Moviebill*, 10 May 2019. moviebill.com/stories/star-trek-deep-space-nine-what-we-left-behind-ira-steven-behr-interview/.

Bernardi, Daniel. "*Star Trek* in the 1960s: Liberal-Humanism and the Production of Race." *Science Fiction Studies*, vol. 24, no. 2, 1997, pp. 209–225.

Duant, Tina, and Tina Nguyen. "Homeless Camps Weighed in L.A. Industrial Area." *Los Angeles Times,* 14 October 1994. www.latimes.com/archives/la-xpm-1994-10-14-mn-50276-story.html.

Erigha, Maryann. "Do African Americans Direct Science Fiction or Blockbuster Franchises? Race, Genre, and Contemporary Hollywood." *Journal of Black Studies*, vol. 47, no. 6, 2016, pp. 550–569.

Fanon, Frantz. *The Wretched of the Earth.* Translated by Richard Philcox. Grove Press, 1963.

Ferguson, Kathy E. "This Species Which Is Not One: Identity Practices in *Star Trek: Deep Space Nine.*" *Journal of Theory, Culture and Politics*, vol. 15, no. 2, 2002, pp. 181–195.

Foucault, Michel. "Society Must Be Defended." *Lectures at the College de France 1975–1976*, edited by Mauro Berton and Allessandra Fontana. Translated by David Macey. Picador, 1997, pp. 239–264.

Gilmore, Ruth Wilson. *The Golden Gulag: Prisons, Surplus, Crisis, and Opposition in Globalizing California.* California UP, 2007.

Gonzalez, George A. Star Trek *and the Politics of Globalism*. Palgrave Macmillan, 2018.

Hassler-Forest, Dan. "*Star Trek*, Global Capitalism, and Immaterial Labour." *Science Fiction Film and Television*, vol. 9, no. 3, 2016, pp. 371–391.
"Homelessness and Racial Disparity." *National Alliance to End Homelessness,* October 2020, endhomelessness.org/homeless-in-america/what-causes-homelessness/inequality.
Jameson, Fredric. "Progress Versus Utopia: Or, Can We Imagine the Future?" *Science Fiction Studies*, vol. 9, no. 2, 1982, pp. 147–158.
Kendi, Ibram X. "How to Be an Antiracist: On Why We Need to Fight Racism the Way We Fight Cancer." *YouTube*, 13 Aug. 2019, youtu.be/_oQXki0hG9w.
Kwan, Allen. "Seeking New Civilizations: Race Normativity in the *Star Trek* Franchise." *Bulletin of Science, Technology & Society*, vol. 27, no. 1, 2007, pp. 59–70.
Mbembe, Achille. "Necropolitics." *Biopolitics: A Reader*, edited by Timothy Campbell and Adam Sitze. Duke UP, 2013, pp. 161–192.
Pearson, Roberta, and Máire Messenger Davies. Star Trek *and American Television*. U of California P, 2014.
Robinson, Cedric J. *Black Marxism: The Making of a Radical Tradition*. U of North Carolina P, 1983.
VanDerWerff, Emily. "*Star Trek: Deep Space Nine* Accidently Predicted the 2020s by Writing about the 1990s." *Vox*, 16 February 2021. www.vox.com/culture/22273263/star-trek-deep-space-nine-past-tense-prediction-2024.
Zoglin, Richard. "A Bold Vision." Star Trek, *Inside the Most Influential Science-Fiction Series Ever. Time Special Edition*. Meredith Corporation, 2021, pp. 6-13.

The Unkillable Idea
of Benny Russell

Afrofuturist Temporalities
and "Far Beyond the Stars"

DYLAN REID MILLER

> "You can deny me all you want, but you cannot deny Ben
> Sisko. He exists. That future, that space station, all those
> people, they exist in here. In my mind. I created it. And every
> one of you know it…. That future, I created it, and it's real!"
> —"Far Beyond the Stars"

In a pivotal and deeply poignant scene in the *Star Trek: Deep Space Nine* (1993–1999) episode "Far Beyond the Stars," author Benny Russell (Avery Brooks) has his story "Deep Space Nine" pulped by his racist publisher. Even the most outspoken of his coworkers, suspected communist Herbert Rossoff (Armin Shimerman), says nothing in his defense as Benny is fired for attempting to tell the story of a Black man dreaming of a better future, one where Benjamin Sisko, the central character of the show's main plot (also played by Avery Brooks), can be the Black captain of a starbase. This metanarrative forces the watcher to consider the afrofuturist content in *Deep Space Nine* and how sharply it contrasts with the content of other properties; the interaction of Sisko and Benny's lives as members of the African diaspora with the technological advancements of the universe stands apart from the sociopolitical orientation of the franchise as a whole, which focuses on a future dominated by the same cultural hierarchy as our present.

Star Trek has long been lauded for its political messaging in episodes like "Let That Be Your Last Battlefield" and "The Outcast," as well as for its diverse casting, particularly in *The Original Series* in the 1960s. This diversity is, however, only skin deep; the shows are predicated on an Earth that has been politically and culturally united under present-day hegemonic structures. Its vision of a united Earth ostensibly collapses hierarchical organizations of race, gender, and sexuality upwards until the only culture left is the "apolitical" neutrality of white cisheteropatriarchy. Rarely do the franchise's characters of color demonstrate an affinity or connection to their cultural backgrounds, in contrast to their white counterparts, and although this allows them to be visible as individual subjects worthy of recognition, it unintentionally reinforces the notion that the social construction of race is about skin color first and foremost, instead of a network of complex cultural practices that are generatively produced. Even where *Star Trek* has attempted to engage with the cultural backstories of its characters, it has failed to recognize the context of its production. This is especially evident in the case of Chakotay (Robert Beltran) in *Star Trek: Voyager* (1995–2001), and broadly in the series' treatment of indigenous identity. In the book *As We Have Always Done*, Leanne Betasamosake Simpson writes of the ways in which capitalism and colonialism have affected the territories of her nation, the Michi Saagiig Nishnaabeg. Not only have settler-colonial practices resulted in a dispossession of Nishnaabeg people's ancestral land, but also of their cultural intelligence generated through their attachment to, and relationship with, that territory:

> Because settler colonialism is the system that maintains this dispossession in the present, we need to be clear that our attachment to land is not up for negotiation, and that a radical resurgence within grounded normativity necessarily means the dismantling of settler colonialism and the return of indigenous lands [44].

Grounded normativity is a reference to Glen Sean Coulthard's *Red Skin, White Masks*, defined by Simpson as "ethical frameworks generated by these place-based practices and associated knowledges" (22). Indigenous knowledge cannot be decoupled from the land upon which it developed; in contrast, settler-colonial conceptions of land reduce its significance to that of a resource or commodity. By centering a settler-colonial perspective as an ostensible default for all of humankind, the so-called post-racial future of the *Star Trek* universe cannot or will not allow space for respectful depictions of colonized peoples, let alone conceive of the possibility for decolonization as a mechanism by which Earth could be "united."

In nearly every appearance of an indigenous tribe, nation, or individual, these communities and people have been further dispossessed from the land in which their grounded normativity is based. *The Original Series* episode "The Paradise Syndrome," *The Next Generation* episode "Journey's End," Michael A. Martin's novel *Beneath the Raptor's Wing*, and Chakotay's lore in *Voyager* all depict indigenous people who have either been forcibly removed from their planets or who have voluntarily left as the only way to maintain their sovereignty. Similarly, Black characters that appear in most *Star Trek* series fall victim to the side effects of liberal identity politics, namely the recognition of identity by a settler-colonial state as a method by which colonial subjects are produced and placed into social hierarchies to uphold that state. As Lisa Alexander says in "The Framing of Blackness in *Star Trek: Deep Space Nine*," most science fiction, including earlier iterations of *Star Trek*, seemed to send the message that "if black characters wanted to be integrated into multicultural and relatively equal spaces then they had to leave connections to black history and culture behind" (152). Nyota Uhura (Nichelle Nichols) of *The Original Series* was not given a first name until the 1982 tie-in book *Star Trek II Biographies* by William Rotsler, and no mention is made of her birthplace or cultural heritage beyond speaking Swahili. Though canonically of Somali descent, *Star Trek: The Next Generation's* Geordi La Forge (LeVar Burton) is allotted very little screen time to explore his heritage, especially when compared to Captain Jean-Luc Picard's conspicuous displays of French identity. Treating Uhura, La Forge, and Chakotay as disruptions in a white status quo, Coulthard says, "rests on the problematic background assumption that the settler state constitutes a legitimate framework within which Indigenous [and in this case Black] peoples might be more justly included, or from which they could be further excluded" (36). In addition, by situating identity in singular characters, the shows fail to recognize that identity categories are constructed through the participation of bodies over time in the practices that constitute that category, rather than being the innate and unchanging identities of individuals in isolation from each other.

Captain Benjamin Sisko, in stark contrast, places emphasis on remembering the anachronistic racism of the *Star Trek* universe and on engaging with the cultural heritage of his Creole background. He regularly cooks Creole food for his son and his crew, which he was taught to do by his father, a chef and restaurateur, and in several episodes, there is a focus on Sisko's devotion to keeping alive the knowledge of anti–Black racism on Earth, despite bigotry being ostensibly eliminated by the twenty-fourth century. Scholars have previously written about how Sisko's intentional Blackness changes the way that *Deep Space Nine* thinks about science fiction storytelling; in "'Explorers'—*Star Trek: Deep Space Nine*," Micheal Pounds argues that "at the centre of [*Deep Space Nine*] is an intention to use its lead character's complicated identity through which his ethnicity is threaded as a narrative engine for generating stories that might go beyond broken warp coils, trans mats and food processors" (215). Unlike *Star Trek's* other colonized characters, Sisko does not exist in an isolated timespace that turns characters into representatives of race only through the color of their skin. Rather, he is embedded deeply in race as it is socially constructed and engaged in the generative process of participating in and shaping Creole culture.

Timespace, rather than spacetime, is the analytical lens through which this essay views Sisko's experiences. Spacetime, the model of conventional Western physics, governs the *Star Trek* franchise's mechanical realities; the four dimensions of space and time are perceived as interconnected, with the former three (length, width, depth) being manipulable variables, and the latter (time) an inviolable constant. The technology of *Star Trek* depends on some rules of general relativity being bent for the sake of its premise, like the ability of starships to travel at warp (speeds faster than light). However, it does not ask the viewer to consider a different set of rules entirely, only to allow for an advancement in technology that has allowed humanity to alter them. Thus, leading with time rather than space in this phrase is an attempt to shift our priorities and allow for non-linear considerations of temporal reality. Ontology, the philosophy of being, concerns itself with the identification and categorization of that which exists within spacetime; in contrast, timespace is an integration of Jacques Derrida's concept of hauntology into our understanding of existence as we perceive it. Hauntology is used to describe an ontological disjunction where locating the origins of history finds itself dependent on an "always-already absent present." It draws its name from atemporal Marxist thought, specifically the opening line from *The Communist Manifesto*, "a spectre is haunting Europe—the spectre of communism" (Marx and Engels 47). The communism that is haunting colonizer and settler-colonial nations is a specter and thus is not present, but neither is it absent, at once in the past and the present, outside the flow of linear temporality (Macksey and Donato 254). In *The End of History and the Last Man*, Francis Fukuyama claims that the victory of bourgeois liberal democracy over the USSR in the 1980s brought about the titular "end of history," cementing contemporary Western socioeconomic and political structures as the best and final stage of human development; however, when it comes to imagining a revolutionary, decolonized future for humankind, as Benny Russell says, "you cannot kill an idea" ("Far Beyond the Stars").

Colonizers tend to treat historical events as situated only in the past, rather than processes that have fundamentally shaped the landscape of political and economic realities that rule the present moment, and in turn the future is often presented as an abstract and inaccessible temporal location rather than a site of change and possibility. Whereas it is difficult for us to conceptualize time as scientifically or physically non-linear, a divergence from *cultural* perceptions of time as a series of distinct and disconnected events is essential to disrupt settler-colonial futurity by acknowledging the presence of all moments as inseparably interconnected. Just because racism is theoretically an anachronism in *Star Trek*'s twenty-fourth century does not mean that the people of color that live in it are unaffected by the fact it once existed. Spacetime requires the presence of an object to measure time; timespace is intended to make room for what is absent as an equal partner in the tangible shaping of a space.

In Kara Keeling's "Looking for M—," she writes of a documentary subject who disappears before the film's completion to avoid being deployed to Iraq. This subject was part of an identity of queer Black women self-identified as the "aggressives," and Keeling argues that asking where s/he is serves only the power structures that seek to make hypervisible queer people and people of color in order to uphold colonial, white supremacist logics. Rather, the question to be asked is "when M—'s visibility will enable hir survival by providing the protection the realm of the visible affords those whose existence is valued, those we want to look for so we can look out for and look after them" (Keeling 577). In short, *when* does visibility for the marginalized cease to be for the purposes of identification within hierarchies of oppression, and become instead a recognition of their rights as a human being? This essay explores the ways in which *Deep Space Nine* handles the "when" of visibility for Benjamin Sisko, and how such visibility provides the audience with an example of how structures like race can remain tangible in the absence of hierarchical reinforcement for the purpose of oppression through the past's continued existence in the present. Using Black, indigenous, and queer authors, I discuss his non-linear relationship with time, made literal through his familial and divine ties with the non-linear aliens called the Prophets. As a white person living on stolen land, I will as much as possible avoid recuperating the intelligences of these authors to a white understanding of history and academia; rather, I hope to put the work of the Black creatives on *Deep Space Nine*, primarily Avery Brooks, in conversation with these authors, to create an understanding of how Sisko's Blackness as identity is shaped by his non-linearity in a fictional universe dominated by neoliberal, capitalist, future-oriented philosophies.

Academic consideration surrounding time as a political process with the potential to be a site of disruption was first introduced to me by a series of writings from the mid–2000s that concerned themselves primarily with queer communities; Lee Edelman's *No Future: Queer Theory and the Death Drive* and Judith/Jack Halberstam's *In a Queer Time and Place: Transgender Bodies, Subcultural Lives* in particular outlined the ways in which the structures of dominant social norms are interested in upholding linear futurity as the sole temporal orientation. As Shannon Winnubst points out in "Temporality in Queer Theory and Continental Philosophy," as an extension of her work in *Queering Freedom*, the roots of linear temporality are found in Lockean liberalism and the emergence of modern capitalist labor structures. She points to the works of Edelman, Halberstam, and Sara Ahmed as challenging and analyzing dominant social norms and their foundation on "a temporality that orients us always and only toward the future" and notes that because "we do not often conceive temporality as a constructed aspect of living existence," we often fail to even consider its role in upholding the oppressive structures of colonial and imperialist rule (Winnubst, "Temporality in Queer Theory" 138).

Although Sisko is not canonically queer in the conventional non-academic usage of the term, queer time and similar concepts as a philosophy of cultural intelligence are not limited only to LGBTQ+ communities, though it is worth mentioning that the non-linearity of *Deep Space Nine* also exists in the first on-screen queer kiss in the franchise's history between Jadzia Dax (Terry Farrell) and Lenara Kahn (Susanna Thompson) in the episode "Rejoined," both simultaneously young women and gender-queer beings hundreds of years old through the combining of personality between humanoid host and vermiform symbiont (perhaps unsurprisingly, "Rejoined" was directed by Avery Brooks). Non-linear time as an artistic concept has a much longer history than its academic counterpart and has been especially prevalent in the work of Black authors, from Audre Lorde to Samuel Delaney to Octavia Butler. Alexis Lothian's *Old Futures: Speculative Fiction and Queer Possibility* outlines the afrofuturist traditions of queer speculation upon which this essay is basing its analysis. She discusses, as this essay did in its introduction, the way that speculative fiction is often guided by the cultural politics of Eurocentric Enlightenment philosophers, and ties that to a particular consideration of temporality:

> Istvan Csicsery-Ronay Jr. describes science fiction as an outgrowth of the temporality of European Enlightenment thought and the technological developments of modernity: it is "an expression of the political-cultural transformation that originated in European imperialism and was inspired by the ideal of a single global technological regime...." If the timelines that structure futuristic fiction map an Enlightenment vision of history onto the past, present, and future of the globe, according to a colonial taxonomy of human development that places male, Western European whiteness in the privileged position, then stepping forward in this timeline may be less than appealing for those who are not its official subjects [105].

This is a succinct description of the way that *Star Trek* as a franchise seems to visualize humanity's future, as a step forward using technology without a restructuring of the dynamics of production that developed this technology, nor a reconsideration of the ways in which this technology is used. Legal scholars like Andrew Ferguson have written extensively about how it is possible to already see the inequitable distribution of "progress" based on who has access to this progress and its usage, and an obfuscation of the conditions it perpetuates because of the supposed impossibility of technology to embody bias. The technology of surveillance, such as facial recognition software and artificial intelligence used to determine neighborhoods with a high crime risk, are flawed both on input and output through biased data sets and a failure by the user to critically examine the conclusions drawn.

Thus, afrofuturism as a practice necessarily embodies an evaluation of what "the future" represents within the genre of science fiction. Resistance to modernity as it is culturally understood and imagined, and as it is defined by technological advancement, becomes a site of alternative temporality that turns away from futurity as the only direction in which society can or should travel. *Deep Space Nine* is predicated on and framed by Sisko's ties to an alien race that lives in the first stable wormhole discovered by the Federation, colloquially called the Prophets. They are worshipped as gods by the population of the nearby planet Bajor for their presumed ability to see the future. The reality, as we learn from Sisko's first encounter with them, is that they do not experience time in a linear sense at all; for them, "past," "present," and "future" are undefined terms, meaningless in how they organize and process information and events. Sisko serves as their Emissary to the linear timeline, born to a woman possessed by a Prophet to ensure that he would fulfill this role. At the show's conclusion, he leaves the linear corporeal plane to join them, cementing his physical and metaphorical non-linearity.

Through the narrative conceit of the Prophets, as well as Sisko's repeatedly asserted desire to keep alive cultural traditions and historical knowledge regarding the structures of racism, *Deep Space Nine*'s relationship to temporality stands as an afrofuturist challenge to the rest of the *Star Trek* franchise. An example is the two-part episode "Past Tense," in which Sisko and the British-Sudanese station doctor Julian Bashir (Alexander Siddig) are placed into a so-called Sanctuary District in 2024 after a transporter accident sends them back in time. Sanctuary Districts were intended to function as temporary housing for the homeless while they were evaluated for placement in jobs, but they quickly became overcrowded blocks walled off from the rest of the cities where they were built, and in which the financially destitute and mentally ill live under the watchful eye of law enforcement. Sisko recognizes the time and place of their travel as immediately before a series of riots that changed the Sanctuary District system; when the leader of these riots, Gabriel Bell (John Lendale Bennett), dies because of their presence, Sisko impersonates him in order to serve his revolutionary role and thereby re-create a future without Sanctuary Districts. Meanwhile, the white-passing alien Jadzia Dax, who was also sent back in time, is taken in by an upper-class man who owns a media conglomerate, embodying how twenty-first-century classism cannot be separated from racial dynamics and reaffirming that those with control over technologies, particularly those of surveillance, gain control in futures with settler-colonialist notions of production and futurity.

This is also apparent in Sisko's disdain for the holoprogram depicting a version of Las Vegas in 1962 whitewashed of racism, which he firmly asserts is a "lie" and initially refuses to participate in because of his unwillingness to pretend in its reality ("Badda-Bing, Badda-Bang"). The pre-riot Sanctuary Districts and the Las Vegas hologram are hauntological, the futures that they offer being ever present even as they did not exist. The government of 2024 Earth did not use these districts to reform societal inequality, and a vision of 1962 Las Vegas devoid of racism must always be aware that racism was once there and has been removed. The timespace of these areas will not allow them to ethically be divorced from the specter of racism.

However, of all the thematically non-linear plots and episodes spanning the show's seven season run, none is more suited to this conversation than "Far Beyond the Stars," the episode discussed in the opening to this essay. The episode, directed by Brooks, is a metanarrative in which Sisko is sent hallucinations—likely but unconfirmed to be from the Prophets—of himself as a 1950s science fiction author trying to get a novelized version of the plot of *Deep Space Nine* published in the magazine he works for. The character of the author, Benny Russell, is likewise diegetically hallucinating that he and the people around him are the characters from his writing. Benny's first "Deep Space Nine" story is "pulped" by his publishing company at the last minute, because of its portrayal of a Black captain. This, in conjunction with the police violence committed against Benny and Jimmy, a young Black man from his neighborhood (Cirroc Lofton, who also plays Sisko's son Jake), culminates in an outpouring of emotion that leads to Benny's psychiatric confinement, where we see him in the show's final season.

Timespace and the tangibility of absence it is founded on allows for a conversation about "Deep Space Nine"; though pulped, it continues to influence the world in which it exists. In *Old Futures*, Lothian cites Sheree R. Thomas's anthology *Dark Matter: A Century of Speculative Fiction from the African Diaspora* and explains how "her introduction figures Black writing as an unrecognized shaping force—like the 'dark matter' physicists know is there because of its effects but cannot perceive directly—in the history of modernity and of literary futures" (105). The destruction and denial of Benny's work does not make intangible the way that the readership of the magazine is impacted by it. Benny and his writing are deliberately made absent in the public consciousness, and the lack of him, either in photos of the magazine staff, or as he exists as a part of Sisko, is felt in how the possibility of a future in which Sisko is present ceases to be.

At the end of "Far Beyond the Stars," Benny questions a street preacher (Brock Peters, who also plays Sisko's father Joseph) who has encouraged him to write throughout the episode in hopes of confirming his true self: Benny Russell or Benjamin Sisko. The preacher responds that he is both "the dreamer and the dreamed" ("Far Beyond the Stars"). This sentiment calls back to the suggestion by one of the other magazine writers that the story of *Deep Space Nine* be made the dream of a convict or shoeshine boy wishing for a better life. Furthermore, this is echoed by Sisko when he returns to what is, presumably, the present, by wondering aloud to his father whether Benny Russell is still out there, dreaming of this future. Although the reappearance of Benny in "Shadows and Symbols" allows for a debate regarding which character is "real" in a diegetic sense, the ambiguity of these episodes implores the audience to consider them both as equally real and constructed by each other, as well as the culture that connects them—simultaneously, the "dreamer and the dreamed."

A similar dream, unbridled by hegemonic conceptions of temporality, manifests from within the subtext of "Looking for M—." Keeling places special emphasis on Frantz Fanon's usage of a quote from Marx in his book *Black Skin, White Masks* that illustrates the way in which the past and future fundamentally affect each other: "The social revolution cannot draw its poetry from the past, but only from the future. It cannot begin with itself before it has stripped itself of all its superstitions concerning the past" (Fanon 223). Keeling points out that part of Fanon's project was to "[explode] the temporality of the colonial mode of representation of otherness and [to reveal] a temporality that raises the possibility of the impossible within colonial reality, Black liberation" (565). Through its ambiguity and thematic usage of non-linear time, the series as a whole, and Benny's story in particular, becomes part of this same project, recontextualizing *Deep Space Nine* as Benny's liberation from colonialism's conceptions of spacetime.

Keeling's project to keep M— spatially and temporarily absent because of the "violence underpinning the very terrain of looking" can also be applied to a conversation about definitively locating Benny and Sisko, both within their relative realities, and in terms of realizing either of them as the "real" character (572). Benny's story in "Far Beyond the Stars" begins with a literal denial of visibility; Benny and Kay Eaton (Nana Visitor) are to be excluded from an upcoming photo of the magazine's authors under the assumption that their readership would be unhappy to find out that the staff includes a Black person and a woman. This is followed almost immediately by a moment of hypervisibility as Benny encounters the policemen who will later assault him and kill Jimmy. As he enters their field of vision and becomes observed as a racialized subject, he is ascribed criminality and threatened with arrest. The other figure representative of authority, the magazine's editor Douglas Pabst (René Auberjonois), also observes Benny as a danger as soon as he asserts himself. In the scene where Benny finds out that his story has been pulped, and when he finally abandons the soft-spoken affectation he has adopted for the majority of the episode, Pabst immediately exclaims that he will call the cops. The juxtaposition between the moments where Benny is offered recognition and the moments where he is erased is demonstrative of the ways in which both Black visibility and invisibility are circumstantially weaponized under the mechanisms of control and oppression in a white supremacist state.

The incident results in Benny's involuntary commitment to a psychiatric ward in "Shadows and Symbols," where his Blackness is hypervisible; but even as he is hypervisible, the possibility that he will be seen outside the context of confinement and control is stolen away through the attempt to stop him from writing. He is denied paper or a typewriter, though curiously has retained a pencil, and continues to tell Sisko's story by writing it on the walls. The psychologist Dr. Wykoff (Casey Biggs, who plays Gul Dukat's second-in-command, Damar, in the main storyline) tells him that his writing is "too dangerous" and offers him his freedom if he is willing to paint over the words; concurrently, in his own time, Sisko attempts to open a box that will reopen the wormhole which was closed by the Pah-wraiths, thereby allowing him to speak to the Prophets again. Benny can re-enter society if he is willing to give up the dream—specifically, the moment of the dream that re-establishes its non-linearity. The psychologists do not paint over it for him, because no matter what they do to him, Sisko continues to be real. He cannot be removed from timespace, as his absence will be felt both by those who knew of him and those who are unable to see a future in which he could exist; this is illustrative of the idea that Black people can resist via rejecting white futurity and constructing alternate modes of temporality. If Benny and his work are to be seen within the linear timeline, he must voluntarily sacrifice the potentialities of non-linearity. The existence of Sisko and what he represents, even on the walls of a psychiatric ward, are far more dangerous than the concept of marginalized people operating squarely within the colonial structures of futurity.

Like Keeling's M—, Benny creates—and thereby becomes—Sisko through the rejection of visibility within a settler-colonial framework; in turn, Sisko ultimately joins the Prophets, thereby becoming unlocatable in timespace despite his continued existence. This escape from the spatial fabric of the *Star Trek* universe is the final liberation of his character, just as M— recuses hirself from the violence of the state through hir disappearance: "Precisely because what is visible is caught in the struggle for hegemony and its process of valorization, one cannot want the relative security promised by visibility … the first question that must be asked of M— is not where is s/he but when might s/he be" (Keeling 577). Benny can only exist when Sisko exists; by his resistance, Sisko exists any-when, thereby representing the unkillable idea of afrofuturism. As the *Star Trek* franchise continues to expand, the specters of Benny and Sisko will haunt it, reminding the audience of futures beyond what settler-colonial thinking can imagine.

WORKS CITED AND CONSULTED

Alexander, Lisa Doris. "Far Beyond the Stars: The Framing of Blackness in *Star Trek: Deep Space Nine*." *Journal of Popular Film & Television*, vol. 44, no. 3, 2016, pp. 150–158. EBSCO-host, doi:10.1080/01956051.2016.1142418.

Coulthard, Glen Sean. *Red Skin, White Masks*. U of Minnesota P, 2014.

Derrida, Jacques. *Specters of Marx: The State of the Debt, the Work of Mourning and the New International*. Crane Library at the University of British Columbia, 2011.

Edelman, Lee. *No Future: Queer Theory and the Death Drive*. Duke UP, 2004.

Fanon, Frantz. *Black Skin, White Masks*. Translated by Charles Lam Markmann. Grove Press, 1968.

Ferguson, Andrew Guthrie. *The Rise of Big Data Policing: Surveillance, Race, and the Future of Law Enforcement*. NYU Press, 2017. JSTOR, www.jstor.org/stable/j.ctt1pwtb27.

Fukuyama, Francis. *The End of History and the Last Man*. Penguin, 1992.

Halberstam, Judith. *In a Queer Time and Place: Transgender Bodies, Subcultural Lives*. NYU Press, 2005.

Keeling, Kara. "Looking For M—." *GLQ: A Journal of Lesbian and Gay Studies*, vol. 15, no. 4, 2009, pp. 565–582. doi:10.1215/10642684-2009-002.

Lothian, Alexis. *Old Futures: Speculative Fiction and Queer Possibility*. NYU Press, 2018.

Macksey, Richard, and Eugenio Donato. *The Languages of Criticism and the Sciences of Man: The Structuralist Controversy*. Johns Hopkins UP, 1979.

Martin, Michael A. *The Romulan War: Beneath the Raptor's Wing*. Pocket Books, 2011.

Marx, Karl, and Friedrich Engels. *The Communist Manifesto*. Pluto Press, 2017.

Pounds, Micheal Charles. "'Explorers'—*Star Trek: Deep Space Nine*." *African Identities*, vol. 7, no. 2, 2009, pp. 209–235. EBSCOhost, doi:10.1080/14725840902808892.

Rotsler, William. *Star Trek II Biographies*. Wanderer Books, 1982.

Simpson, Leanne Betasamosake. *As We Have Always Done: Indigenous Freedom Through Radical Resistance*. U of Minnesota P, 2017.

Thomas, Sheree R. *Dark Matter: A Century of Speculative Fiction from the American Diaspora*. Warner Books, 2000.

Winnubst, Shannon. *Queering Freedom*. Indiana UP, 2006.

_____. "Temporality in Queer Theory and Continental Philosophy." *Philosophy Compass*, vol. 5, 2010, pp. 136–146.

(Un)Radical Feminism

Gender and the Limits of Imagination

ROWAN BELL

Near the beginning of *What We Left Behind* (2019), a documentary detailing the making of *Star Trek: Deep Space Nine* (1993–1999), there is a segment which recounts the show's positive impact on its female fans. In a series of stirring sound bites, women and girls of all ages report how the show has inspired them and provided them with strong, well-written, and emotionally complex female role models. It is a touching moment in the documentary, and one that hits home for a lot of female *Star Trek* fans. Historically, women have not always been made to feel at home in science fiction culture, and *Star Trek* does not have the best record on this point. For many of the fans presented in the documentary, *Deep Space Nine* represented exciting and empowering new possibilities. The film drives home this point with an action montage of the women featured in the show: Kira Nerys (Nana Visitor), Jadzia Dax (Terry Farrell), Ezri Dax (Nicole de Boer), Kasidy Yates (Penny Johnson Jerald), Keiko O'Brien (Rosalind Chao), and Leeta (Chase Masterson). The music over this montage is Meredith Brooks' "Bitch," a song about being changeable but nonetheless demanding love—and a testament to late twentieth-century tropes about White American women.

Deep Space Nine thought it was ahead of its time on gender issues; and in many ways, it was correct. It joined a growing trend of science fiction and fantasy television featuring powerful female leading characters. The show ran concurrently with *Buffy the Vampire Slayer* (1997–2003), *Xena: Warrior Princess* (1995–2001), and *The X-Files* (1993–2018), and just preceded *Firefly* (2002–2003) and the new *Battlestar Galactica* (2004–2009). Far from the Lois Lanes and Barbarellas of the mid-twentieth century, Buffy (Sarah Michelle Gellar), Xena (Lucy Lawless), Scully (Gillian Anderson), Kira, and Dax were fully developed characters with their own interests,

135

who (mostly) went around fully clothed and (mostly) did not need men to get things done. The impressiveness of these advancements is somewhat mitigated by the low height of the bar. It did not take much to improve on existing tropes, and it should not be revolutionary to introduce a female character who is an independent person. Still, it was a relatively good time to be a nerdy feminist. At least things were moving in the right direction.

Star Trek has always been motivated by an enchanting idealism about human possibility. It shows us a world where we have moved beyond categories which oppress and divide us; where we have eliminated money, and with it poverty, class warfare, bigotry, and material injustice; and where, in the words of Jean-Luc Picard (Patrick Stewart), "we work together to better ourselves and the rest of humanity" (Star Trek: First Contact). It allows us to imagine for a moment what the world would be like if humans were united and equal, and in so doing, reflects back to us the ways in which we are not. In the 1960s, this took the form of including Nyota Uhura (Nichelle Nichols), a Black woman, on the bridge of the Enterprise—a radical statement which provoked White American rage, particularly when the show featured American broadcast television's first interracial kiss ("Plato's Stepchildren"). In the 1990s, this manifested with a Black man as captain, and a host of strong, nuanced, stereotype-smashing female characters. We get Kira, a tough-as-nails, immensely capable First Officer whose anger is righteous and powerful; Dax, a brilliant, funny, and profoundly wise 300-year-old scientist whose unapologetic sexuality is never a character flaw; Kasidy Yates, a take-no-bull freighter captain who is nonetheless an ideal romantic partner; Keiko O'Brien, a wife and mother whose career and interests are portrayed as valuable and worthy; and Leeta, initially a vapidly pretty "dabo girl" who turns out to be skilled, smart, and self-sufficient—to name a few.

Quite generally, the political bar that Star Trek sets for itself is sky-high. Unlike shows set in the present day, a mythic past, a dystopian future, or an alternate reality, Star Trek uniquely purports to show us what our ideal future would be. It is our choices which might lead to the United Federation (or not), our possibilities which might be realized in this egalitarian paradise (or not). This is often made explicit. Wise humans frequently make references to the problems of Earth's history, generally when comparing them to some morally backwards alien culture; the people of this planet oppress their working class, or kill each other over minor differences in religious belief, or divide their population according to irrelevant physical features—but Terrans have moved past all of that. Nearly every Star Trek show has featured at least one episode portraying a familiar Earth set within a few decades of the show's airdate, just to illuminate the contrast. Deep Space Nine, by far the grittiest of the classic series, pulls no punches in this regard. In "Past Tense" and "Far Beyond the Stars," the show offered explicit takes on income inequality, homelessness, segrega-tion, police brutality, and anti–Black discrimination in twentieth-century America—rare direct hits in a narrative that typically cloaks its political points in analogy and thought experiment. It explicitly aims to show us what stands in the way of a better future: old-fashioned American racism, classism, and capitalism.

And sexism. Right?

Certainly, *Deep Space Nine* is not afraid to discuss sex inequality. The show even features an explicit struggle for feminist rights, when Ishka (Andrea Martin, later Cecily Adams) decides to take on the Ferengi laws forbidding women to wear clothes or earn profit. Ishka's efforts, and their effect on the bewildered men in her life who previously took misogyny for granted, are at times funny and heartfelt, at times disappointing, and at times deeply problematic. Still, narratives like this make it clear that *Deep Space Nine* was striving to support women's rights—even if those attempts sometimes missed the mark.

In an early episode, "Sanctuary," the crew of Deep Space 9 meets an alien race known as the Skrreeans. Skrreean culture is matriarchal, and the women have all the social power—a fact that does not escape the crew's notice. The viewer is introduced to a woman named Haneek. Haneek is unambiguously the head of her household; she has two male mates, who are childlike, submissive, and obey her without question. When interacting with the station's senior officers, Haneek is surprised to see men involved in the business of negotiation. She reveals that all Skrreean leaders are women: "Men are far too emotional to be leaders. They're constantly fight-ing amongst themselves. It's their favorite thing to do" ("Sanctuary"). This predictably unsettles the men in the room, much to Dax's amusement.

The point here is well taken. When women are criticized for being "too emotional," or this feature is used to explain their subordinate status, it is usually done by explicitly or implicitly contrasting women's emotionality with men's rationality and clear-headedness. If these characterizations of men and women were accurate, it would seem natural, or right, that men are in charge of things; if we must decide between "emotional" leaders and "rational" ones, the choice is clear. There are other implicit cultural beliefs about men, however, which should undermine this framework. In Western society, we are told that men are more aggressive, more competitive, and more violent than women. Oddly enough, these characteristics are rarely presented as being impediments to good leadership. To put the point differ-ently: there are plenty of emotions associated with being a man, and those emotions are just as likely to cloud judgment as any associated with being a woman. Even if our cultural beliefs about the natural emotional states of men and women were true, they would not justify excluding women from leadership roles. To call women "emotional" sounds like a mere description, but it is not. It is a way of justifying unequal power relationships, and upon inspection, it fails. The Skrreean role reversal gives the viewer just enough information to work this out on their own. It is a clever piece of writing, and a classic *Star Trek* way to question the viewer's assumptions.

A striking point about this episode, however, is that despite the reversal of *power* in Skrreean gender roles, other aspects of those roles remain quite fixed. Skrreean women wear flowing pastels and makeup on their faces and keep their hair long. Skrreean men wear pants, no makeup, and short hair. Haneek's stereotypes about men are very familiar to a modern human sensibility. She and Kira bond over their mutual dislike of a dress in a shop. In short, the women are recognizably *women* and the men recognizably *men* by turn-of-the-millennium human standards. This is not unique to Skrreean culture, of course. Most aliens encountered in various *Star Trek* series roughly follow some version of binary gender roles.

It is not clear why this should be the case. One of the cornerstone insights of feminist theory is that gender is socially constructed. This means, among other things, that the particular norms and trappings of some genders are entirely dependent on the social context. For example, what counts as *woman* or *feminine* in a modern White household in the American Midwest will be very different than it was a few centuries ago, or on a different continent, or even next door, in the home of members of another race, culture, or class. This is excellent evidence that the concepts that we recognize as "woman" and "feminine" are not fixed or natural, but rather are constructs which can and do change. Attempts to define them according to particular features tend to privilege one group over another. For example, an understanding of femininity and women as "soft" and "delicate" privileges White, western, upper-class women, and indicates that women who do meet those standards are *better* at being women than those who do not.

Concepts of "woman" and "feminine" here are clearly more confused than they seem. As Simone de Beauvoir sardonically asks,

> Is femininity secreted by the ovaries? Is it enshrined in a Platonic heaven? Is a frilly petticoat enough to bring it down to earth? Although some women zealously strive to embody it, the model has never been patented. It is typically described in vague and shimmering terms borrowed from a clairvoyant's vocabulary [3].

Beauvoir's point is this: we think that we know what "femininity" means, but it starts to fall apart when we try to define it. It probably is not a nebulous supernatural phenomenon, and it is equally unlikely to be "secreted by the ovaries." And, as noted above, it is not something that can be defined by reference to particular features, because which features count as "feminine" can and do change radically. We take "femininity" for granted, but we do not really know what it is.

One important point here is that "woman" and "feminine" are *social* phenomena. We cannot define them with reference to biological features. For one thing, not all women have the same biological features; trans women, intersex women, or cisgender women who have had hysterectomies and mastectomies are all women and can all be feminine. Independently of any of these considerations, however, gender categories exist in the social world and are not biological. Wearing a dress or being the primary caregiver of children is not necessarily connected to the chromosomes or body parts one has. Even if there is a strong correlation between these two kinds of things, they can still be understood and analyzed independently. Beauvoir famously stated, "One is not born, but rather becomes, woman" (283). Some have read this as distinguishing between *sex*, or one's set of biological reproductive features, and *gender*, or the social meaning of those reproductive features. Although Beauvoir scholars agree that she did not intend this point, it nevertheless caught on (Ásta 54). Put simply: there are fixed realities about the body (sex), but the social meaning of that body (gender) is not at all fixed. Rather, it is determined by human culture. Another way to say this is that sex is a *material fact*, but gender is a *social fact*. That does not mean gender does not have real, material consequences. Social facts are still facts. Rather, it means that gender is not *essential* or *innate*. Femininity is not "secreted by the ovaries." What counts as feminine, and as a woman, depends on where and who you are.

It is surprising, then, that the egalitarian future imagined by *Star Trek* showrunners is so stringently gendered. Why is it that so many alien females have longer hair, more delicate features, and more jewelry and makeup than the males? Moreover, why do so many alien cultures seem to have *patriarchies*—including the Klingons, who are in other ways exceptions to the above points? Why is it so unexpected when the Skrreeans are matriarchal?

Here is an answer that might spring to mind. Common-sense wisdom suggests that facts about gender come from innate sex properties. That is, one might think that females are inclined to certain kinds of social behaviors, while males are inclined to others. Perhaps females naturally want to be prettier while males naturally want to be stronger; perhaps males are inclined to leadership roles while females are inclined to caregiving roles; and so on. This view is known as *biological essentialism*, because it makes claims about male and female "essential" features. Biological essentialism is a popular view, in part because we observe such strong correlations between biological features and gendered behavioral patterns.

If biological essentialism is right, we can apply it to all species who have males and females. The biological essentialist can even make room for some gender-nonconformity if they keep their statements vague and probabilistic. Individual people, cultures, or races who do not follow the gendered patterns can be written off as anomalies.

In 1859, almost a century before Beauvoir's *The Second Sex* was published, Harriet Taylor Mill and John Stuart Mill were writing about this very subject. In *The Subjection of Women*, they argue,

> I deny that any one knows, or can know, the nature of the two sexes, as long as they have only been seen in their present relation to one another. If men had ever been found in society without women, or women without men, or if there had been a society of men and women in which the women were not under the control of the men, something might have been positively known about the mental and moral differences which may be inherent in the nature of each. What is now called the nature of women is an eminently artificial thing—the result of forced repression in some directions, unnatural stimulation in others…. Men, with that inability to recognise their own work which distinguishes the unanalytic mind, indolently believe that the tree grows of itself in the way they have made it grow, and that it would die if one half of it were not kept in a vapour bath and the other half in the snow [136–137].

Mill and Mill's point is that we live in a deeply and rigidly gendered society in which females are trained to certain behaviors since birth—specifically, towards behaviors that encourage and justify the subordinate status of women. That makes it impossible to know what is innate or "natural" for them. The only observations that we have about gender and sex have been made under social conditions that are historically geared towards oppressing women. We therefore cannot make any justified claims about what the "nature" of women might be.

In her book *Delusions of Gender*, psychologist and philosopher Cordelia Fine argues that existing research is unable to conclusively show inherent differences between male and female brains. There are differences in adulthood, but since the brain is shaped by experience, those differences might not be innate. Fine lists the following report from a self-described feminist mother, who had recently discovered her unborn baby's sex was male:

> He was a boy. He was "stronger" now than the child I had known only one minute before. He did not need to be addressed with such light and fluffy language, such as "little one." … Thus, I lowered my voice to a deeper octave. It lost its tenderness. The tone in my voice was more articulate and short, whereas, before, the pitch in my voice was high and feminine. I wanted him to be "strong" and "athletic," therefore, I had to speak to him with a stereotypical "strong," "masculine" voice to encourage this "innate strength" [193].

In short, we expect and train children to be boys and girls even *before they are born*. As such, how are we supposed to know what their essential properties are?

It is important to understand what exactly is being said here. The argument is not that biology does not give rise to any natural tendencies, nor is it that males and females do not have innate differences. The point is, rather, about *what we know* about those differences. Maybe natural sex and gender differences exist; maybe they do not. Maybe they look like we would expect them to look; maybe they do not. Yet we cannot be sure because, as philosophers would say, we lack *epistemic access* to them. We simply do not know.

The feminist critique is not just that gender is epistemically dubious. It is also morally bad, for two reasons. First, it is exclusionary. Attempts to identify particular "natural features" of gender tend to privilege a "default" picture of women or men—typically, a White, cisgender, middle- or upper-class, non-disabled, European, English-speaking one. Claims about essential features tend to rely on gender stereotypes, and gender stereotypes tend to erase people who are marginalized: people of color, disabled people, poor or working-class people, non–European people, and trans, queer, and gender-nonconforming people. Essentialism about gender therefore promotes a falsely homogenous picture of gender and excludes people who do not fit the bill.

Second, gender enables systemic sexism. One striking commonality among gender roles is that women tend to be associated with features that justify their subordination. For example, there is an old patriarchal argument that women should not be granted equal rights or social power because they are too intellectually or emotionally unstable to handle them. Consider the tired but far-from-forgotten joke that a woman president would fall apart under pressure if she were menstruating. These observations illuminate a dark truth about gender roles. If women essentially have properties that are suitable for subordinate roles, or essentially *lack* properties that are suitable for leadership roles, then their subordinate status would be natural, too, and by extension both unchangeable and appropriate. However, biological essentialism is unfounded; we have no good reason to think that women essentially have any particular properties. Feminists argue that there is a better explanation for women's status. The association between women and inferior features is social, not biological. It is not an accident that women tend to be constructed as, for example, nurturing, unintelligent, or emotionally unstable. Essential features do not produce gendered subordination; gendered subordination produces the illusion of essential features. Gender works to justify social hierarchy. It makes patriarchy appear to be a natural consequence of biological sex. As Mill and Mill ask, "Was there ever any domination which did not appear natural to those who possessed it?" (127).

Feminist analysis therefore argues that gender cannot be understood without understanding power. Feminist philosophers sometimes call this the "debunking project" (Haslanger 132–136; see also Ásta 45–47). Gender masquerades as natural and innate in order to justify an unequal social order, when, in reality, gender helps to produce and maintain that social order. To achieve equality, we should *debunk gender essentialism*. That is, we should expose gender as *not* natural, but constructed, contingent, and oppressive.

It is striking, then, that *Deep Space Nine* is so gender essentialist. Not only do almost all of the alien races have a clear sex binary—and if they do not, attention is called to it immediately, and the strangeness of this is the focus of the episode—but almost all of them have recognizable men and women, and no other options. *Star Trek: The Next Generation* (1987–1994) was at least willing to entertain the possibility that some of these things are not fixed in some non-humans. Consider Q (John de Lancie) suggesting that he might have appeared to Picard as a woman ("Qpid"); Data (Brent Spiner) allowing his constructed child to choose their own gender presentation ("The Offspring"); or the well-intentioned but deeply problematic portrayal of a primarily androgynous race with some marginalized gendered individuals ("The Outcast"). *Deep Space Nine*, by contrast, did not question gender, and in many cases seems to have reinforced it.

Consider the Founders. They are *literal* fluid beings with no fixed bodies of any kind. Yet they still seem to have fixed binary sexes and genders. Odo (René Auberjonois), for example, has a gender-conforming heterosexual male identity. It is implied that he patterned his face and hair after the scientist who found him, but this is never addressed or questioned. Moreover, the Female Changeling (Salome Jens) is billed and referred to as just that—the Female Changeling. Every Founder we meet has a recognizable binary human-like gender. The introduction of a race of shapeshifters into *Star Trek* canon presents an exciting possibility to break some hardline gender barriers, but these possibilities go entirely unrealized.

A more promising case is the Trill. Through symbiosis with a worm-species, many Trills carry the memory of multiple lifetimes within them. Jadzia Dax is a woman, but many of her past hosts were men. Commander Benjamin Sisko (Avery Brooks), who knew her previous male host, continues to call her "old man"; but when Jadzia is replaced by Ezri, she resists this moniker, protesting, "Don't call me that! I'm not the old man" ("Afterimage"). Some fans have taken the Dax character as a metaphor for transgender experience, pointing in particular to cases where people who knew Dax through lifetimes accept her new identity and pronouns without question (Coates). Given *Deep Space Nine*'s somewhat dismal track record on queer issues, it is unlikely that this metaphor was intended. Still, one might take this as an encouraging exploration of gender possibilities.

In her essay on identity in *Deep Space Nine*, Kathy Ferguson argues, along these lines, that Dax's "embodied situation" is one of "gender slippage" (178). According to Ferguson, Dax's experience in both male and female bodies lends them a changeable lived gender experience that does not treat gender or sex as defining or even particularly important. Dax thus represents an opening up of possibilities that are often not available to us Earth-bound humans, whose gendered experiences are often attributed to "nature" (178). Kathy Ferguson points to various cases where Jadzia offers parenting advice to Sisko as both a mother and a father, or a moment when Ezri references her inability to remember her own gender/sex ("Prodigal Daughter"), as evidence that the being Dax itself does not have a stable gender or sex identity. According to Ferguson, insight into Trill norms and practices throughout the show serves as a parallel to our own practices of gender policing, and the character of Dax is a "gender-bending doubled creature" whose calm attitude towards the multiplicity and changeability or her self and body is "simultaneously, attractively strange and strangely familiar" (187).

However, Ferguson also notes that there are two features of Dax which de-radicalize the narrative. First, each Dax host with whom we become closely familiar, and thus every major Trill character in *Deep Space Nine*, is presented and meant to be interpreted as women. Male Trill characters, even Dax hosts, are relatively underdeveloped. Furthermore, Ferguson argues that, given a tendency to equate gender in general, and particularly gendered excess, fluidity, or expression in general with femininity and women, it is much harder to imagine a man or a male figure representing this "gender slippage" than a woman or a female figure (179). Second, the gender categorization of each host of Dax is taken to be binary and unambiguous. Curzon Dax, the host prior to Jadzia, was a womanizing "man's man." Both Jadzia and Ezri are relatively gender-conforming women. Both primarily engage in sexual and romantic relationships with men, with the notable exception of Jadzia's relationship with another joined Trill woman, Lenara Kahn ("Rejoined"). However, as Ferguson points out, this relationship occurs because Dax and Kahn were married in a previous life, at which time the Dax symbiont had a male host and the Kahn symbiont a female one. This potentially transgressive lesbian relationship therefore rests safely on heterosexual foundations (183–184). Moreover, each Trill that we meet is referred to with a gender-specific binary pronoun, and we are presumably supposed to understand them as having a gender corresponding to their sex assigned at birth. In short, the show "recoups the radical uncertainty of the Trills' embodied situation"—or at least tries to—by repeatedly insisting that, even for Trills, gender and sex are closely aligned and recognizable by our own binary, heteronormative, dominant gender matrix (179).

Trill gender ambiguity is further undercut by the fact that the Dax character frequently reinforces gender stereotypes in her own way. She tends to take gender roles at face value, and even makes wry observations about the natures of men and women. Consider this exchange:

SARINA: (to O'Brien) I remember you. You're Julian's best friend.
O'BRIEN: Well, we get on all right.
BASHIR: For the most part.
SARINA: Why are you pretending that it's not true?
DAX: Because they're men. And men have trouble expressing their feelings ["Chrysalis"].

The judgment about "men" here is offered without qualification. Even if we understand Dax as making a point about typical behavior, rather than about men's natures, this raises questions. Why do men, apparently across cultures and planets, have trouble expressing their feelings? The feminist answer is: most likely because they are responsive to norms about masculinity, and because women are tasked with the emotional labor. Yet if that is true, it starts to look like the *Star Trek* universe has not progressed much in this regard. Does masculinity still demand that boys should hide their feelings? How feminist is this future if someone as old, wise, and well-gender-traveled as Dax still trades in harmful binary gender stereotypes?

Of course, a story can never fully escape the confines of the time in which it was created, and *Deep Space Nine* is no exception. One can write off many of these instances as ignorance or bias, endemic to the culture in which it was embedded. Yet it is precisely the unreflective manner in which these scenarios are presented, the way gender is taken for granted, that sheds light on the deeper issue. One of the magnificent things about science fiction is the blank slate it provides a writer's imagination. The narrative is not bound by the confines of real-world barriers, whether physical or social. The only rules are those of good storytelling. As Ferguson puts it,

Science fiction enhances our capacity to see beyond the familiar by imagining compelling stories and characters based in ways of living that defy the categories readers/viewers bring to them…. Politically robust science fiction can recruit us into an imaginary universe in which we are invited to refuse normalizing violence by extending legitimacy to bodies and identities otherwise considered "false, unreal, and unintelligible" (Butler 1999a: xxiii) [173].

Given these possibilities, the gender essentialism of *Deep Space Nine* comes off as, at best, unimaginative. In leaving many gender assumptions unquestioned, *Deep Space Nine* presents us with an implicit gender theory. It is in the nature of sentient species, it suggests, to bifurcate, not only into male and female sex roles, but into *men* and *women*. In a universe full of possibility, *Deep Space Nine* falls prey to the myth of gender inevitability.

Deep Space Nine does feature one explicitly feminist storyline—and its presentation of this narrative is particularly telling. In *Deep Space Nine*, the Ferengi are depicted as a comically mercenary race of extreme capitalists whose entire social order and moral code are constructed around the earning of profit. They are unsurprisingly also sexist. Their law forbids females from wearing clothes, leaving the house, or participating in public life or economic exchange in any way. An early episode ("Rules of Acquisition") features a young Ferengi woman named Pel (Hélène Udy) posing as a man in order to get a job at Quark's bar. It is revealed that if her masquerade is discovered, she could be imprisoned, along with anyone who has done business with her. Quark (Armin Shimerman) and his brother Rom (Max Grodénchik) discover her deception and are forced to help her hide so that they do not face punishment themselves. The viewer is encouraged to empathize with Pel and the plight of other Ferengi females, and to question Quark and Rom's moral motivations.

These themes are illustrated in greater detail in the Ferengi feminist storyline. When we meet Ishka, Quark and Rom's mother, not only is she wearing clothes, she is secretly *earning profit* ("Family Business"). She is later revealed to be dating the Grand Nagus (Wallace Shawn), leader of the Ferengi empire ("Ferengi Love Songs"). She then convinces the Nagus to join her cause, and he passes a law granting females equal rights under Ferengi law ("Profit and Lace"). The penultimate episode of the series ("The Dogs of War") features the appointment of Rom—perhaps the most compassionate and equal-minded Ferengi of all time, and almost certainly their only Marxist—as Grand Nagus, indicating that the progressive reforms on Ferenginar will only continue.

It is worth noting, cynically, that both Ishka and Pel are primarily motivated by the desire to participate in hyper-capitalist Ferengi society, rather than to change it. As Rom observes, "Ferengi workers don't want to stop the exploitation, we want to find a way to become the exploiters" ("Bar Association"). Jacob Held points out that Grand Nagus Zek's ultimate support of Ishka's feminist goals is also motivated by profit. That is, "It's good business. He isn't concerned with equitable treatment, fairness, or respect. Rather, it makes good economic sense to grant women equal rights: equal rights to work, earn money, consume, and foster economic growth" (118). Feminist political philosophers have argued that the combination of capitalism and systemic sexism leads to the economic dependence of women on men, as well as disproportionate burden of unpaid labor for women (Ann

Ferguson). If this is right, it seems that true women's liberation is unlikely to be achieved on Ferenginar without a radical change in Ferengi economic and social practices—rather the opposite of Ishka's goals.

Nevertheless, the story of the Ferengi feminist uprising is surprisingly heartfelt, and for the most part strikes a decent balance between humor and earnest if heavy-handed political commentary. Yet it is by no means anything new. Ferengi misogyny is a caricature. It lampoons only the most extreme forms of sex discrimination, and leaves the subtler, more pervasive forms untouched. Narratively, Ishka's struggle for equal rights is fun; politically, it comes off as preaching to the choir, and unfortunately not saying much of interest. By the 1990s, it was a well-struck point with most of the American television-viewing audience that women should be treated equally. The gap still yawns between this belief and real equality. In a show that has been both celebrated and panned for questioning idealistic Federation principles, and whose gray characters and tough ethical dilemmas distinguish it as among the most nuanced of *Star Trek*'s offerings, the moral of *Deep Space Nine*'s feminist storyline just boils down to "Sexism is bad." And that is just not a very interesting, challenging, or satisfying point of conclusion.

Nevertheless, most of this storyline lands reasonably well. There is one outlying episode, however, which does not. "Profit and Lace" is a study in political and comedic misfires. In the episode, Quark is forced to pose as a Ferengi woman in order to convince a male politician to support his mother's feminist cause. There is potential here for a nuanced, incisive story about walking a mile in high-heeled shoes. What is instead delivered is a litany of tired gender tropes, with all of the potentially interesting or insightful ideas instead passed off as tasteless jokes. Quark is emotionally overwhelmed by the new hormones; he thinks his hips look too big; despite being a typically shrewd and calculating businessman, he suddenly cannot remember the "facts and figures" necessary to complete the task; he develops a conscience, and magnanimously decides not to sexually harass an employee; and several of the male Ferengi in the episode seem literally unable to resist sexually harassing him. All of this is played exclusively for laughs, and not particularly subtle ones. The punch lines suggest that femininity is ridiculous; that homosexuality is hilarious; that gender variance is a joke; and, most saliently, that "female hormones" make one more sensitive and caring, but unintelligent and unstable. The result is deeply sexist, misogynistic, homophobic, and transphobic.

Philosopher Talia Bettcher identifies two alternating characterizations of trans women in the public view: the "deceiver" who successfully "passes herself off" as a woman and tricks men into homosexual acts; and the "pretender," the unconvincing "man in a dress" who is worthy of, alternatively, contempt and pity (47). These characterizations are used to justify and excuse violence against trans women. "Profit and Lace" manages to represent both. Quark's female persona is first portrayed as the "pretender"—lumbering, indelicate, and unconvincing. By the climax of the episode, though, he has evolved into the "deceiver"; he first "dupes" and then seduces a Ferengi political leader, thereby winning his support and ensuring that Ferengi women's equal rights are protected.

"Profit and Lace" is infamous among *Deep Space Nine* fans. Darren Mooney of *The M0vie Blog* writes,

> It could reasonably be argued that the toxicity of *Profit and Lace* is not even quarantined. The episode is so bad that it becomes a retroactive taint upon *Deep Space Nine*'s attempts to develop and flesh out the Ferengi.

This is an excellent point, but the stain is not limited to the Ferengi storyline. "Profit and Lace" single-handedly undoes much of the goodwill to which *Deep Space Nine* otherwise might be entitled on gender issues. Ferengi society, with its characteristic greed, selfishness, bigotry, and exploitation, could serve as a dark mirror of the worst parts of humanity. In "Profit and Lace," it instead becomes a fun-house mirror, distorting the cautionary tale into an unsettling joke. The Ferengi equal rights amendment should have been the high point of the show's only explicitly feminist narrative. Instead, it is remarkably un-feminist.

Deep Space Nine needs better feminism than this. It *wants* to be feminist; it *wants* to be progressive; it *wants* to meet its own high bar; and it is easy to see how hard it is trying. In some ways, it succeeds. The major female characters on the show are leaps and bounds beyond anything in previous *Star Trek* shows. As shown in *What We Left Behind*, thousands of fans have been genuinely inspired by them. Take Major Kira, whose journey from uncompromising, war-hardened extremist to emotionally healthy leader and diplomat is beautifully written. The show valorizes, rather than punishes, her anger; she gains nuance but does not lose power. Kira is just the kind of stereotype-breaking female hero that viewers need. Still, *Deep Space Nine* finds excuses to sexualize her. In "Our Man Bashir" and "His Way," provocatively-clad holographic versions of Kira are hypersexual and seductive. In the Mirror Universe episodes ("Crossover," "Through the Looking Glass," "Shattered Mirror," "The Emperor's New Cloak"), Kira's alter-ego is a sly pansexual villain in a shiny silver catsuit. Predictably, "pansexual" here is presented as synonymous with "manipulative" and "evil." In "Badda-Bing, Badda-Bang," it is not a hologram or an alternate but Kira herself in the slinky gown—apparently able to flip the switch to "smokey-eyed seductress" at a moment's notice. Narratively, this can be enjoyable; it is always fun to see one's favorite characters behave in unexpected ways. It is conspicuous, however, that in each of these episodes, the part Kira ends up playing is some combination of the problematic sexist stereotypes from which her character in general refreshingly escapes.

In *Down Girl: The Logic of Misogyny*, philosopher Kate Manne makes an important distinction between *misogyny* and *sexism*. Manne argues that there are two separate phenomena at work in the oppression of women, which need different names. *Misogyny* is the "enforcement branch" of the patriarchal social order. It is about policing gender and gender expectations. Misogyny punishes women who do not fulfill their prescribed social role and rewards those who do; for example, a woman who does not want to have children might be criticized or mocked, but a woman who does have children and devotes herself to being a mother might be celebrated—provided she does it in a socially acceptable way, of course. By contrast, *sexism* is the "justificatory branch" of the patriarchal social order. Sexism consists of a set of beliefs about what is natural. A sexist belief might be that women are "naturally suited" to be caregivers. As Manne puts it,

> Sexist ideology will often consist in assumptions, beliefs, theories, stereotypes, and broader cultural narratives that represent men and women as importantly different in ways that, if true and known to be true, would make rational people more inclined to support and participate in patriarchal social arrangements [79].

Sexism trades on commonly held assumptions about what men and women are "really" like; if these assumptions were correct, then many sexist arrangements in society would make sense. As noted above, given the gendered conditions we actually have, one cannot know what is natural. Ironically, however, sexist thinking is used to justify *enforcing* gender roles: the norms of masculinity and femininity are enforced from birth, and those who do not comply are often harshly punished. This punishment is what Manne calls *misogyny*.

To its credit, *Deep Space Nine* does not often openly punish its women. Contrast this with the common science fiction trope of torture, abuse, rape, or murder of strong female characters: Ellen Ripley (Sigourney Weaver) from the *Alien* films; River Song (Alex Kingston) from *Doctor Who* (2005–present); and most of the female characters from *Buffy The Vampire Slayer* are all salient examples. A cynic might note, however, that *Deep Space Nine*'s women do not face punishment because they do not really challenge their roles. Manne argues that the primary distinguishing feature of a "woman's role" is to be a man's moral support: *good* women are the ones who provide deserving men with care, comfort, and sex, and *bad* women are the ones who do not—or, worse, the ones who ask for those things *from men* when the men do not offer them. In various ways, the female characters of *Deep Space Nine* are often "good women." Jadzia Dax is Sisko's mentor and emotional support, and throughout her relationship with Worf (Michael Dorn) she serves as a buffer, a sounding board, and a counselor for his emotional development. Ezri Dax is an actual counselor. Even when she is not performing this role, Worf, Dr. Bashir (Alexander Siddig), and Quark all work out their grief about Jadzia's death through her. Kasidy Yates frequently does the emotional labor in her relationship, such as running interference when Sisko will not communicate with his friends and family ("Take Me Out to the Holosuite"). Keiko O'Brien is the primary caregiver of the O'Briens' children, and in volunteering to be a schoolteacher she takes responsibility for most of the children on the station. Interestingly, however, she is insistent about having her needs met and pursuing her own career, and the show often seems determined to vilify her for this. She is portrayed as spiteful and demanding, and Miles (Colm Meaney) is often angry and bitter with her; at one point she is possessed by an evil Pah-wraith to manipulate Miles into treason, literally becoming the villain ("The Assignment").

The sexism and misogyny of *Deep Space Nine* is generally subtle, and far from unique in the genre or the broader culture. The show primarily errs by omission. It fails to challenge common sexist assumptions. It provides strong female characters but finds small ways to return them to their expected roles, by sexualizing them or casting them as emotional support. It assumes that in a galaxy populated with thousands of unique alien races, the overwhelming majority will be sorted into binary gender categories which almost perfectly mirror human ones. This reinforces the flawed idea that gender is natural and corresponds perfectly to biological sex. Not only do we lack good epistemic reasons to accept this biological essentialism, we also have good moral reasons to reject it: it is exclusionary, culturally biased, and serves to make oppressive gender roles seem natural and normal. Yet *Deep Space Nine* leaves biological essentialism undisputed, even when it has excellent opportunities to question it.

Deep Space Nine's representation of gender demonstrates an inability to deliver on its own promises. *Star Trek* is meant to show us an ideal future, a world beyond human bias and division. Why, then, is the gender division still so stark? *Deep Space Nine* may be the only *Star Trek* series to utter the word "feminist" ("Profit and Lace"). Why, then, is its feminism so short-sighted? We cannot, of course, expect showrunners to be fully literate in feminist theory; but in a universe which advertises limitless possibilities, *Deep Space Nine*'s failure to question harmful gender assumptions is, at best, a testament to its lack of imagination.

Works Cited and Consulted

Ásta. *Categories We Live By: The Construction of Sex, Gender, Race, and Other Social Categories*. Oxford UP, 2018.

Beauvoir, Simone de. *The Second Sex.* Translated by Constance Borde and Sheila Malovany Chevallier. Vintage Books, 2009.
Bettcher, Talia Mae. "Evil Deceivers and Make-Believers: Transphobic Violence and the Politics of Illusion." *Hypatia*, vol. 22, no. 3, 2007, pp. 43–65.
Butler, Judith. *Bodies That Matter.* Routledge, 1993.
_____. *Gender Trouble.* 1990. Routledge, 2007.
Coates, Lauren. "How Transgender *Star Trek* Fans Came to View Jadzia Dax as Their Own." *The Mary Sue,* 4 September 2019, www.themarysue.com/jadzia-dax-transgender-star-trek-fans/. Accessed 26 May 2020.
Dembroff, Robin. "Real Talk on the Metaphysics of Gender." *Philosophical Topics*, vol. 46, no. 2, 2018, pp. 21–50.
Dembroff, Robin, and Cat Saint-Croix. "Yep, I'm Gay: Understanding Agential Identity." *Ergo: An Open Access Journal of Philosophy*, vol. 6, 2019, pp. 571–599.
Ferguson, Ann. "Feminist Perspectives on Class and Work." *The Stanford Encyclopedia of Philosophy* (Fall 2016 Edition), edited by Edward N. Zalta. 28 September 2016, plato.stanford.edu/entries/feminism-class/. Accessed 28 May 2020.
Ferguson, Kathy E. "This Species Which Is Not One: Identity Practices in *Star Trek: Deep Space Nine.*" *Judith Butler's Precarious Politics: Critical Encounters,* edited by Terrell Carver and Samuel A. Chambers. Routledge, 2008, pp. 173–187.
Fine, Cordelia. *Delusions of Gender: The Real Science Behind Sex Differences.* W.W. Norton, 2010.
Haslanger, Sally. *Resisting Reality: Social Construction and Social Critique.* Oxford UP, 2012.
Held, Jacob. "'The Rules of Acquisition Can't Help You Now': What Can the Ferengi Teach Us About Business Ethics?" Star Trek *and Philosophy,* edited by Jason T. Eberl and Kevin S. Decker. Carus Publishing, 2008, pp. 117–128.
Manne, Kate. *Down Girl: The Logic of Misogyny.* Oxford UP, 2018.
Mill, John Stuart. *On Liberty and The Subjection of Women.* 1859. Wordsworth Editions Limited, 1996.
Mooney, Darren. "*Star Trek: Deep Space Nine*—Profit and Lace (Review)." *The M0vie Blog,* 22 May 2017, them0vieblog.com/2017/05/22/star-trek-deep-space-nine-profit-and-lace-review/. Accessed 28 May 2020.
Serano, Julia. *Whipping Girl.* Seal Press, 2007.

Filmography and Other Media

Brooks, Meredith. "Bitch." *Blurring the Edges*, Capitol Records, 1997. *Spotify,* open.spotify.com/track/3i6qNxyVgIdUZTTi5m25EM.
What We Left Behind: Looking Back at Star Trek: Deep Space Nine, directed by Ira Steven Behr and David Zappone. 455 Films, 2019.

Sisko's Conversion Experience and the Secularism of William James

Exploring Faith, Religion, and the Visions of the Prophets

DREW CHASTAIN

Deep Space Nine (1993–1999) is distinctive as a *Star Trek* series for its sustained exploration of religion, faith, and spirituality. The space station's unique setting helps make this possible. Rather than cruising all about the galaxy like the starships of the other *Star Trek* series, the space station Deep Space 9 maintains a position near the planet Bajor, where the Bajoran people have cultivated a rich religious tradition for tens of thousands of years, based upon visions received from the Orbs of the Prophets. Shaped like hourglasses, the Orbs are said to have fallen from the sky, carrying messages from the Prophets, who the Bajorans treat as divinities. In "Emissary," the origin of the Orbs is discovered when the nearby wormhole opens. Inside the wormhole, Commander Benjamin Sisko (Avery Brooks) makes first contact with the wormhole aliens the Bajorans call the "Prophets," a non-corporeal species who live inside the wormhole and outside of linear time. This encounter initiates a new stage in Sisko's life as the Emissary of the Prophets, a figure foretold by the Prophets and eagerly anticipated by the Bajorans.

The narrative dynamic set up between a Starfleet officer, the wormhole aliens, and the Bajoran people enables *Star Trek* storytellers to navigate the tensions between Bajoran religiosity and Starfleet secularism, also revealing ways in which spirituality and faith are possible without religion. Having a secular Starfleet background, Sisko is not thrilled at first to play the religious role of the Emissary and is quite happy to hand over the position to a Bajoran claiming the title in the episode "Accession." Yet after it is made clear to everyone that the wormhole aliens view Sisko as the true Emissary, Sisko warms up to the idea, finally showing full commitment to the role in the "The Rapture." In this episode, Sisko experiences a sacred vision that brings him close to grasping the full truth of the universe from a non-linear temporal perspective like that experienced by the wormhole aliens. This is a profoundly transformative spiritual experience for Sisko, and it can also be seen as Sisko's climactic conversion experience, setting up a foundation for his faith in the Prophets.

Given Sisko's continued commitment to the path of the Emissary through the remainder of the series, it is tempting to view *Deep Space Nine* as making a pro-religious break from the secular humanist ethos of *Star Trek* established by Gene Roddenberry in *The Original Series* (1966–1969) and *The Next Generation* (1987–1994). Although *Deep Space Nine* closely explores religious phenomena and takes spiritual experiences seriously, the series also displays the downside of religion, primarily epitomized by Winn Adami (Louise Fletcher). Winn is at first a Bajoran Vedek, or priest, and eventually becomes Kai and (briefly) acting First Minister, functioning as both a religious and political leader to the Bajorans. Winn represents someone who is religious, but not sufficiently spiritual, whose expressions of faith—despite a lifetime of study—ring hollow, and who is often politically and personally motivated by envy and vengeance. Winn's character also illustrates the dogmatic dangers of religion. As with the texts of real-world religions, the Bajoran prophecies are open to interpretation, and Winn's interpretations are regularly influenced by provincialism, self-interest, and spiritual ignorance.

Complicating the question of whether *Deep Space Nine* is pro-religious, the world of *Star Trek* is rife with supernatural or paranormal phenomena, which has been true since *Star Trek* got its start. Under the guidance of Roddenberry, the very first three episodes of *The Original Series* featured aliens or humans making use of psychic powers.[1] All that is needed for the paranormal to be accepted into the secular world of *Star Trek* is the mere possibility of a scientific explanation, even if sufficient explanation is rarely given in the storyline itself. The same is true for *Deep Space Nine*, although much of the supernatural phenomena in this series are more characteristically religious in nature, such as sacred visions or demonic possessions. Yet when it comes to the question of faith, *Deep Space Nine* does not straightforwardly endorse religious faith, instead producing a dialogue about the nature and value of religious and secular varieties of faith. When Sisko cultivates faith owing to a spiritual experience, this is not the religious kind of faith criticized by secularists—faith without evidence or faith against evidence. Sisko's newfound faith is based on the existence of a special kind of alien species living in the wormhole which can provide linear, corporeal beings with ecstatic enlightenment experiences. Sisko and the space station's Starfleet crew need not reject their scientific commitments to see the validity of Sisko's faith in the Prophets, because there is surely a scientific explanation for Sisko's experiences, even if the space station's science officers have trouble understanding them fully.[2]

In *The Varieties of Religious Experience*, philosopher and psychologist William James relates faith to conversion experience in a way that helps bring Sisko's conversion into focus. James describes sudden conversion experience as ecstatic, very much like Sisko's, involving what James explicitly refers to as a "faith-state." Interestingly, William James and *Deep Space Nine* share the goal of finding a line separating spiritual experience from dogmatic religion. While James is more pro-religious than *Star Trek*, James also allows for a kind of spiritual faith that does not take the additional step of dogmatic belief without evidence.[3] James' account of the conversion experience helps us to see how Sisko's sacred vision supports faith and also how this kind of faith is set apart from more problematic forms of religious faith.

The Varieties of Vision Experience in Deep Space Nine

Sisko is only one among many who has visions on *Deep Space Nine*. Throughout the series, numerous characters do, including Jadzia Dax (Terry Farrell), Quark (Armin Shimerman), and Kira Nerys (Nana Visitor). These visions can be roughly sorted into three kinds: episodic, interactive, and rapturous. The first two are by far the most common. An episodic vision transports the individual to another place and perhaps even another time, at least mentally, as if the character is lucidly dreaming while rendered unconscious to present surroundings. For instance, in one of the simplest and most serene visions of the series, Jadzia looks into the Orb of Prophecy and Change in "Emissary" and briefly returns to her past experience of receiving the Dax symbiont into her body for the first time. Yet not all episodic visions take the individual to a remembered event, and some involve more metaphorical elements. In "The Collaborator," Vedek Bareil (Philip Anglim) has three separate episodic visions, all of which seem to foretell his own death in symbolic ways typical of a dream. The episode "Far Beyond the Stars" consists almost entirely of one long episodic vision transporting Sisko deep into the past to 1950s Earth, well beyond his own personal memory. As Sisko experiences it, the vision lasts for days, though he is unconscious for only a few minutes back on the space station. In "Wrongs Darker Than Death or Night," Kira consults the Orb of Time, intentionally seeking out a long episodic vision of the past in order to determine whether her mother truly did have an affair with Gul Dukat (Marc Alaimo) during the Cardassian occupation of Bajor.

An interactive vision is also episodic in nature and can access the memories of the one having the vision, but an interactive vision is distinctive in that it involves direct interchange with the wormhole aliens. Although they exist outside time as non-corporeal, non-linear beings, the wormhole aliens are able to interact with linear, corporeal beings by inducing a vision and adopting the personae of various individuals known to the one having the vision. During his first contact with the wormhole aliens in "Emissary," Sisko interacts with them by speaking to his son Jake (Cirroc Lofton) and his deceased wife Jennifer (Felecia Bell) and many others in a variety of experiential settings generated by Sisko's own past memories, such as his memory of being attacked by the Borg on the *Saratoga*. Through this interactive vision, Sisko comes to understand who the wormhole aliens are and helps them to grasp the corporeal and linear limitations of human existence. In "Prophet Motive," Quark has a different objective in his interactive vision, which the Ferengi experiences as taking place in his own bar and other places with which he is acquainted, involving interaction with the personae of Doctor Julian Bashir (Alexander Siddig), his brother Rom (Max Grodénchik), and others. Having deduced that the wormhole aliens are the ones responsible for transforming Grand Nagus Zek (Wallace Shawn) into an uncharacteristically compassionate, altruistic person, Quark seeks to persuade the wormhole aliens to change Zek back to his money-hungry, self-interested personality.

Both episodic and interactive visions can serve practical goals, as when Kira seeks information about her mother's involvement with Dukat, or when Quark hopes to have Zek returned to his normal self. Yet both kinds of visions can also trigger strong emotional reactions and inspire clarifying revelations. In his first Orb vision in "Prophet Motive," Quark has a dreamlike experience featuring the Grand Nagus, who blithely taunts Quark about his fears and anxieties. Then Quark receives the clue that leads him to the conclusion that the wormhole aliens are the ones who molded Zek into a benevolent being. The most deeply psychotherapeutic vision of the series is Sisko's extended interactive vision with the wormhole aliens in "Emissary." To interact with corporeal beings, the wormhole aliens regularly select memories of people and places that are charged with significance for the one having the vision. Using this method, the wormhole aliens repeatedly return Sisko to the traumatic memory of his unsuccessful attempt to save Jennifer's life on the *Saratoga*, revealing that the loss of his wife still weighs very heavily on him. In the course of this interactive vision, Sisko collapses into tears and comes to realize just how much he is holding on to the past. Through his communion with the wormhole aliens, Sisko is able to achieve a state of catharsis, and this in turn enables him to accept his assignment as commander of Deep Space 9, to which he had initially been resistant, owing to his emotional blockage.

The third, rapturous kind of vision amplifies the emotional and revelatory aspects of visions made possible by the wormhole aliens. The most remarkable rapturous vision of the series is the one experienced by Sisko in "The Rapture." In this episode, the Cardassians return a 20,000-year-old painting of the lost Bajoran city of B'hala. It is prophesied that the lost city can only be found by someone who has been touched by the Prophets, and, having developed a taste for his role as Emissary to the Prophets, Sisko quickly becomes obsessed with the painting. Ancient symbols that appear on a *bantaca* spire in the painting reveal B'hala's location, but only one side of the spire is clearly presented, so Sisko has the painting scanned into the station's computer, then recreates the spire in three dimensions on the holodeck. When Sisko goes to save the holodeck program, he receives a shock from the console that knocks him unconscious. Thereafter, Sisko experiences heightened luminescence and occasional sharp headaches which correlate with a deeper and deeper meditative engagement with the ancient puzzle of B'hala. When Kira wakes Sisko from a trance on the holodeck, Sisko reports that he was actually there at B'hala, as in an episodic vision, hearing the temple chimes, smelling the burning *bateret* leaves, and tasting the incense on the wind. Even more remarkably, Sisko says he could also see the past and the future and "the pattern that held it all together" ("The Rapture"). Kira explains that Sisko is experiencing what Bajorans call a *pagh'tem'far*, or sacred vision.

Episodic and interactive visions can be exciting at times, but not like this rapturous kind of vision. Sisko is so committed to the vision that he is willing to endure debilitating headaches and even risk death to see the vision through to the end. After Sisko follows a hunch and finds the lost city of B'hala underground on Bajor, he insists on letting the effects of the shock continue. Chief Medical Officer Bashir says that Sisko needs to have his neural sheaths re-polarized to avoid death, but Sisko resists life-saving treatments because something extraordinary is happening to him. His romantic partner Kasidy Yates (Penny Johnson Jerald) is upset that Sisko is risking his life for a "mystical journey" instead of prioritizing his son, Jake ("The Rapture"). When Admiral Charlie Whatley (Ernest Perry, Jr.) arrives on the space station to participate in welcoming Bajor to the Federation, he finds that Sisko is preoccupied with his *pagh'tem'far* rather than attending to all of his duties. Sisko arrives late to a meeting to finalize Bajor's admission, and, against Federation objectives, Sisko dramatically proclaims that Bajor must not join the Federation, then collapses in a seizure. With Sisko's life at risk, Jake asks Bashir to end the visions to save his father's life. Waking to find that his sacred vision has ended, Sisko is forlorn, crying, "No! You took them away! … I almost had it, almost understood it all. Now it's gone" ("The Rapture").

After his sacred vision, Sisko continues to be deeply committed to the Prophets for the remainder of the series. In "The Reckoning," he allows the evil wormhole aliens, known as the Pah-wraiths or False Prophets, to maintain possession of his son's body in order to fulfill a prophecy, trusting that the true Prophets know what is best. When the wormhole collapses at the end of the sixth season, Sisko travels to the deserts of Tyree to find the Orb of the Emissary, led by little more than an internal hunch and faith in the Prophets. Ultimately, Sisko sacrifices himself in flames to prevent Dukat and the Pah-wraiths from gaining victory over the Prophets. Sisko's increase in faith follows from a certain kind of spiritual experience which finds its first big climax in "The Rapture." William James also describes how an increase in faith can emerge from a dramatic spiritual experience. Although such experiences commonly lead to religious faith in God and faith in associated religious doctrines, James does not think that the value of faith rests on such dogmatic commitments, a conclusion very much in line with the secular *Star Trek* ethos of *Deep Space Nine*.

William James on Conversion Experience

In *The Varieties of Religious Experience*, a monumental work compiling a series of twenty lectures delivered in 1901 and 1902, James provides a thorough philosophical investigation of the experiential side of religion, being less concerned with the complexities of religious belief and doctrine. As a psychologist, James is also very aware of the most recent developments in neurology. He aims to explain to a science-minded, non-religious readership how religious faith is acquired and also what makes faith valuable. In a pair of lectures entitled "Conversion," James explores the experiential aspect of an individual's sudden transformation to a life of faith, relying upon numerous historical, first-person accounts of Christian conversion experiences.[4]

The first feature of a sudden conversion experience is the surrendering of one's will to what is experienced as a higher power, or some form of external control. This self-surrender is precipitated by the individual's prior struggle with despair, melancholy, or sin. For there to be such a sudden shift in life orientation, James concludes that the one who achieves conversion must have been nurturing two different identities within the individual. There is first the melancholy egoic self that dominates the individual's consciousness prior to conversion, and then there is also the more ecstatic divinely-oriented self that is being nurtured beneath the surface of consciousness in the subconscious mind. James says that, while an individual is under the control of the melancholy self, it cannot be an act of will that initiates the profound change in life orientation, but instead it must be a moment of self-surrender. The eruption of the ecstatic self is made possible when the melancholy self releases control, allowing the new self to take over completely.

Importantly, James' psychological explanation leaves open whether there really is a higher power involved in the conversion experience, since the internal process can be understood entirely in psychological terms. This dramatic internal process also explains how the individual could experience sudden conversion as being caused by some external control, even if this is not really the case. The individual experiences the self being overtaken by something else, but what takes over may well have come from the individual's own subconscious mind. While respecting the fully secular psychological explanation, James himself favors the notion that God could still be responsible for a conversion experience. He supposes that when God influences a conversion in an individual, such divine influence enters in through the subconscious mind (439–444). Yet James does not deliver a final answer on the existence of God, and, as will be seen, he also does not derive the value of faith from God's existence, but instead from a secular source.

Various aspects of what James describes can be found in Sisko's transformation from Starfleet Officer to Emissary. When Sisko first arrives at the space station, he is still very much in a state of grieving over the death of his wife Jennifer. In his first interactive vision with the wormhole aliens, Sisko experiences a psychotherapeutic breakthrough, enabling him to finally accept his wife's death. This helps set the stage for Sisko's full abandonment to ecstasy in his *pagh'tem'far* in "The Rapture." Sisko experiences this sacred vision as a form of external control by the wormhole aliens, initiated by the shock he receives from the holodeck console. Sisko has been "touched by the Prophets," and the experience continues until Jake asks Bashir to restore balance to Sisko's neurophysiology out of concern for his father's life. Whereas James leaves it open whether there really is a God externally influencing conversion experiences, the writers of *Deep Space Nine* are able to fictionally suppose that there is a scientifically-explicable source of external control, so that Sisko's conversion experience is more than just an internal psychological process. Yet this is not the same as embracing religion. The *pagh'tem'far* induced by the wormhole aliens provides an imaginative way to explore the value of faith that comes out of spiritual experience, but without having Sisko adopt faith in God *per se*, and certainly without Sisko needing to accept any dogmatic aspect of religion.

In order to assess the secular value of faith, several other features of James' description of conversion experience are also important, all of which closely correspond to Sisko's experience. Rounding out his analysis, James says that four features of conversion experience constitute what he calls a "faith-state": (i) the loss of worry; (ii) the perception of truths not known before; (iii) the appearance of newness in the world; and (iv) the ecstasy of happiness (219–225). All of these features can be found in Sisko's sacred vision in "The Rapture." As for loss of worry, in addition to being unconcerned about his own death, Sisko exhibits little worry about his relationship with Kasidy Yates when she returns from serving prison time for her role in assisting the Maquis. Putting the past behind them, Sisko invites Kasidy to join him in his search for B'hala on Bajor. Sisko is most definitely perceiving truths not known before, as he relates to Kira on the holodeck, and Sisko also later reports to the admiral that he is having continual "moments of insight, flashes of understanding" ("The Rapture"). Along with newly perceived truths, the universe itself now shows up as something new and fresh. To explain to Kasidy and Jake how he could possibly risk death for his sacred vision, Sisko says, "The baby I'm holding in my hands now is the universe itself, and I need time to study its face" ("The Rapture"). Lastly, all of these changes are wrapped in an aura of ecstasy. His *pagh'tem'far* is apparently of the highest order, both intellectually and aesthetically. With a deep, luxuriant tone in his voice, he confesses to Kira that the sacred vision "felt wonderful" ("The Rapture"). Also emphasizing this aspect of a conversion experience, James concludes that "the joyous conviction itself, the assurance that all is well with one" deserves "the name of faith *par excellence*" (218).

The correspondence between Sisko's experience and James' description of the faith-state within conversion experience is remarkably resonant. Still, it can be wondered what value the experience has if it does not have its source in a benevolent and trustworthy higher power, like God, or even the wormhole aliens. Though James himself is inclined to theism, his secularism rises to the surface when he addresses the value of faith. He argues that the external origin of the faith-state does not decide its value. Instead, the value of faith is decided by the fruits, or effects, of the conversion experience:

> If the *fruits for life* of the state of conversion are good, we ought to idealize and venerate it, even though it be a piece of natural psychology; if not, we ought to make short work with it, no matter what supernatural being may have infused it [211; emphasis original].

Also acknowledging that intense conversion experiences do not last forever, James makes a comparison to an intense experience of love in order to bring out the beneficial fruit of conversion experience:

> Love is, for instance, well known not to be irrevocable, yet, constant or inconstant, it reveals new flights and reaches of ideality while it lasts. These revelations form its significance to men and women, whatever be its duration. So with conversion experience: that it should for even a short time show a human being what the high-water mark of his spiritual capacity is, this is what constitutes its importance [228].

That is, the primary importance of such a spiritual experience is not contained in what a person of faith may claim about the nature of reality, but rather in what such an experience shows about the potential vitality of life. Even when life takes a negative turn, the memory of the ecstatic experience remains, inspiring trust in the value of living. This effect can be seen in Sisko. When Jadzia is killed by Dukat, Sisko retreats to New Orleans to take some time to reflect and help his father with his restaurant. Though morose, as he was when he first arrived to Deep Space 9, Sisko maintains the faith that something can be done to reopen the wormhole. Eventually, he is on the ecstatic vision path once again, walking through the desert on Tyree in search of the Orb of the Emissary.

Of course, Sisko's faith involves both ecstatic subjective experiences and his trust in the god-like wormhole aliens who have knowledge of the future and who also intended that Sisko be born just so that he can fulfill his destiny of conquering the Pah-wraiths. So, in this science fiction storyline aimed at fascinating and entertaining television audiences, there is more to Sisko's faith than an ecstatic subjective experience. Still, this additional imaginative science fiction can be seen as a device for exploring the intense psychological role that faith plays in a human life, while also showing how the value of spirituality can be understood in secular terms. In real life, we may have faith in ourselves, in other people, in nature, or in ideas that are unrelated to religion. *Deep Space Nine* and William James both help us to see that the heightened subjective experience of faith in such things is a large part of the value of that faith.

Overall, *Deep Space Nine* is certainly putting a positive spin on non-religious spirituality. Another exploration of the value of spiritual experience in *Deep Space Nine* can be found in the storyline developed around the character of Odo (René Auberjonois), a shapeshifter who discovers that his own people live on the other side of the wormhole in the Gamma Quadrant. When he finally meets a member of his own species, Odo learns that he is able to link with other shapeshifters, which involves the actual merging of their malleable shapeshifting substance, leading to an experience of subjective union that radically transforms Odo's life and personality. Once again, a science fiction framework enables the presentation of the value of spiritual experience by supposing the existence of an extraordinary—but presumably scientifically possible—alien. This is not the same as being pro-religion. While vouching for the value of spirituality in a world of science, *Deep Space Nine* also lays out a secular critique of religion, with particular focus on its dogmatic and controlling aspects, and its vulnerability to abuse.

The Problem of Dogmatism in Religion

Given Sisko's triumph at the end of the series, *Deep Space Nine* can be interpreted as glorifying faith. Because of his faith in the Prophets, Sisko finds the Orb of the Emissary and defeats the Pah-wraiths. Yet faith is presented in a negative light as well. Sisko himself struggles with faith in "Penumbra" when he is told by the Prophets that he must not marry Kasidy Yates. In an interactive vision with the persona of his mother Sarah (Deborah Lacey), Sisko complains to the Prophets, "You don't care how I feel. All you care is that I do what you want" ("Penumbra"). The secular ethos of Starfleet holds autonomy sacred, as codified in the Prime Directive, which forbids interference with the natural development of other cultures. An underlying critique of religion in *Star Trek* is that religion requires rational beings to abdicate free self-determination in their obedience to a higher life form whose worthiness of worship is questionable owing to that very demand. When religion becomes a glaring obstacle for free will, faith receives a negative assessment.

In *Deep Space Nine*, another problem of religious faith that is revisited repeatedly is more specifically the problem of faith in prophecy, which comes out most vividly in "Destiny." The stage is set when Vedek Yarka (Erick Avari) warns Sisko that the Prophets do not want the commander to bring a Cardassian science team aboard the station to help deploy a communications relay on the other side of the wormhole, because doing so "will bring destruction on us all" ("Destiny"). Yarka cites the Third Prophecy revealed to Trakor by the Orb of Change over 3,000 years ago: "When the river wakes, stirred once more to Janir's side, three vipers will return to their nest in the sky. When the vipers try to peer through the temple gates, a sword of stars will appear in the heavens. The temple will burn, and the gates will be cast open" ("Destiny"). Yarka takes the vipers to be a reference to the Cardassians, but Kira observes that there are only two Cardassians coming to the station, not three, suggesting that Yarka has arrived at a mistaken interpretation. Though Yarka insists that there will be three, Sisko and Kira are both fairly skeptical—until a third Cardassian unexpectedly joins the science team. Incredulity further crumbles when they discover a comet on the other side of the wormhole that could aptly be described as a "sword of stars."

Speaking Bajoran to Bajoran, Yarka tells Kira she must prioritize her faith over Starfleet's mission and influence Sisko to believe in the prophecy, because, without her faith, what does Kira have left? Yarka represents a superlatively religious type, who views faith not as one virtue to be balanced among many other virtues, but as the most fundamental virtue of all, absolute and unlimited. When Sisko learns that Kira is now taking the prophecy seriously, he agrees with her that a rational, secular Starfleet officer can accept that the wormhole aliens see the future and that they also could have transmitted knowledge of the future to someone like Trakor thousands of years ago. For Sisko, however, the problem remains that Trakor's prophecy is contained in "an ancient text that's been translated and retranslated over the centuries, words that were couched in metaphor to begin with" ("Destiny"). This is where a critique of Vedek Yarka's faith emerges, aimed more particularly at fundamentalist strains of religion that take metaphorical language of ancient texts literally or adhere to rigid interpretations of religious language having vague or multivalent meanings.

The action of the episode intensifies as it appears that Sisko's inattention to prophecy will lead to the destruction of the wormhole, but in the end disaster is averted and the installation of the communications relay is successful.

In an ironic twist, Kira helps Sisko to see that the prophecy had been fulfilled nonetheless, the three vipers not being the Cardassians, but instead the comet fragments that Sisko guided through the wormhole. Also, they brought the comet fragments through using a subspace field around the shuttlepod, which might look like a "sword of stars" to Trakor thousands of years ago. The problem of prophecy is not that there can sometimes be unavoidable fates or destinies, but that the faithful who believe in a prophecy, or some other aspect of a religious text or doctrine, can be too certain of their interpretations, closed off to critical reevaluation. *Deep Space Nine* would have us conclude that this is not the kind of faith that should be counted as a virtue.[5]

Another critique of religious fundamentalism is found in an earlier episode "In the Hands of the Prophets," which provides the first introduction to the character of Winn, who continues to represent the problematic side of religion for the remainder of the series. Vedek Winn confronts Keiko O'Brien (Rosalind Chao) while she is teaching a class on the science of the wormhole to the children on the space station, ultimately declaring that Keiko's scientific interpretation is blasphemy. Winn presents herself as defending the faith and speaking for the Prophets, insisting that Keiko should not teach anything about the wormhole at all if she does not take seriously Bajoran spiritual beliefs about the Prophets. Winn's view ultimately incites a terrorist bombing of the school, which demonstrates the violent extremes of religious fundamentalism. Through the voice of Sisko, however, *Deep Space Nine* finds a way to distinguish a critique of fundamentalist faith from a complete rejection of faith. When Jake tells Sisko that thinking of the wormhole as a Celestial Temple for the Prophets is "dumb," Sisko defends faith and warns against becoming like those who are so scientifically-minded that they are closed to other interpretations, just as the religious fundamentalists are. In his defense of faith, Sisko tells Jake, "For over fifty years, the one thing that allowed the Bajorans to survive the Cardassian occupation was their faith. The Prophets were their only source of hope and courage" ("In the Hands of the Prophets").

Two sides of the phenomenon of faith are being distinguished here: the emotional side, relating to the will to live; and the dogmatic side, relating to belief. In what he tells Jake about faith, Sisko is affirming the emotional side, which gets its value from the loss of worry and joyous conviction that it provides, enabling hope and courage. At the same time, like William James, Sisko can imagine someone with this kind of faith being open to different views of reality, because the value of faith is derived primarily from the life-affirming emotions inspired by what James calls a "faith-state," not dogmatism. In a faith-state, there is surely some measure of belief in the general possibility of future success, happiness or contentment, but no need for the precise dogmatic assertions of religious doctrine or interpretations of prophecy.

A critique of dogmatic faith is made once again in "Accession," when Bajoran poet Akorem Laan (Richard Libertini) is transported from the past by the Prophets. Akorem claims to be Emissary and declares a reinstatement of the Bajoran religious practice of the *D'jarras*, a caste system that had been abandoned during the Cardassian occupation. Obedient to the Emissary, most Bajorans immediately make the change, which soon results in one Bajoran killing another on the space station in response to a violation of the rules of the *D'jarras*. The culture of the Federation is of course opposed to such inegalitarianism and its murderous effects. It is made clear in this episode that the value of faith is not derived from dogmatism when the Prophets convey that they consider Sisko, not the religious traditionalist, to be the true Emissary.

The importance of maintaining critical thinking within the context of faith is illustrated in yet another way relating directly to vision experiences, when Kai Winn has her first interactive visions with the wormhole aliens in "'Til Death Do Us Part" and "Strange Bedfellows." Though Winn had experienced visions through the Orbs, as anyone can, never had the Prophets spoken to her directly in an interactive vision. Yet, as she soon discovers, it really is not the Prophets speaking to her, but instead the False Prophets, or Pah-wraiths, raising the concern that not even the visions that are so central to Bajoran faith can be trusted. James also warns against adopting too trusting an attitude toward the contents of spiritual experiences themselves, observing that the "super-normal incidents, such as voices and visions and overpowering impressions of the meaning of suddenly presented scripture texts, the melting emotions and tumultuous affections connected with the crisis of change, may all come by way of nature, or worse still, be counterfeited by Satan" (211–212). For James, it is not the supernatural origin of visions that constitutes the value of faith, nor the dogmatic adherence to the content of visions. The fruit of faith is its energizing and emboldening effect on the human spirit.

This is an aspect of faith and spirituality that can be championed by a secular *Star Trek* ethos, but which must also be guided by additional ethical principles that respect the value of autonomy, equality, and critical rationality. If not, spirituality can still be a faulty guide, as in the case of Kai Winn. Though at first she is disgusted to discover that she has been deceived by the evil Pah-wraiths, Winn soon accepts her allegiance to the False Prophets, because the Pah-wraiths at least provide her with purpose, while the true Prophets ignore her. In this case, not only dogmatism, but also extreme egoism, spoils the fruits of spirituality. Unfortunately, religious institutions are all too vulnerable to the manipulation of religious leaders who are not themselves spiritually and ethically enlightened or motivated, such as Kai Winn, and also her accomplice Dukat, who deceitfully influences many Bajorans to follow the Pah-wraiths in "Covenant." The problems with religion are many, but religion does not have a monopoly on spirituality or faith.

Conclusion

Deep Space Nine imagines a secular Starfleet officer who undergoes a profoundly spiritual conversion experience without sacrificing his scientific or ethical sensibilities and also without formally becoming a follower of any religious leader or dogma. Sisko himself unwittingly becomes a religious leader as the Emissary but does not seriously demand that others have faith in him for the sake of his own personal gain. The kind of faith Sisko achieves through his various visions is a faith in life and a faith in the wormhole aliens, who, over time, prove themselves worthy of that trust. *Deep Space Nine* suggests that a secular future still has room for an interest in spiritual experience, and that not all aspects of spirituality are religious relics of the past. As James writes, "Were we writing the story of the mind from the purely natural-history point of view, with no religious interest whatsoever, we should still have to write down man's liability to sudden and complete conversion as one of his most curious peculiarities" (205). Thanks to *Deep Space Nine*, the peculiarity of conversion experience has been written into the world of *Star Trek*.

NOTES

1. Those first three episodes are "The Man Trap," "Charlie X," and "Where No Man Has Gone Before." Amazing psychic powers and other paranormal phenomena show up in *The Original Series* in at least a dozen other episodes with little or no attempt at providing a scientific explanation. In "Turnabout Intruder," Spock (Leonard Nimoy) observes, "This crew has been to many places in the galaxy. They've been witness to many strange events. They are trained to know that what seems to be impossible often is possible given the scientific analysis of the phenomenon" ("Turnabout Intruder").

2. Not everyone is agreed on whether—or to what extent, or in what ways—*Star Trek* can be considered anti-religious. While critiquing religion, *Star Trek* also uses religious mythic themes to enhance storytelling, favorably explores forms of spirituality and supernaturalism that are difficult to distinguish from religion and may even exhibit something like a religious commitment to secularism. The tension between religion and secularism in the world of *Star Trek* is stimulatingly addressed by Thomas Richards in chapter 4 of *The Meaning of* Star Trek (1997); Mike Hertenstein in chapter 7 of *The Double Vision of* Star Trek (1998); Jon Wagner and Jan Lundeen in *Deep Space and Sacred Time:* Star Trek *in the American Mythos* (1998); and Ross S. Kraemer, William Cassidy, and Susan L. Schwartz in *Religions of* Star Trek (2003). Helpful articles on the topic include those by Paul Linford (1999), Darcee L. McLaren and Jennifer E. Porter (1999), Michael A. Burstein (2006), Kevin S. Decker (2016), and James F. McGrath (2015, 2016). Roddenberry's own views on God and religion can be found in a candid interview with Terrence Sweeney (1985). In her very insightful book *The Ethics of* Star Trek (2001), Judith Barad relates Sisko's adoption of the role of Emissary to Søren Kierkegaard's prioritizing of the religious stage over the ethical stage (chapter 9). The present essay complements Barad's work by exploring the ways in which spiritual experience leads to Sisko's conversion and faith, although I suggest a non-religious framework for understanding this. In passing, Douglas Cowan suggests viewing William James' account of mystical experience as a model for the spiritual experience that Sisko undergoes, but I have instead fastened onto James' similar and related account of conversion experience, rather than mystical experience (155).

3. James is also known for his arguments in favor of belief without evidence, or "the will to believe," which is explored by another *Star Trek* philosopher, Heather Keith, in "The Second-Coming of Kahless: Worf's 'Will to Believe.'"

4. That James is so greatly influenced by Christianity is fitting because, as it happens,

Christianity is the religion that probably most influences the mythic crafting of the Emissary storyline in *Deep Space Nine*, as argued by Barad (chapter 9) and Cassidy (Kraemer et al. 85, 90–91). While *Star Trek* storytellers are critical of various religious attitudes and structures, they also borrow heavily on the rich mythic frameworks provided by real world religions, as observed by Richards (Chapters 3–4) and also Schwartz: "*Star Trek* really *does* want the best of both worlds—the secular humanistic confidence in the triumph of reason, and the emotional and transforming experience of myth" (Kraemer et al. 157; emphasis original).

    5. Paul Linford is critical of *Deep Space Nine* for its caricature of religion, which is reduced almost entirely to the Bajorans' faith in prophecies. Linford says, "The prophecies do not seem to offer moral teaching, myth, or eschatology," also observing that the Prophets lack powers of creation and that their religious doctrine lacks any soteriology, or account of salvation, further distancing Bajoran religion from much more complex Western religions (78). Linford may be correct that *Deep Space Nine* does not give full consideration to the potential value of religious doctrine and practice, but at the same time, the fictional reduction of religion to belief in prophecies elegantly focuses the problem of interpretation that the series wants to highlight in order to sort out the pros and cons of faith. However, in a chapter devoted to the series, Cowan questions the validity of Linford's and others' skepticism of *Deep Space Nine*'s various depictions of religious transcendence (150–152).

Works Cited and Consulted

Barad, Judith, with Ed Robertson. *The Ethics of* Star Trek. Harper Perennial, 2001.

Burstein, Michael A. "We Find the One Quite Adequate: Religious Attitudes in *Star Trek*." *Boarding the Enterprise*, edited by David Gerrold and Robert J. Sawyer. BenBella, 2006, pp. 87–99.

Cowan, Douglas E. *Sacred Space: The Quest for Transcendence in Science Fiction Film and Television*. Baylor UP, 2010.

Decker, Kevin S. "'The Human Adventure Is Just Beginning': *Star Trek*'s Secular Society." *The Ultimate* Star Trek *and Philosophy: The Search for Socrates*, edited by Kevin S. Decker and Jason T. Eberl. John Wiley & Sons, 2016, pp. 326–39.

Hertenstein, Mike. *The Double Vision of* Star Trek: *Half-Humans, Evil Twins, and Science Fiction*. Cornerstone Press Chicago, 1998.

James, William. *The Varieties of Religious Experience*. Barnes & Noble Classics, 1902.

Jindra, Michael. "*Star Trek* Fandom as a Religious Phenomenon." *Sociology of Religion*, vol. 55, no. 1, 1994, pp. 27–51.

Keith, Heather. "The Second-Coming of Kahless: Worf's 'Will to Believe.'" Star Trek *and Philosophy: The Wrath of Kant*, edited by Kevin S. Decker and Jason T. Eberl. Open Court Publishing, 2008, pp. 173–184.

Kraemer, Ross, William Cassidy, and Susan L. Schwartz. *Religions of* Star Trek. Basic Books, 2003.

Linford, Paul. "Deeds of Power: Respect for Religion in *Star Trek: Deep Space Nine*." Star Trek *and Sacred Ground: Explorations of* Star Trek, *Religion, and American Culture*, edited by Jennifer E. Porter and Darcee L. McLaren. SUNY Press, 1999, pp. 77–100.

McGrath, James F. "Explicit and Implicit Religion in *Doctor Who* and *Star Trek*." *Implicit Religion*, vol. 18, no. 4, 2015, pp. 471–84.

_____. "A God Needs Compassion, but Not a Starship: *Star Trek*'s Humanist Theology." *The Ultimate* Star Trek *and Philosophy: The Search for Socrates*, edited by Kevin S. Decker and Jason T. Eberl. John Wiley & Sons, 2016, pp. 315–25.

McLaren, Darcee L., and Jennifer E. Porter. "(Re)Covering Sacred Ground: New Age Spirituality in *Star Trek: Voyager*." Star Trek *and Sacred Ground: Explorations of* Star Trek, *Religion, and American Culture*, edited by Jennifer E. Porter and Darcee L. McLaren. SUNY Press, 1999, pp. 101–115.

Richards, Thomas. *The Meaning of* Star Trek. Doubleday, 1997.

Sweeney, Terrence A. *God*. Winston, 1985.

Wagner, Jon, and Jan Lundeen. *Deep Space and Sacred Time:* Star Trek *in American Mythos*. Praeger, 1998.

Traversing/able Sacred Space

The Bajoran Wormhole as Spiritual Journey

Michael G. Cornelius

When Starfleet Commander (later Captain) Benjamin Sisko (Avery Brooks) and his Science Officer Jadzia Dax (Terry Farrell) discover a stable, artificially-constructed wormhole in Bajoran space, the duo do more than simply set off the chain of events that would frame the overarching storyline of *Star Trek*'s most narratively rich and complex series. The discovery of the Bajoran wormhole wholly transforms the entire area around it, changing not just the destinies of those peoples who worked and lived in the vicinity of the wormhole, but altering the very nature of (the) space in that region itself. The significance of this altered space varied for the different species and cultures in proximity to the wormhole. As Douglas R. Edward observes, "How a people interpret their geographic surroundings illuminates how they perceive their world and their place in it" (72). Thus the diverse species and cultures who dwell within proximity of the wormhole interpret the meaning of this spatial transfiguration through the values and principles that define their cultures. For the Federation, the wormhole represents new avenues for exploration, new places to seek out "new life and new civilizations." Opening up an entirely new discourse in potential knowledge, the wormhole represents an opportunity to discover, reflecting the oft-repeated mantra in the series that the twenty-fourth-century goal of humanity was to continually expand their base of knowledge of the universe. For the Ferengi, the wormhole reflects new opportunities for commerce, new civilizations to trade with and exploit. In a business conference held at Deep Space 9, the Ferengi Grand Nagus Zek explains that "truly lucrative business opportunities" have become difficult to find in the Alpha Quadrant, because the Ferengi reputation, a "reputation that has been tainted by the lies of our competitors," has hindered their ability to engage in commerce. However, as Zek triumphantly explains, "But no thanks to the discovery of the wormhole we can finally avoid such false-hoods. The Gamma Quadrant, gentlemen. Millions of new worlds on our very doorstep. The potential for Ferengi business expansion is staggering" ("The Nagus").

For the Cardassians, the wormhole denotes a new opportunity to demonstrate their cultural and military superiority in the quadrant, a chance to rehabilitate a self-view that had been damaged by their recent withdrawal from Bajor itself. Securing control of the wormhole signifies the possibility of a victory over the Bajorans after suffering a defeat that had wounded the psyche of the entire nation. As a "major" power in the Alpha Quadrant, their defeat at the hands of guerrilla insurgents signaled weakness; taking control of the wormhole would have provided a powerful counter-narrative to the Bajoran tale of freedom. Lastly, for the Dominion, the wormhole embodies new threats from new species, species who may challenge the Dominion's need to control and dominate the lives of others as a means to assuage their xenophobic fears of "solids." Prickling their inherent and long-standing fear of Others, the Dominion sees the worm-hole as a threat—not just to their borders, but to their very being.

Each society thus views the wormhole differently based on those values—learning; avarice; superiority; xenophobia—that, in the series, come to hallmark and broadly define their people. Yet what unites each of these views is that the wormhole's sudden appearance is grounded in representations of newness—new ideas, new opportunities, new hazards, but always new potentialities, all of which recognizes the manner in which the landscape around them has suddenly altered. This "newness" is what reshapes both space and the actions and minds of those who experience it. Yet for the Bajoran people the wormhole embodies nothing new, but stands instead as perceptible proof of a far more ancient ideal—their faith. For the Bajorans, the wormhole is the Celestial Temple, the home of their gods, and the narrative events of *Deep Space Nine* indicate that the wormhole is indeed the homespace of those same entities who have sent the Bajorans their consecrated orbs, who have communed with them through visions, and who have—whether purposefully or otherwise—encouraged their worship. To the Bajorans, the wormhole is, first and foremost, not a commercial opportunity nor a Northwest Passage to a far point of the galaxy; it is not a prospect to affirm their cultural or political authority. It is their Mount Olympus, the area where their gods dwell, the most sacred place in their entire religion. Despite this, though—or perhaps because of it?—it remains a wormhole, two fixed points in space, a passage through which thousands of ships have traversed, all simply in the effort to get from one side of the galaxy to the other. For the Bajorans, the wormhole is sacred space; but to the other species of the Alpha and Gamma Quadrants, it is a shortcut. This juxtaposition of two seemingly radically opposed concepts creates a dialectical tension over the usage of a space that, seemingly, should not be easily parsed nor managed. Most religious groups share their sacred spaces only under very specific conditions; one would imagine that few would relish viewing such reverential spaces being used by non-believers as a bypass, as a means only to some other, non-religious end. Yet this is precisely the spatial condition set forth in *Deep Space Nine*. The Bajorans never object to the usage of the wormhole as a wormhole; on the contrary, they embrace the traversable nature of this most sacred site. Why do a people who—in the world of *Star Trek*—are defined by their religiosity embrace such a secular usage and purpose of their most sacred site? To put it more bluntly, why let the heathen into the gates of heaven? The answer may very well be indicated in that exact question. Though most Alpha and Gamma Quadrant species may only see travel through the wormhole as traversing two points in space, for the Bajorans, travel through the Celestial Temple must be viewed as a spiritual journey. In sharing their sacred space, the Bajorans may also hope to share their sacred journey and, ultimately, their spirituality and faith. Embracing interstellar traffic becomes a form of evangelism; ultimately, the Bajorans accept the secular use of the Celestial Temple because, in the end, they believe it may result in varying forms of ecclesiastic conversion.

Transforming Space

Prior to the discovery of the wormhole, Deep Space 9—and Bajor— are hardly the center points of the universe. Julian Bashir (Siddig El Fadil), Chief Medical Officer on Deep Space 9, identifies the region as "frontier"-like and describes it as, "The farthest reaches of the galaxy. One of the most remote outposts available. This is where the adventure is. This is where heroes are made. Right here, in the wilderness" ("Emissary"). His description rankles the station's Bajoran First Officer, Major Kira Nerys (Nana Visitor), who pointedly rejoins, "This wilderness is my home" ("Emissary").

In reality, Bajor and Deep Space 9 are both—the frontier, and someone's home. Space is inscribable; the father of spatial theories, Yi-Fu Tuan, notes this facet of spatial dynamics thusly in his seminal work *Space and Place: The Perspective of Experience*: "Space is transformed into place as it acquires definition and meaning" (136). Here, Tuan uses the common descriptors of "space" and "place" as a type of linguistic taxonomy, noting a distinction between undefined, non-demarcated space and defined, demarcated place. The distinction between the two rests on the manner in which the area is defined and delineated by human presence. Those environs that have no meaning to any group of peoples are "space," while those that have meaning—that have personal, physical, social, and/or cultural relevance—are "place." The key tenet here is the inscription of meaning onto an area or environment through a deliberate human act of will. Whether the area has meaning for an individual person (as the site of a significant memory, for example) or the entire planet is irrelevant, since the interpretation of space begins and (in many ways) ends on the individual level. It is individual beings who espy a space and make it place; whether this distinction is cultural and universal or personal and singular hardly matters to the individual person who is making this interpretation in the first place. As such, space—or place—falls squarely into the eye of the beholder. Whereas Dr. Bashir views Deep Space 9 and the surrounding climes as the "frontier," Major Kira, in her own interpolation of the space, sees it as her "home." Both are right, and even if Bashir's view may be ill-informed (as personal and cultural interpretations often are), it does not negate the existence and essence of his construct of the space before him, for him.[1]

Space always exists in this manner, as construable to individuals and, as such, as existing in differing planes of reality depending very much on the person or persons who are viewing and interpreting said reality. One Terran's "frontier" may be another Bajoran's "home," but the same was true during the era of European exploration, when "new" lands were "discovered," or during the great frontier expansion in the American West during the nineteenth century, when white settlers moved into "new" territories that had been home to indigenous peoples for millennia. The interpretation of space is highly dependent on those who view it and the needs of those individuals. The young, enthusiastic doctor espies in the "frontier" a chance to make a name for himself, to cast his own identity in the semblance of some semi-legendary Western hero of folklore who came before him. The Bajoran major rankles not only because the place where she was reared, her homespace, was described as rough and remote and backwoods (with all the unpleasant implications that such associations carry for both the environ and the people who call it home) but also because, in the midst of the Cardassian withdrawal, the Bajoran people are fractured and divided. Her home is threatened by internal conflict and existential crises, by a people who differ on their very definition of what constitutes "home" and, as such, the word carries more spatial meaning that she may perhaps imagine.

All of this changes, though, upon the discovery of the wormhole. Immediately upon its discovery, Kira underscores its value: "That wormhole might just reshape the future of this entire quadrant" ("Emissary"). Her choice of word here—"reshape"—is telling. Kira immediately sees the spatial significance of the wormhole. This significance is reinforced in a conversation later in the episode that Sisko has with the Captain of the starship *Enterprise*, Jean-Luc Picard (Patrick Stewart):

SISKO: We're not done with the Cardassians yet, not with the strategic importance of that wormhole.

PICARD: Well, you've put Bajor on the map, Commander. This will shortly become a leading center of commerce and scientific exploration. And for Starfleet, one of our most important posts ["Emissary"].

Like Kira, Picard uses spatial metaphors ("put Bajor on the map") to describe the cultural and spatial significance of the wormhole. Its meaning is more than commercial or exploratory, and these spatial descriptors only highlight the wormhole's import by re-imagining the space around it. In re-"shaping" the quadrant, Kira is suddenly re-imagining the homespace around her, a space she previously and quite trenchantly defended. This is, perhaps, because Kira can now imagine a redefinition of home that could unite her fractured people. Picard, as well, in noting that the wormhole has "put Bajor on the map," emphasizes the manner in which spatial reconfiguration can alter cultural perception. Bajor's spatial elevation has broad implications—for its people, for the Federation, for the other powers of the Alpha Quadrant—implications that Picard and Sisko are only too aware will bring them unforeseen difficulties as well.

It is a relatively easy thing to physically transform space. Humanity has been doing just that for thousands of years, clearing forests for crop land, building villages on empty terrains, constructing vast cities where, only a short time before, there may have been nothing but desert and a few hardscrabble dwellings. It is far more difficult to alter the *perception* of space, particularly on a cultural level. Such a transformation requires broad cultural concurrence, an agreement between differing parties that the meaning of the space is now something different than what it was.

Religioscapes—sacred, religious spaces—are one product of cultural concurrence. As Mircea Eliade writes, "Every sacred space implies a hierophany, an irruption of the sacred that results in detaching a territory from the surrounding cosmic milieu and making it qualitatively different" (26). An "irruption" indicates an abrupt or violent alteration. This is not to state that the formation of religioscapes is inherently a violent act—not at all. Rather, it emphasizes the wholesale and occasionally sudden transformation of space when it converts from secular to sacred space. This is significant because, as Sigurd Bergmann observes, "Religions…[are] ritualizations which depend on space and [in turn] reshape it" (11). What is important here is the ritualistic nature of religioscape and the widespread recognition of this ritual by individuals both within and without the religious community. Sacred spaces do not happen accidentally; they are culturally inscribed through a form of ritualized practice that must be systematized by one group and yet recognized by an even broader constituency. The result is the alteration of space, at least metaphorically, through belief.

As George Wolfe notes, "Since the dawn of civilization, humans have had a need for sacred gathering places—spaces designated for worshipping the omnipotent force or forces to which we all inevitably succumb" (400). He adds that such space reflects the belief that humans became separated from God through either ignorance (as asserted in Eastern philosophy) or the transgression of Divine Law as depicted in Judaism, Christianity, and Islam. It therefore became necessary to prepare appropriate, holy, and protected places for people to again draw near the Divine (401). Margaret Morse agrees: "Pious objects and spaces operated as focal points for ritualized action, where contact with the divine was made possible. Serving both devotional and didactic needs, they shaped the spiritual and moral character of the family" (184). These spaces, then, are more than just areas for the faithful to gather or places to construct a house of worship. Sacred spaces shape the mores and values of congregations and communities. It makes culture, and, in turn, makes those who dwell within said culture. This is not to suggest that the only factor that shapes a culture is religion; while this may be true in isolated or segregated religious communities, religion is only one facet for creating and shaping culture. As a cultural factor, though, religion's importance and its influence should not be undervalued. This is certainly true of the Bajorans, whose faith is perhaps the defining characteristic ascribed to their culture. While the tenets of the Bajoran faith are never clearly elucidated in *Deep Space Nine*, the wholesale presence of the Bajoran faith is visible everywhere. The Bajorans have sacred objects (the orbs) and spaces (shrines and monasteries), even on Deep Space 9; a structured religious class with vedeks and a kai; and a system of governance that is at least partially theocratic, with the Vedek Assembly acting as a branch of government and the kai wielding tremendous political influence and power. The Bajoran people adorn themselves with ornamentations that signal their faith (especially on their ears) and often intersperse traditional greetings and farewells with religious sentiment. These manifestations of religion reflect a culture that is deeply connective to the construct of faith itself. Sisko emphasizes the importance of the Bajoran faith when he tells his son, Jake (Cirroc Lofton), "for over fifty years, the one thing that allowed the Bajorans to survive the Cardassian occupation was their faith. The Prophets were their only source of hope and courage" ("In the Hands of the Prophets"). Jake, who has been raised in the secular humanist values of the Federation, scoffs at the notion of faith:

> JAKE: But there were no Prophets; they were just aliens that you found in the wormhole.
> SISKO: To those aliens, the future is no more difficult to see than the past. Why shouldn't they be considered Prophets? ["In the Hands of the Prophets"].

When Jake scoffs at his father's response, Sisko tells him, "it's a matter of interpretation. It may not be what you believe, but that doesn't make it wrong" ("In the Hand of the Prophets").

Sisko's notion that it is all a "matter of interpretation" reflects—but also devalues—the nature of religion and the way in which it can shape cultural thought. The Bajorans do not believe that their faith is the by-product of "interpretation"; yet because their beliefs are not universally shared aboard Deep Space 9 or across the universe, others may see their faith or religion as only a cultural product. The Federation respects the religious values of others and embraces a multicultural, multi-religious, multi-species pluralism—provided said cultures do not impinge upon their own core values. Ultimately, though, the Federation view of the Bajorans and Bajor itself is perhaps somewhere between the dreamy "wilderness" notions of Dr. Bashir and the "commerce and scientific exploration" of Captain Picard— all descriptors situated deeply within the cultural values of the Federation, and not Bajor.

This is why sacred space can be so important to a culture or society. Wolfe writes that, "The sanctuary is the part of any shrine in which one finds refuge from the world" (403). For the Bajorans, their faith provided respite and shelter from the harsh treatments of the Cardassians— even if only psychically—and still provides relief from Federation values as well, when such relief may be warranted. After all, "religions happen in spaces" (Bergmann et al. 1). These spaces can be physical or metaphysical. The entrenched faith of the Bajoran oppressed Sisko discusses with his son was not always found in a sacred shrine. As Miguel Herrero de Jáuregui observes, "The definition of [human] spiritual states as physical spaces is very common in religion" (597). He adds: "In ancient Greece the description of spiritual states as 'places' is famously found in Plato, who depicts the process of philosophical knowledge as a sacred journey, a kind of inner pilgrimage or *theoria*, towards the contemplation of truth" (597). Indeed, it is something of a misnomer to note that Sisko and Dax "discovered" the wormhole. The Bajorans had always believed in the Celestial Temple; it was always psychic space for them, always as real as any religioscape. Whether it physically existed or not made little difference to them. As a site of faith, it *did* exist, regardless of form. Thus Sisko's argument that the Bajoran faith allowed them to survive fifty years of oppressive Cardassian occupation reflects the notion that the Bajorans always had a space, a sacred space, that the Cardassians could never reach—a space within their own selves.

Whether physical or metaphysical, the demarcation of sacred space is important to any faith community. Indeed, humanity has a tendency to classify the entirety of the world based on spatial boundaries and functions, as does any individual person. Yet the delineation of sacred space comes about in no small part by its juxtaposition against non-sacred, worldly spaces. This results in the bifurcation of territory: "certain areas of space are sacred and, correspondingly … other areas are worldly" (North and North 3). Sacred spaces are juxtaposed against the spaces we work in, live in, travel to and from—in short, sacred spaces are juxtaposed against all other spaces humans may encounter. This suggests that sacred religioscapes possess a significance beyond other spaces. Thus the wormhole as religioscape is far more meaningful to the Bajorans than to anyone else. This, however, begs a rather pertinent question: if the Celestial Temple is the most sacred religioscape for Bajorans, and the Bajorans have the "rights" to said space, why do they allow—well, pretty much anyone—to enter their sacred space?

Sharing Sacred Space

Sacred space is destination space.

Unless they belong to a religious caste, people do not inhabit religioscapes. Most individuals who visit sacred spaces tend to do so for particular, ritualistic reasons. These rituals affirm their faith, strengthening the bonds of believer to creed, in a communal setting shared between believers. It is a place where people go, sometimes on set schedules, to perform particular ceremonies and rituals. As such, the practice of religion is both private and public. It is private in the sense that it occurs in spaces that are distinct from all other (worldly) spaces, usually out of the gaze of those who are not members of the faith community. It is public in that community membership is usually not restrictive; that is to say, while many faith traditions have structures designed to keep others out, those same structures are designed to process new believers who may become part of the faith community. Still, in general, entering into a faith tradition requires more work than simply passing through a threshold (though there are exceptions to this), and thus one could argue that sacred spaces tend to be more exclusive than inclusive.

Yet the lines between exclusivity and inclusivity, and the ways in which sacred spaces can be used for non-sacred functions, have long been blurred. When religious buildings dominated landscapes, these spaces were often used for non-sacral reasons: for safety; for commerce; for education. Yet this obfuscation of spatial intent and purpose was not always welcomed. All four gospels of the Christian Bible tell the story of Jesus cleansing the temple in Jerusalem, clearing it of all commercial activity:

> On reaching Jerusalem, Jesus entered the temple courts and began driving out those who were buying and selling there. He overturned the tables of the money changers and the benches of those selling doves, and would not allow anyone to

carry merchandise through the temple courts. And as he taught them, he said, "Is it not written: 'My house will be called a house of prayer for all nations'? But you have made it 'a den of robbers'" [Mark 11:15–17].[2]

As David Seeley reports, "The temple act would ... have been out of keeping with Jesus' style. We hear of no other instance of his employing physical violence" (60). As puzzling as Jesus' vociferous and strident reaction has been to Biblical scholars, the intent of this scene has also eluded them. Richard H. Hiers writes that some scholars believe that "when Jesus attacked the money changers and traders he was indirectly attacking the sacerdotal hierarchy which sponsored these concessions.... Several other writers have also suggested, in effect, that Jesus intended, by purifying the Temple, to prepare Israel for coming of the Kingdom of God" (83). In seeking greater meaning, scholars have left behind perhaps the most obvious objection Jesus seems to be lodging here, which is not truly towards the utilization of sacred space as commercial space, but rather towards the utilization of sacred space as *something else*, as worldly space, for something other than the ritualistic purpose for which it was designed. Hiers agrees: "what he [Jesus] finds objectionable is the presence of these merchants and traders *in the Temple*" (83, italics original). It is not the act here that is most upsetting; it is the location.

Despite these protestations, though, there has long existed a dialectical tension between the use of sacred space as sacred space and its use as something else. For example, many great cathedrals today exist as tourist destinations. Indeed, they are often first and foremost an attraction; while exhortations for visitors to remain quiet and reverent in such spaces reflect their sacred pasts, charging an admission fee and even allowing people to tour the facility while religious ceremonies are occurring obscures the fundamental purpose of such space.

In their exploration of shared religious spaces, Robert M. Hayden and Timothy D. Walker suggest that, "Consideration of shared religious space is ... generally tightly delimited and often unilaterally defined, seeing the space as a single site and the sharing as a manifestation of tolerance, even as mutual embrace of the other, at present or in a very recent moment in time" (400). They add:

> Our work has led us to think that the best way to understand shared religious sites is by looking at them as nodes in structures of social interactions between populations that distinguish themselves and each other as different, on religious grounds, through time. As a node, a single site is not isolable from the social networks, of varying scale, that interact at it [407].

Hayden and Walker's conception of shared sacred space is largely syncretistic, wherein an amalgamation of religious ideas or values co-exist within a particular setting. This could happen when one denomination allows another to utilize part of its church-space for a ceremonial purpose, or when a particular site becomes consecrated to more than one faith group. In Jerusalem, the Western Wall, or Wailing Wall, as it is also known, is sacred to Muslims, Jews, and (to a lesser extent) Christians. Whereas the space has different meaning to each group, in this particular instance, they co-exist in a sense of spatial tolerance, each group making an allowance for the presence of the other(s).

When Jesus routed the money-changers, however, he was not decrying shared sacrality, but the encroachment of non-sacred (and in this case commercial) ventures into sacred space. This is the tension found in cathedrals today, where believers kneel in reverent prayer while tourists take pictures of stained glass windows. This would also (seemingly) reflect the tension in the use of the Bajoran Celestial Temple as a pathway for commerce, exploration, and military conquest. And yet this tension does not seem to really exist. In fact, far from objecting to the encroachment of other species into the Celestial Temple, the Bajorans seem to welcome the mass of spaceships that traverse their sacred space.

Traversing Sacred Space

In *Star Trek* canonicity, the custody of wormholes seem to work under basic spatial property principles, suggesting that the "rights" to a wormhole belongs to whomever controls the space it is in. In *The Next Generation* episode "The Price," a wormhole is found near the Barzan home world. Seeing this as both a natural resource and a lucrative opportunity, the Barzans open negotiations with the Federation, the Caldonians, the Chrysalians, and eventually the Ferengi for the rights to administer the wormhole for them. No one contests the claim of the Barzans to administer the wormhole, nor does anyone try to take it by force, even though the Barzans are, by their own admission, ill equipped to defend their own territory against larger, more aggressive forces. Nonetheless, this seems to establish basic *Star Trek* principles regarding wormhole control—less "finders keepers" and more "whose backyard is it in."

When the wormhole is uncovered during *Deep Space Nine*'s pilot episode, Kira realizes right away the importance of establishing Bajoran authority over it: "The Bajorans have to stake a claim to [the wormhole]. And I have to admit that claim will be a lot stronger if there's a Federation presence to back it up" ("Emissary"). It is evident that Kira is concerned that the Cardassians will endeavor to stake their own claim to the wormhole by force (they are lurking about in warships outside the station). It is also clear that she is concerned that the Federation may claim the wormhole as their own to control, when she notes that the role of Starfleet is only to "back up" the Bajorans, not override or overrule them.

Once their claim is clearly established, the religious significance of the wormhole is not lost to the Bajorans: "I remember when I first saw the gate of the Celestial Temple—I was on the Promenade. When it burst into view, this whirlpool of color and light, the people all around me were in awe. They said they could feel the love of the Prophets washing over them" ("Strange Bedfellows"). These words are uttered by Kai Winn (Louise Fletcher), a malignant religious presence who speaks here ironically, because she herself experiences no such feeling upon viewing the wormhole's aperture. And yet her words, hollow as they may be, only echo the significance of the wormhole to everyday Bajorans, who feel the direct presence of their gods simply upon viewing it.

To suggest the Bajorans view the wormhole as only a religioscape is perhaps somewhat naïve. Clearly, Kira and the Bajoran provisional government are keenly aware that the attention brought by the wormhole may benefit the Bajoran economy and the Bajoran people, both of which are struggling mightily at the series' onset. Yet commercial and diplomatic attention entails as many potential problems as it does potential benefits. These problems are detailed as the series unfolds, especially when a malevolent political power from the Gamma Quadrant threatens the entirety of the Alpha Quadrant, at one point planning to cause the Bajoran sun to go supernova, collapsing the wormhole and utterly destroying the entire Bajoran system, killing millions ("By Inferno's Light"). So, again, the question must be posed: why do the Bajorans allow practically anyone entry into their most sacred Celestial Temple?

Perhaps what is significant here, from a religio-cultural perspective, is that the Celestial Temple is less a destination than it is a passage. Though a sacred site, it is not an end, nor a beginning, but a middle point in any journey that involves travel from the Alpha to the Gamma Quadrant. It is a point of passage—but a highly significant, unique point of passage. As Robert M. Torrance observes, such points of passage can hold tremendous significance for spiritual rituals and journeys:

> [It is] not the beginning or end points, the separation or incorporation, which these rites have in common—rites of birth, marriage, initiation, or death begin and end in wholly different biological and social conditions—but passage itself, the critical crossing of a threshold that is not a line but a region, a temporal and spatial in between, "autonomous" because not governed by conventions prevailing before and after the crossing. Each passage, to be sure, presupposes a goal— it is a passage to something—but no goal entirely subsumes the passage to it (autonomy cannot be subsumed under law, or movement under fixity) or finally

terminates the process of crossing, since every end point is potentially a point of departure…. What the rite of passage celebrates above all is passage itself [10].

What Torrance contends here is that while the commencement and completion of religious ceremonies and religious quests hold significance, it is usually at some midpoint in the journey when the quester discovers her or his spiritual awakening. It is the journey that matters most, because it is the journey—not the termination of the journey—that creates the impression of spiritual awakening. The Bajorans are not a spiritually exclusive people. They openly share their faith with others; in short, in their own way, they evangelize. Whether or not outsiders may wholly join the Bajoran faith is difficult to answer, given what limited knowledge of the religion we possess. They may partake, however, in Bajoran religious festivals, have orb experiences, and participate in Bajoran ecclesiastic ceremonies. While the Bajoran evangelical tradition may seem less irksome than other forms of fervent religious recruitment, it is nonetheless a part of their faith tradition. As Lesslie Newbigin observes, "The *evangel* is for the *oikoumene*," a Greek word meaning "the inhabited world" (146). This is especially relevant here; for the Greeks, the *oikoumene* meant the Greek world only, and excluded those not of Greek society; for others, though, including the Bajorans, the *oikoumene* may mean all inhabited worlds, suggesting that their faith is for any who wish to observe.

By allowing easy access to the Celestial Temple, the Bajorans may believe they are sharing their faith with the other cultures of the Alpha and Gamma Quadrants. This may not be as far-fetched as it seems. After all, narratives of travels, journeys, and quests are frequently about the search for identity. As Marta Mazurkiewicz observes, in such narratives "a protagonist … makes an actual or metaphoric journey, experiencing many obstacles and difficulties but finally achieving a better understanding of himself and of the society in which he lives" (47–48). Iain Chambers agrees: "Our sense of being, of identity and language, is experienced and extrapolated from movement: the 'I' does not pre-exist this movement and then go out into the world" (24). Spiritual journeys reflect a particular identity shift, from non-believer to believer. Many faith traditions believe not only in the righteousness of their creeds, but that it is their duty to share their faith with outsiders. Changing one's faith is changing one's identity; to do either, Chambers would argue, requires movement, travel, a journey into the world outside of one's self and one's familiar environs.

This is not to suggest that a non-believer would make a single trip through the wormhole and suddenly become a full-fledged acolyte of the Prophets, especially if that individual was not raised in the Bajoran spiritual tradition. Nonetheless, the spatial identity of the wormhole as the Celestial Temple would be well known to those who travel within it, and the phenomenon itself would likely give travelers pause and create sensations of awe and wonder as they first pass through. The knowledge that the wormhole is, indeed, sacred space, even if it is not the particular sacred space of the individual passing through at any given time, may be enough to create a sense of correlation between these different factors: spirituality, faith, and space.

There is clear evidence that these journeys do impact individuals in tremendously spiritual ways. Sisko himself enters the wormhole as a non-believer and re-emerges as Emissary of the Prophets, an important religious figure in Bajoran theology. Though he is at first reluctant to accept his role as Emissary, over time Sisko embraces his place in the Bajoran faith tradition, to the point where he is willing to place his faith and trust in the Prophets and allow the potential sacrifice of his own son in a celestial battle between a Prophet and the Pah-wraith Kosst Amojan ("The Reckoning"). Sisko's journey through the wormhole leads to his own spiritual journey, one in which he communes directly with the Bajoran deities. Sisko's slow but ecstatic conversion story is rather distinctive, though its essentials—a spiritual quest, communion with deities, a belief in a greater, ecclesiastic purpose—are hardly in and of themselves unique. Such experiences are the tenets of most spiritual journey narratives, and the identity shifts that come with these types of faith-based experiences are precisely the purpose of evangelizing—to create more believers.

Conclusion

In *Evangelicalism in Modern Britain*, David Bebbington outlines his "evangelical theological quadrilateral" to denote the definitory qualities of Evangelical Christians. These are: primacy of the Bible; conversion; atonement theology; and justification through deeds (Kandiah 52; Bebbington 1–19). Sisko's religious trajectory in the series demonstrates the prioritization of Bajoran prophetic texts (Sisko himself utters a prophecy in "The Rapture" that comes to pass in "By Inferno's Light"); his own conversion narrative; numerous atonement narratives (even Winn attempts religious atonement in the end, sacrificing herself to save the Emissary and the Prophets in the series finale, "What You Leave Behind"); and as for justification through deed, eventually *Deep Space Nine* reveals that Sisko was actually created through the efforts of the Prophets to win their final, apocalyptic battle with the Pah-wraiths.

Though it seems unlikely that other trips through the wormhole will create as direct a conversion experience as Sisko's, it cannot be ignored that by sharing their sacred space with others, the Bajoran people are also sharing their religion as well. To travel through the Celestial Temple is to spend time in a holy shrine of the Bajoran faith, to spend time in their sacred space. As Hayden and Walker note,

> Religioscapes as we define them are inherently fluid: people move, taking their religious practices with them, and potentially changing the built environment as well, in ways that reflect their beliefs. Yet the religioscape also reflects the connections between people who regard themselves as holding the same beliefs, or are regarded by others as doing so [408].

The journey through the wormhole creates and sustains these connections. For Sisko, the journey results in him becoming an important religious figure for the Bajoran people, their Emissary of the Prophets. Others may not be as affected, but it is difficult to venture into any sacred space and not feel the weight of its sacrality. This is because, ultimately, the spatial identities of such places are not defined by what they contain nor how they function, but by the faith traditions they reflect and inspire. It may seem odd that the Bajorans allow anyone to traverse their most sacred religioscape, to travel through the Celestial Temple simply to move from one point in the galaxy to another. And yet perhaps they do this because they know that such movement through sacred space always carries with it tremendous significance, and that such journeys are not just informative, but formative. Ultimately, the Bajorans are doing more here than sharing their space; they are also sharing their faith.

Notes

1. Bashir is, of course, being influenced by the Federation's decidedly colonialist bent. For more on *Star Trek* and colonialism, see Bishop, Whitney, and Ono, among others.

2. The same scene appears in all four gospels (Matthew 21:12–17; Luke 19:45–48; John 2:13–16). It occurs a week before Jesus's death and is one of the more scholarly-debated incidents in the Bible.

Works Cited and Consulted

Bebbington, David. *Evangelicalism in Modern Britain: From the 1730s to the 1980s.* Unwin Hyman, 1989.

Bergmann, Sigurd. "Nature, Space and the Sacred: Introductory Remarks." *Nature, Space and the Sacred: Transdisciplinary Perspectives*, edited by Sigurd Bergmann, P.M. Scott, M. Jansdotter Samuelsson, and H. Bedford-Strohm. Ashgate, 2008, pp. 9–18.

Bergmann, Sigurd, et al. "Editorial." *Nature, Space and the Sacred: Transdisciplinary Perspectives*, edited by Sigurd Bergmann, P.M. Scott, M. Jansdotter Samuelsson, and H. Bedford-Strohm. Ashgate, 2008, pp. 1–8.

Bishop, Bart. "*Star Trek* into Colonialism." *The Kelvin Timeline of* Star Trek, edited by Matthew Wilhelm Kapell and Ace G. Pilkington. McFarland, 2019, pp. 58–71.

Chambers, Iain. *Migrancy, Culture, Identity.* Routledge, 1994.

Edward, Douglas R. *Religion and Power: Pagans, Jews, and Christians in the Greek East.* Oxford UP, 1996.

Eliade, Mircea. *The Sacred and the Profane: The Nature of Religion.* Translated by Willard R. Trask. Harcourt, 1959.

Hayden, Robert M., and Timothy D. Walker. "Intersecting Religioscapes: A Comparative Approach to Trajectories of Change, Scale, and Competitive Sharing of Religious Spaces." *Journal of the American Academy of Religion*, vol. 81, no. 2, June 2013, pp. 399–426.

Herrero de Jáuregui, Miguel. "The Construction of Inner Religious Space in Wandering Religion of Classical Greece." *Numen*, vol. 62, 2015, pp. 596–626.

Hiers, Richard H. "Purification of the Temple: Preparation for the Kingdom of God." *Journal of Biblical Literature*, vol. 90, no. 1, Mar. 1971, pp. 82–90.

Kandiah, Krish. "Lesslie Newbigin's Contribution to a Theology of Evangelism." *Transformation*, vol. 24, no. 1, January 2007, pp. 51–60.

Mazurkiewicz, Marta. "Bildungsroman All'Italiana: The Formation Novel in Italian Post-War Fiction." *The European Connection*, vol. 16, 2012, pp. 47–58.

Morse, Margaret. "Creating Sacred Space: The Religious Visual Culture of the Renaissance Venetian *Casa*." *Renaissance Studies*, vol. 21, no. 2, 2007, pp. 151–184.

Newbigin, Lesslie. "Cross-Currents in Ecumenical and Evangelical Understandings of Mission." *International Bulletin of Missionary Research*, vol. 6, no. 4, 1982, pp. 146–151.

North, John, and Philip North. "Introduction." *Sacred Space: House of God, Gate of Heaven.* Edited by John North and Philip North. Continuum, 2007.

Ono, Kent A. "Domesticating Terrorism: A Neocolonial Economy of *Différance*." *Enterprise Zones: Critical Positions on* Star Trek, edited by Taylor Harrison, Sarah Projansky, Kent A. Ono, and Elyce Rae Helford. Westview Press, 1996, pp. 157–185.

Seeley, David. "Jesus' Temple Act Revisited: A Response to P.M. Casey." *The Catholic Biblical Quarterly*, vol. 62, no. 1, January 2000, pp. 55–63.

Torrance, Robert M. *The Spiritual Quest: Transcendence in Myth, Religion, and Science.* U of California P, 1994.

Tuan, Yi-Fu. *Space and Place: The Perspective of Experience.* U Minnesota P, 1977.

Whitney, Allison. "Love at First Contact: Sex, Race and Colonial Fantasy in Star Trek: First Contact." *The Sex Is Out of this World: Essays on the Carnal Side of Science Fiction*, edited by Sherry Ginn and Michael G. Cornelius. McFarland, 2012, pp. 62–85.

Wolfe, George. "Inner Space as Sacred Space: The Temple as Metaphor for the Mystical Experience." *Crosscurrents*, 2002, pp. 400–411.

Epilogue

SHERRY GINN

Following the cancellation of *Star Trek: Enterprise* (2001–2005) in 2005, fans lamented the fate of the franchise and had to be content with reruns. This, of course, is no difficulty, as each of the previous series can be found on multiple networks and platforms. For example, BBC America currently airs multiple episodes of *The Next Generation* (1987–1994) and *Deep Space Nine* (1993–1999) weekly and in order, immediately restarting each upon finishing the final season, totaling seven for each. In addition, series in the first set of six[1] can be found on CBS Access (*The Original Series* [1966–1969]), *The Next Generation, Enterprise*) and Netflix and Amazon Prime (all but *The Animated Series*, 1973–1974). Like another science fiction series—one also with a fifty-plus year history, whose fans were rewarded when *Doctor Who* was rebooted in 2005—*Star Trek* fans were similarly rewarded in 2017 with the premiere of *Star Trek: Discovery* (2017–present).[2] An instant critical success, *Discovery* appealed to both Trekkies and Trekkers.[3] A fourth season of the series is in production as of this writing. In fact, in total, four *Star Trek* series are currently in production—*Discovery, Lower Decks* (2020–present), *Picard* (2020–present), and *Strange New Worlds* (announced May 2020, currently filming)—and rumors abound that more are in the works. Fifty-plus years from its first broadcast, *Star Trek* shows no sign of stopping or slowing down.

This glut of *Trek*-related television begs the question: Why? What makes *Star Trek* such an enduring text? And why now? There are many answers to these questions, from the appeal of the cast members to the writing to the production values to the allure of a future vastly different (read: simpler, calmer, better) from the one in which we are living at this moment in time. As a matter of fact, these words are being penned during the coronavirus pandemic, a terrifying scourge that has killed millions of people around the globe. The future as envisioned in the various *Star Trek* franchises, especially the ones set in the maturity of the United Federation of Planets, is one in which poverty, totalitarianism, and disease, along with the various -isms of racism, fascism, sexism, ageism, ableism, etc., are largely archaic nouns whose definitions could be found in a dictionary and not as much in the real world (or so it seems). *Star Trek* offers the promise of paradise and, perhaps even more appealing, offers a sense of inevitability that humanity's ultimate outcome is, in fact, utopian. It is not so much hope for the future but the absolute certitude that the future is hopeful. Thus, for many *Star Trek* viewers, the future is bright and shiny (an affirmation I say every day to myself in the shower). It is a future in which we would like to live, right now. As a recent *Time Special Edition* publication about *Star Trek* noted, "Decades after its premiere, *Star Trek* thrives on the idea that there is always something beyond our understanding waiting to be discovered … even after all of these years, fans are still eager to engage with their favorite captains on the bridge" (5).

I was there from the very beginning, with *The Original Series*, and I am still here, eagerly waiting for whatever iteration of the series comes next. That does not mean that I have liked everything in the fifty-five-years-plus franchise's history, but I can appreciate the optimism of those who set out to produce a series about our future, one in which humankind not only survives, but thrives. There are certainly days when I despair and wonder what the hell is going on outside my door. As I write these words, I take note of the fact that I re-watched "Treachery, Faith and the Great River" last night. This is the episode where Odo learns about the plague killing his people, and I thought how ironic that I am watching this episode at a time when the people of the world are dying of the coronavirus. This episode was broadcast over twenty years ago, and yet Odo's response upon learning about the plague resonated deeply with me; its significance, like so many episodes of *Deep Space Nine*, is in illustrating yet another way the series was not only different from *The Original Series* and *The Next Generation*, but also very much prescient about our own time—themes that we hope have been illustrated in the essays contained in this book.

I also make note of this fact because of the virus' effect on those people who planned to contribute to this collection. My coeditor and I received nearly sixty abstracts for this collection and began this book with an expectation of receiving twenty-five essays. We realized that some of those essays might not fit into our vision of the collection; anytime one puts together a collection like this one, some essays simply do not come together. Plus, we knew that life would intervene for a few authors, who would find themselves unable to complete their works as well. Life (and death), however, had different notions for all of us. For a brief time, we thought we would have to cancel the project altogether. Happily, the intrepid authors contained in this collection persevered. The collection does not say everything we wanted it to say. We would have loved to have essays about Dax or Worf or Dukat, or more on gender, or essays on class. We would have liked more on *Deep Space Nine*, period. We started this project not only because Michael and I believe *Deep Space Nine* to be the best of the *Trek*s, but because we felt it had a lot to say—about *Star Trek*; about serialized story-telling; about the future and the past and thusly, always, the present—that it had not been studied in quite the way it should be. Some of that work is done in this collection; there is more to do. There are still "strange new worlds" to discover about *Deep Space Nine*. Then again, in a narrative as rich as this, perhaps there always should be.

Where We Were and Where We Are Going

If anyone were to believe that fans have no power, they only had to watch television during the week of April 18, 2021 (see Hamilton, for example).[4] The owners of six English Premier League football clubs announced that they, along with club owners in Spain and Italy, were creating a Super League that would include fifteen permanent teams that could never be relegated from the League, with five slots that could be filled through some type of annual qualifying event.[4] The outcry from English fans was swift and vocal, and within forty-eight hours, all six PL teams had withdrawn from the Super League, as had several of the European clubs.

Of course, such a "fan-atic" response is nothing new to Trekkies. In their recent book *The Voyages of Star Trek: A Mirror on American Society though Time*, Kathleen M. Heath and Ann S. Carlisle trace the years between *The Original Series* and *The Next Generation*, when *Star Trek* fans kept the franchise alive by producing fanzines and fan-fiction as well as convening conventions for devotees of the show. It was during this hiatus that a sub-culture of *Star Trek* fans emerged; they were referred to as Trekkies, and the term was originally meant to be derogatory, comparing *Star Trek* fans to rock groupies. However, the devotion of the Trekkies could not be dismissed so easily; they generated millions of dollars in revenue for companies that marketed *Trek*-themed merchandise. Paramount executives realized that they were missing out on the revenue generated by this phenomenon and quickly rectified their mistaken belief that *Star Trek* was not a lucrative product. Paramount also jumped on the film bandwagon, releasing four *Star Trek* films between 1979 and 1986. Yet, what the fans truly wanted was another *Star Trek* series, and their wishes were granted in 1987 when *The Next Generation* was produced.

I was an avid viewer of *The Next Generation* from the beginning. As a matter of fact, that was my Saturday night date with my boyfriend (now husband): dinner and *Star Trek*. Yet as I look back now, with a more criti-cal eye, I do find myself asking: where was the drama? The idea of a future with no poverty and war along with respect and dignity guaranteed for all humans is simplistically utopian. Yet is it compelling? As noted in our introduction, *Deep Space Nine* is the favorite iteration of *Trek* for both me and my coeditor. But how did we get there from *The Next Generation*? Is the movement from utopian to anti-utopian (if not nearly dystopian) prog-ress or regress? Did *Star Trek* narratively advance while hope for the future degenerated? What does such movement say about those of us consum-ing these texts? Why are we so enamored of destroying paradise? And what does it say about the editors of this volume that the *Star Trek* series that (at least to that point in time) did the most work to disrupt the utopian vision of the franchise is, by and far, our favorite?

I keep thinking about all of this as I sit in my office chair and look out-side my window. I retired from academia in 2018. I missed the infamous Spring 2020 "pivot" from in-person teaching to online teaching. I missed stu-dent technology catastrophes, the fraught of moving from communicating in person to never seeing a soul; I missed having to wholly shift my pedagogy from an in-person mode to digital media. At home, I was relatively safe in my retirement, in my house, in my own world. I could work on my books, con-sume all the popular culture I wanted, and think. The world is struggling all around me, and yet, somehow, I have the luxury of rest and contemplation.

I saw the struggles; witnessed them fairly close up. I saw my former colleagues push themselves to the brink to prepare classes for students; I had many a conversation with my coeditor, still a full-time professor, and watched, as time continued to pass, as he grew more and more exhausted, as the lines on his face grew more apparent and the aspect of his eyes ever wearier. One of our authors would send us a revised essay and I would pounce on it, delighted for distraction and mental exercise in my cozy, safe world; and every time I would send it on to Michael, I almost felt apolo-getic, adding more to a plate I knew was already overly full.

And yet, as I stare at the tail end of this project, as the world slowly returns to whatever new normal will emerge from this tragedy, as we all argue over what this all means, I keep thinking of that young(er) version of me and her boyfriend watching *The Next Generation*; and I keep thinking of who I am, now, older, hopefully wiser, definitely settled, and I keep think-ing about *Deep Space Nine*. A pandemic is a funny thing. We all found our-selves stuck: stuck inside, stuck indoors, stuck in moments of time in our lives without any real sense of how to advance, to get to that next phase. It is hard to make progress when you cannot leave the house. And yet, in our confinement, in my cozy office nook, I had time to reflect, to contemplate, to rest. And I find myself thinking about where this entire project started, and where this book starts. With *Star Trek*. With *The Next Generation* and *Deep Space Nine*. With perpetual motion and perpetual rest.

It is apt, I think, to describe the current state of the world—at least at the time I am authoring these words—as a perfect imbalance of perpetual motion and perpetual rest. I think of Michael, who teaches and works every day, all day, seven days a week, from a little desk in a corner of his guest bedroom. He never moves, and he never stops moving. He can never stop being, so he can never be. In some ways, he is *The Next Generation*. Helping that one student to save her grade or convincing that colleague not to just quit in frustration—these are the frantic acts of heroism, small as they may seem, that define *Star Trek*. Humanity helping others, seeking out newness and making it better. And yet, here I am, at rest, with the luxury of time and my own thoughts. And so I am able to see things as he and so many others simply do not have the time to do. At least, my thinking tells me as such. And, of course, I keep thinking about *Deep Space Nine*.

When I first started watching, Kira quickly became my favorite character (as evidenced by my essay about her in this collection). I remember liking the fact that the actors were more diverse than the other *Treks* (although still not as diverse as it could have been for the 1990s). But now, in the midst of all this pandemic, I find myself thinking about Sisko more than any other character. Benjamin Sisko is a widower with a teenage son when he assumes command of *Deep Space Nine*. He was portrayed by Avery Brooks, a Black actor best known to audiences (and certainly to me) from the television series *Spenser: For Hire* (1985–1988). He was a strong leader who commanded the respect of his crew, and his relationship with his son was both loving and caring. As a matter of fact, Sisko's portrayal had a "strong positive impact on the image of a Black man in American culture," belying the stereotype of the absentee Black father (Heath and Carlisle 55). *Deep Space Nine* still presented mostly White characters (even the aliens were White), and its representation of women was dismal compared to the strides toward equality that women were making socially and politically in 1990s United States (Heath and Carlisle). But it had Sisko, the captain, a wounded man, an ideal father, and a messianic figure.

It is no surprise that the *Star Trek* captains are amongst the most revered and celebrated figures in the entire pantheon of the series. They each contain a particular essence, a mystique, that also encapsulates their series. And what would they make of this, our time period? What would they make of the pandemic? Picard, no doubt, would need to solve this. Right away. He would work tirelessly with his tireless crew to technobabble a way out of it. Janeway would likely try the same, though her approach would perhaps be a bit more hardscrabble and homemade, and we would no doubt have to "talk things out" at some point, too.

Kirk—well, Kirk would certainly punch any man who refused to wear a mask in the grocery store. But what of Sisko? What of the Emissary to the Prophets, what of the father of Jake Sisko, what of one of the most significant Black figures from television in the entire last decade of the twentieth century? What would he do now? I think, in some ways, he would do what I am doing. Rest. That is not to say he would not work to solve any problem—of course he would, he is Starfleet—but Sisko, and *Deep Space Nine*, recognizes the virtue of rest. The rest of contemplation and thought. The virtue of, sometimes, doing nothing. More than any other *Star Trek* captain, Sisko would learn to live in this moment. Because, as the sum of his existence has taught him, there is nothing else to truly do.

It is fascinating—or, perhaps more appropriately, it is *telling*—that Sisko ends the series lost somewhere in time. In the final episode of the series, Sisko appears to Kasidy Yates in a vision. He is in the Celestial Temple, he tells her. He is with the Prophets. "When will you be back?" she asks. "It's hard to say," he replies. "Maybe a year. Maybe … yesterday" ("What You Leave Behind"). When I first saw the episode, Sisko's response, enigmatic as it is, seemed fitting, considering the non-linear nature of the Prophets and, indeed, as Sisko confirms in the same conversation, his own existence. And yet, now…. I find myself understanding what he meant even more. Now, after nearly a year-and-a-half of the pandemic, after life (mine, my coeditor's, yours) having become … what it is…. I understand these words even more. A year. Yesterday. Forever and nothing, all at once. Perpetual motion and perpetual rest. The shrewd captain seeks to understand both and attempts to—if not master—then to navigate them as well and wisely as one can.

Forever Trek

Every summer the *Star Trek* Convention is held at the Rio All Suites Hotel and Casino in Las Vegas, Nevada. I have attended—more than once. The year 2021 was billed as the 55-Year Mission Tour and marked the 100th birthday of Gene Roddenberry. Over one hundred special guests confirmed their appearance. Pandemic or not, this is something I could not miss.

Although I have only attended three of these conventions—one being the 25th anniversary celebration for *Deep Space Nine*[5]—I view each of these occasions as both particularly special memories and particularly special opportunities. The psychologist in me cannot help but notice the ways in which fans and actors interact with one another. Many of them greet each other by name, indicating a long-standing relationship in a somewhat low-key environment (as opposed to attempting to meet and greet one's favorite actor in a venue such as Dragon Con, with its fifty-thousand-plus attendees). Many of those who attend the convention in Las Vegas also go on "Star Trek: The Cruise." As a matter of fact, "Star Trek: The Cruise V," scheduled for February 26–March 5, 2022, sold out. With tongue planted firmly in cheek, the cruise bills itself as an "unconventional voyage" and, as Sabrina Mittermeier remarks about The Cruise III, the experience allows for a more intimate experience for the fan, a way to connect with the actors as well as with other fans in a more relaxed and congenial atmosphere than at a standard hotel convention, a way to build a community sustained even after the event concludes (1377).

Conventions and cruises all seem to act as signals, indicators of a return to "normal," a reversion to the mean. Then again, *Star Trek* was never about what is "normal." It always was an ideal. An ideal, like a convention where a fan and an actor who played a character that means the world to that fan can interact. An ideal, like the Earth of the future. An ideal, like the office of a retired academic, working on a book about *Star Trek: Deep Space Nine* while a pandemic—and the world—rages on outside her.

Or an ideal like community. These conventions and cruises are places where people from all over the world—people of all stripes and types—intermingle together with alien beings (*Star Trek* actors and writers) in peace, harmony, and a spirit of bonhomie. Of course, fandom does not always provide a safe space for those who wish to express their love of their favorite shows. Fans can, and do, argue about—well, just about *everything*—when it comes to their favorite shows, including what it means to *be* a fan (exactly how many details does one have to know about a particular episode of a particular series in order to be considered a "true" fan, after all?). For every fan who embraces a newest iteration of *Star Trek*, there are those who cry "doom!" and lament that the series is finally reaching some sort of unnatural conclusion. Some fans are vociferous in their praise of *Discovery*, for example, while others are just as vocal in their condemnation (see Mittermeier and Spychala); yet the series has just finished its third season.

This is, of course, the nature of fandom and the nature of those things that have meaning—personal, cultural, (sometimes) reverential meaning. Our book only adds to this debate, because, at its best, to debate and interrogate our fandoms is to seek to understand them. It is to build community. It is to build that utopian future. It may seem odd to suggest this, but humanity's best hope for a *Star Trek*–like future may very well be the existence of *Star Trek* itself—the existence of narratives that tell us it is okay to imagine a world better than this one, and that provide hope that this great human experiment of ours may end well after all. And as important as it is to tell these narratives, it is just as important to critique them. To poke holes in them. And to learn how to deal with these narratives, holes and all. Because that is the true essence of *Deep Space Nine*. It does not reject the utopian nature of the *Star Trek* mythos. It does not reject paradise. It merely reminds us that to get there will require real work, real examination, real moments of real rest where we look—not to the farthest reaches of the galaxy—but into the further corners of the human soul.

Star Trek has come a long way since its inception in the 1960s, just as we, as a people, have. *Discovery* is the most diverse, female-forward *Star Trek* cast yet. Progress. Here is hoping that the next iterations will be just as engaging and just as frustrating as the ones that came before. Here is also hoping that we, as a people, will continue to embrace that most inspiring yet difficult axiom: "Infinite Diversity in Infinite Combinations," the very basis of Vulcan philosophy, acknowledging the infinite potentialities the universe holds (first noted in *The Original Series*, "Is There in Truth No Beauty?"). Such potentials might include a pandemic, a convention, a friendship, a hopeful future, perpetual motion, perpetual rest—or, indeed, maybe even a television series, one that can teach us something about the infinite possibilities of the universe—theirs, and ours.

Live Long and Prosper.

Notes

1. The first set of six includes *The Original Series*, *The Animated Series*, *The Next Generation*, *Deep Space Nine*, *Voyager*, and *Enterprise*.

2. *Doctor Who* first aired in November 1963. Its premiere was delayed one day because of the assassination of U.S. President John F. Kennedy. Twenty-six seasons aired until 1989, when production ceased. A feature-length made-for-television film aired in 1996 as an attempt to relaunch the franchise, but it was unsuccessful. Russell T. Davies approached the BBC in the early 2000s about a relaunch of the series, which happened in 2005. The series continues as of this writing. *Doctor Who* fans thus had to survive a sixteen-year hiatus with only re-runs and one film. *Star Trek* fans had to survive a twelve-year hiatus with only re-runs and no films that featured actors from the original six series.

3. The term "Trekkie" was first used as a pejorative term, much like "groupie," to describe *Star Trek* fans. I proudly use the term because I was a Trekkie from episode one, back in 1966. Younger fans prefer the term "Trekker," perhaps because of the negative connotation of Trekkie. I will not go into the many arguments that rage among fans about this issue; after all, "Infinite Diversity in Infinite Combinations" ("Is There in Truth No Beauty?").

4. Although the Super League's architects attempted to recruit teams in France (e.g., Paris Saint-Germain) and Germany (e.g., Bayern Munich), teams in those countries refused to join.

5. I admit that the primary reason I went to the Las Vegas convention in 2018 was because Jeffrey Combs would be attending. I learned about the *Deep Space Nine* celebration later, but I attended it, getting to meet Nana Visitor as well as other actors from the series, including Marc Alaimo (Dukat), Max Grodénchik (Rom), Chase Masterson (Leeta), and Cirroc Lofton (Jake). I am also incredibly happy that I got to chat with Aron Eisenberg (Nog) that night; he died in 2019. I was also in the audience when the surprise we had been promised appeared: Sir Patrick Stewart announcing his return in/as *Picard*. The screams from those who were not in the ballroom at the time were quite loud (really, they were very loud). After such an amazing experience I had to be there in 2021 as well.

Works Cited and Consulted

Geraghty, Lincoln, ed. *The Influence of* Star Trek *on Television, Film and Culture*. McFarland, 2008.

Hamilton, Tom. "Super League Collapses: How Fan Reaction, Revolt Helped end English Clubs' Breakaway." ESPN. www.espn.com/soccer/blog-espn-fc-united/story/4366927/super-league-collapses-how-fan-reactionrevolt-helped-end-english-clubs-breakaway. Retrieved 23 April 2021.

Heath, Kathleen M., and Ann S. Carlisle. *The Voyages of* Star Trek: *A Mirror on American Society Though Time*. Rowman and Littlefield, 2020.

Hills, Matt. *Fan Cultures*. Routledge, 2002.

Jenkins, Henry. "Textual Poachers." *The Fan Fiction Studies Reader*, edited by Karen Hellekson and Kristina Busse. U of Iowa Press, 2014, pp. 26–43.

Lamb, Patricia Frazer, and Diana L. Veith. "Romantic Myth, Transcendence, and *Star Trek* Zines." *The Fan Fiction Studies Reader*, edited by Karen Hellekson and Kristina Busse. U of Iowa P, 2014, pp. 96–115.

Lively, Robert L., ed. *Exploring* Star Trek: Voyager: *Critical Essays*. McFarland, 2020.

Mittermeier, Sabrina. "(Un)Conventional Voyages?—*Star Trek*: The Cruise and the Themed Cruise Experience." *The Journal of Popular Culture*, vol. 52, no. 6, 2019, pp. 1372–1386.

Mittermeier, Sabrina, and Mareike Spychala, eds. *Fighting for the Future: Essays on* Star Trek: Discovery. Liverpool UP, 2020.

Star Trek: Inside the Most Influential Science-Fiction Series Ever. Time Special Edition. Meredith Corporation, 2021.

Star Trek Deep Space 9 *Illustrated Handbook*. CBS Studios, 2020.

Appendix A

List of Deep Space Nine Episodes by Season[1]
Episode Number[2] / Title / Writer / Director /Air Date

Season One

1.01, 02 / Emissary, Parts I and II / Rick Berman (story) and Michael Piller (story & teleplay) / David Carson / 3 Jan. 1993

1.03 / Past Prologue / Kathryn Powers / Winrich Kolbe / 10 Jan. 1993

1.04 / A Man Alone / Gerald Sanford (story) and Michael Piller (story & teleplay) / Paul Lynch / 17 Jan. 1993

1.05 / Babel / Sally Caves and Ira Steven Behr (story) and Michael McGreevey and Naren Shankar (teleplay) / Paul Lynch / 24 Jan. 1993

1.06 / Captive Pursuit / Jill Sherman Donner (story & teleplay) and Michael Piller (teleplay) / Corey Allen / 31 Jan. 1993

1.07 / Q-Less / Hannah Louise Shearer (story) and Robert Hewitt Wolfe (teleplay) / Paul Lynch / 7 Feb. 1993

1.08 / Dax / Peter Allan Fields (story & teleplay) and D.C. Fontana (teleplay) / David Carson / 14 Feb. 1993

1.09 / The Passenger / Morgan Gendel (story & teleplay) and Robert Hewitt Wolfe and Michael Piller (teleplay) / Paul Lynch / 21 Feb. 1993

1.10 / Move Along Home / Michael Piller (story) and Frederick Rappaport, Lisa Rich, and Jeanne Carrigan-Fauci (teleplay) / David Carson / 14 Mar. 1993

1.11 / The Nagus / David Livingston (story) and Ira Steven Behr (teleplay) / David Livingston / 21 Mar. 1993

1.12 / Vortex / Sam Rolfe / Winrich Kolbe / 18 Apr. 1993

1.13 / Battle Lines / Hilary J. Bader (story) and Richard Danus and Evan Carlos Somers (teleplay) / Paul Lynch / 25 Apr. 1993

1.14 / The Storyteller / Kurt Michael Bensmiller (story) and Kurt Michael Bensmiller and Ira Steven Behr (teleplay) / David Livingston / 2 May 1993

1.15 / Progress / Peter Alan Fields / Les Landau / 9 May 1993

1.16 / If Wishes Were Horses / Nell McCue Crawford and William L. Crawford (story & teleplay) and Michael Piller (teleplay) / Robert Lagato / 16 May 1993

1.17 / The Forsaken / Jim Trombetta (story) and Don Carlos Dunaway and Michael Piller (teleplay) / Les Landau / 23 May 1993

1.18 / Dramatis Personae / Joe Menosky / Cliff Bole / 30 May 1993
1.19 / Duet / Lisa Rich and Jeanne Carrigan-Fauci (story) and Peter Allan Fields (teleplay) / James L. Conway / 13 June 1993
1.20 / In the Hands of the Prophets / Robert Hewitt Wolfe / David Livingston / 20 June 1993

Season Two

2.01 / The Homecoming / Jeri Taylor (story) and Ira Steven Behr (story & teleplay) / Winrich Kolbe / 26 Sept. 1993
2.02 / The Circle / Peter Allan Fields / Corey Allen / 3 Oct. 1993
2.03 / The Siege / Michael Piller / Winrich Kolbe / 10 Oct. 1993
2.04 / Invasive Procedures / John Whelpley (story & teleplay) and Robert Hewitt Wolfe (teleplay) / Les Landau / 17 Oct. 1993
2.05 / Cardassians / Gene Wolande and John Wright (story) and James Crocker (teleplay) / Cliff Bole / 24 Oct. 1993
2.06 / Melora / Evan Carlos Somers (story & teleplay) and Steven Baum, Michael Piller, and James Crocker (teleplay) / Winrich Kolbe / 31 Oct. 1993
2.07 / Rules of Acquisition / Hilary J. Bader (story) and Ira Steven Behr (teleplay) / David Livingston / 7 Nov. 1993
2.08 / Necessary Evil / Peter Allan Fields / James L. Conway / 14 Nov. 1993
2.09 / Second Sight / Mark Gehred-O'Connell (story & teleplay) and Ira Steven Behr and Robert Hewitt Wolfe (teleplay) / Alexander Singer / 21 Nov. 1993
2.10 / Sanctuary / Gabe Essoe and Kelley Miles (story) and Frederick Rappaport (teleplay) / Les Landau / 28 Nov. 1993
2.11 / Rivals / Jim Trombetta and Michael Piller (story) and Joe Menosky (teleplay) / David Livingston / 2 Jan. 1994
2.12 / The Alternate / Jim Trombetta (story) and Bill Dial (story & teleplay) / David Carson / 9 Jan. 1994
2.13 / Armageddon Game / Morgan Gendel / Winrich Kolbe / 30 Jan. 1994
2.14 / Whispers / Paul Robert Coyle / Les Landau / 6 Feb. 1994
2.15 / Paradise / Jim Trombetta and James Crocker (story) and Jeff King, Richard Manning, and Hans Beimler (teleplay) / Corey Allen / 13 Feb. 1994
2.16 / Shadowplay / Robert Hewitt Wolfe / Robert Scheerer / 20 Feb. 1994
2.17 / Playing God / Jim Trombetta (story and teleplay) and Michael Piller (teleplay) / David Livingston / 27 Feb. 1994
2.18 / Profit and Loss / Flip Kobler and Cindy Marcus / Robert Wiemer / 20 Mar. 1994
2.19 / Blood Oath / Peter Allan Fields / Winrich Kolbe / 27 Mar. 1994
2.20 / The Maquis, Part I / Rick Berman, Michael Piller, and Jeri Taylor (story) and James Crocker (story & teleplay) / David Livingston / 24 Apr. 1994
2.21 / The Maquis, Part II / Rick Berman, Michael Piller, and Jeri Taylor (story) and Ira Steven Behr (story & teleplay) / Corey Allen / 1 May 1994

2.22 / The Wire / Robert Hewitt Wolfe / Kim Friedman / 8 May 1994

2.23 / Crossover / Peter Allan Fields (story & teleplay) and Michael Piller (teleplay) / David Livingston / 15 May 1994

2.24 / The Collaborator / Gary Holland (story & teleplay) and Ira Steven Behr and Robert Hewitt Wolfe (teleplay) / Cliff Bole / 22 May 1994

2.25 / Tribunal / Bill Dial / Avery Brooks / 5 June 1994

2.26 / The Jem'Hadar / Ira Steven Behr / Kim Friedman / 12 June 1994

Season Three

3.01 / The Search, Part I / Ira Steven Behr and Robert Hewitt Wolfe (story) and Ronald D. Moore (teleplay) / Kim Friedman / 26 Sept. 1994

3.02 / The Search, Part II / Ira Steven Behr (story & teleplay) and Robert Hewitt Wolfe (story) / Jonathan Frakes / 3 Oct. 1994

3.03 / The House of Quark / Tom Benko (story) and Ronald D. Moore (teleplay) / Les Landau / 10 Oct. 1994

3.04 / Equilibrium / Christopher Teague (story) and René Echevarria (teleplay) / Cliff Bole / 17 Oct. 1994

3.05 / Second Skin / Robert Hewitt Wolfe / Les Landau / 24 Oct. 1994

3.06 / The Abandoned / D. Thomas Maio and Steve Warnek / Avery Brooks / 31 Oct. 1994

3.07 / Civil Defense / Mike Krohn / Reza Badiyi / 7 Nov. 1994

3.08 / Meridian / Hilary J. Bader and Evan Carlos Somers (story) and Mark Gehred-O'Connell (teleplay) / Jonathan Frakes / 14 Nov. 1994

3.09 / Defiant / Ronald D. Moore / Cliff Bole / 21 Nov. 1994

3.10 / Fascination / Ira Steven Behr and James Crocker (story) and Philip LaZebnik (teleplay) / Avery Brooks / 28 Nov. 1994

3.11 / Past Tense, Part I / Ira Steven Behr (story) and Robert Hewitt Wolfe (story & teleplay) / Reza Badiyi / 2 Jan. 1995

3.12 / Past Tense, Part II / Ira Steven Behr (story & teleplay) and Robert Hewitt Wolfe (story) and René Echevarria (teleplay) / Jonathan Frakes / 9 Jan. 1995

3.13 / Life Support / Christian Ford and Roger Soffer (story) and Ronald D. Moore (teleplay) / Reza Badiyi / 30 Jan. 1995

3.14 / Heart of Stone / Ira Steven Behr and Robert Hewitt Wolfe / Alexander Singer / 6 Feb. 1995

3.15 / Destiny / David S. Cohen and Martin A. Winer / Les Landau / 13 Feb. 1995

3.16 / Prophet Motive / Ira Steven Behr and Robert Hewitt Wolfe / René Auberjonois / 20 Feb. 1995

3.17 / Visionary / Ethan H. Calk (story) and John Shirley (teleplay) / Reza Badiyi / 27 Feb. 1995

3.18 / Distant Voices / Joe Menosky (story) and Ira Steven Behr and Robert Hewitt Wolfe (teleplay) / Alexander Singer / 10 Apr. 1995

3.19 / Through the Looking Glass / Ira Steven Behr and Robert Hewitt Wolfe / Winrich Kolbe / 17 Apr. 1995

3.20 / Improbable Cause / Robert Lederman and David R. Long (story) and René Echevarria (teleplay) / Avery Brooks / 24 Apr. 1995

3.21 / The Die is Cast / Ronald D. Moore / David Livingston / 1 May 1995
3.22 / Explorers / Hilary J. Bader (story) and René Echevarria (teleplay) /
   Cliff Bole / 8 May 1995
3.23 / Family Business / Ira Steven Behr and Robert Hewitt Wolfe / René
   Auberjonois / 15 May 1995
3.24 / Shakaar / Gordon Dawson / Jonathan West / 22 May 1995
3.25 / Facets / René Echevarria / Cliff Bole / 12 June 1995
3.26 / The Adversary / Ira Steven Behr and Robert Hewitt Wolfe / Alexander
   Singer / 19 June 1995

Season Four

4.01, 02 / The Way of the Warrior / Ira Steven Behr and Robert Hewitt Wolfe /
   James L. Conway / 2 Oct. 1995
4.03 / The Visitor / Michael Taylor / David Livingston / 9 Oct. 1995
4.04 / Hippocratic Oath / Nicholas Corea (story) and Lisa Klink (story &
   teleplay) / René Auberjonois / 16 Oct. 1995
4.05 / Indiscretion / Toni Marberry and Jack Treviño (story) and Nicholas
   Corea / LeVar Burton / 23 Oct. 1995
4.06 / Rejoined / René Echevarria (story & teleplay) and Ronald D. Moore
   (teleplay) / Avery Brooks / 30 Oct. 1995
4.07 / Starship Down / David Mack and John J. Ordover / Alexander Singer /
   6 Nov. 1995
4.08 / Little Green Men / Toni Marberry and Jack Treviño (story) and Ira
   Steven Behr and Robert Hewitt Wolfe (teleplay) / James L. Conway / 13
   Nov. 1995
4.09 / The Sword of Kahless / Richard Danus (story) and Hans Beimler
   (teleplay) / LeVar Burton / 20 Nov. 1995
4.10 / Our Man Bashir / Robert Gillan (story) and Ronald D. Moore
   (teleplay) / Winrich Kolbe / 27 Nov. 1995
4.11 / Homefront / Ira Steven Behr and Robert Hewitt Wolfe / David
   Livingston / 1 Jan. 1996
4.12 / Paradise Lost / Ronald D. Moore (story) and Ira Steven Behr and
   Robert Hewitt Wolfe (teleplay) / Reza Badiyi / 8 Jan. 1996
4.13 / Crossfire / René Echevarria / Les Landau / 29 Jan. 1996
4.14 / Return to Grace / Tom Benko (story) and Hans Beimler (teleplay) /
   Jonathan West / 5 Feb. 1996
4.15 / Sons of Mogh / Ronald D. Moore / David Livingston / 12 Feb. 1996
4.16 / Bar Association / Barbara J. Lee and Jenifer A. Lee (story) and Robert
   Hewitt Wolfe and Ira Steven Behr (teleplay) / LeVar Burton / 19 Feb. 1996
4.17 / Accession / Jane Espenson / Les Landau / 26 Feb. 1996
4.18 / Rules of Engagement / Bradley Thompson and David Weddle (story)
   and Ronald D. Moore (teleplay) / LeVar Burton / 8 Apr. 1996
4.19 / Hard Time / Daniel Keys Moran and Lynn Barker (story) and Robert
   Hewitt Wolfe (teleplay) / Alexander Singer / 15 Apr. 1996
4.20 / Shattered Mirror / Ira Steven Behr and Hans Beimler / James L.
   Conway / 22 Apr. 1996

4.21 / The Muse / René Echevarria (story & teleplay) and Majel Barrett Roddenberry (story) / David Livingston / 29 Apr. 1996

4.22 / For the Cause / Mark Gehred-O'Connell (story) and Ronald D. Moore (teleplay) / James L. Conway / 6 May 1996

4.23 / To the Death / Ira Steven Behr and Robert Hewitt Wolfe / LeVar Burton / 13 May 1996

4.24 / The Quickening / Naren Shankar / René Auberjonois / 20 May 1996

4.25 / Body Parts / Louis P. DeSantis and Robert J. Bolivar (story) and Hans Beimler (teleplay) / Avery Brooks / 10 June 1996

4.26 / Broken Link / George A. Brozak (story) and Robert Hewitt Wolfe and Ira Steven Behr (teleplay) / Les Landau / 17 June 1996

Season Five

5.01 / Apocalypse Rising / Ira Steven Behr and Robert Hewitt Wolfe / James L. Conway / 30 Sept. 1996

5.02 / The Ship / Pam Wigginton and Rick Cason (story) and Hans Beimler (teleplay) / Kim Friedman / 7 Oct. 1996

5.03 / Looking for par'Mach in All the Wrong Places / Ronald D. Moore / Andrew J. Robinson / 14 Oct. 1996

5.04 / … Nor the Battle to the Strong / Brice R. Parker (story) and René Echevarria (teleplay) / Kim Friedman / 21 Oct. 1996

5.05 / The Assignment / David R. Long and Robert Lederman (story) and David Weddle and Bradley Thompson (teleplay) / Allan Kroeker / 28 Oct. 1996

5.06 / Trials and Tribble-ations / Ira Steven Behr, Hans Beimler, and Robert Hewitt Wolfe (story) and Ronald D. Moore and René Echevarria (teleplay) / Jonathan West / 4 Nov. 1996

5.07 / Let He Who Is Without Sin… / Robert Hewitt Wolfe and Ira Steven Behr / René Auberjonois / 11 Nov. 1996

5.08 / Things Past / Michael Taylor / LeVar Burton / 18 Nov. 1996

5.09 / The Ascent / Ira Steven Behr and Robert Hewitt Wolfe / Allan Kroeker / 25 Nov. 1996

5.10 / Rapture / L.J. Strom (story) and Hans Beimler (teleplay) / Jonathan West / 30 Dec. 1996

5.11 / The Darkness and The Light / Bryan Fuller (story) and Ronald D. Moore (teleplay) / Michael Vejar / 6 Jan. 1997

5.12 / The Begotten / René Echevarria / Jesús Salvador Treviño / 27 Jan. 1997

5.13 / For the Uniform / Peter Allan Fields / Victor Lobl / 3 Feb. 1997

5.14 / In Purgatory's Shadow / Robert Hewitt Wolfe and Ira Steven Behr / Gabrielle Beaumont / 10 Feb. 1997

5.15 / By Inferno's Light / Ira Steven Behr and Robert Hewitt Wolfe / Les Landau / 17 Feb. 1997

5.16 / Doctor Bashir, I Presume? / Jimmy Diggs (story) and Ronald D. Moore (teleplay) / David Livingston / 24 Feb. 1997

5.17 / A Simple Investigation / René Echevarria / John Kretchmer / 31 Mar. 1997

5.18 / Business as Usual / Bradley Thompson and David Weddle / Siddig El Fadil / 7 Apr. 1997

5.19/ Ties of Blood and Water / Edmund Newton and Robbin L. Slocum (story) and Robert Hewitt Wolfe (teleplay) / Avery Brooks / 14 Apr. 1997

5.20 / Ferengi Love Songs / Ira Steven Behr and Hans Beimler / René Auberjonois / 21 Apr. 1997

5.21 / Soldiers of the Empire / Ronald D. Moore / LeVar Burton / 28 Apr. 1997

5.22 / Children of Time / Gary Holland and Ethan H. Calk (story) and René Echevarria (teleplay) / Allan Kroeker / 5 May 1997

5.23 / Blaze of Glory / Robert Hewitt Wolfe and Ira Steven Behr / Kim Friedman / 12 May 1997

5.24 / Empok Nor / Bryan Fuller (story) and Hans Beimler (teleplay) / Michael Vejar / 19 May 1997

5.25 / In the Cards / Truly Barr Clark and Scott J. Neal (story) and Ronald D. Moore (teleplay) / Michael Dorn / 9 June 1997

5.26 / Call to Arms / Ira Steven Behr and Robert Hewitt Wolfe / Allan Kroeker / 16 June 1997

Season Six

6.01 / A Time to Stand / Ira Steven Behr and Hans Beimler / Allan Kroeker / 29 Sept. 1997

6.02 / Rocks and Shoals / Ronald D. Moore / Michael Vejar / 6 Oct. 1997

6.03 / Sons and Daughters / Bradley Thompson and David Weddle / Jesús Salvador Treviño / 13 Oct. 1997

6.04 / Behind the Lines / René Echevarria / LeVar Burton / 20 Oct. 1997

6.05 / Favor the Bold / Ira Steven Behr and Hans Beimler / Winrich Kolbe / 27 Oct. 1997

6.06 / Sacrifice of Angels / Ira Steven Behr and Hans Beimler / Allan Kroeker / 3 Nov. 1997

6.07 / You Are Cordially Invited / Ronald D. Moore / David Livingston / 10 Nov. 1997

6.08 / Resurrection / Michael Taylor / LeVar Burton / 17 Nov. 1997

6.09 / Statistical Probabilities / Pam Pietroforte (story) and René Echevarria (teleplay) / Anson Williams / 24 Nov. 1997

6.10 / The Magnificent Ferengi / Ira Steven Behr and Hans Beimler / Chip Chalmers / 1 Jan. 1998

6.11 / Waltz / Ronald D. Moore / René Auberjonois / 8 Jan. 1998

6.12 / Who Mourns for Morn? / Mark Gehred-O'Connell / Victor Lobl / 4 Feb. 1998

6.13 / Far Beyond the Stars / Mark Scott Zicree (story) and Ira Steven Behr and Hans Beimler (teleplay) / Avery Brooks / 11 Feb. 1998

6.14 / One Little Ship / David Weddle and Bradley Thompson / Allan Kroeker / 18 Feb. 1998

6.15 / Honor Among Thieves / Philip Kim (story) and René Echevarria (teleplay) / Allan Eastman / 25 Feb. 1998

6.16 / Change of Heart / Ronald D. Moore / David Livingston / 4 Mar. 1998

6.17 / Wrongs Darker Than Death or Night / Ira Steven Behr and Hans Beimler / Jonathan West / 1 Apr. 1998

6.18 / Inquisition / Bradley Thompson and David Weddle / Michael Dorn / 8 Apr. 1998

6.19 / In the Pale Moonlight / Peter Allan Fields (story) and Michael Taylor (teleplay) / Victor Lobl / 15 Apr. 1998

6.20 / His Way / Ira Steven Behr and Hans Beimler / Allan Kroeker / 22 Apr. 1998

6.21 / The Reckoning / Harry M. Werksman and Gabrielle Stanton (story) and David Weddle and Bradley Thompson (teleplay) / Jesús Salvador Treviño / 29 Apr. 1998

6.22 / Valiant / Ronald D. Moore / Michael Vejar / 6 May 1998

6.23 / Profit and Lace / Ira Steven Behr and Hans Beimler / Alexander Siddig / 13 May 1998

6.24 / Time's Orphan / Joe Menosky (story) and David Weddle and Bradley Thompson (teleplay) / Allan Kroeker / 20 May 1998

6.25 / The Sound of Her Voice / Pam Pietroforte (story) and Ronald D. Moore (teleplay) / Winrich Kolbe / 10 June 1998

6.26 / Tears of the Prophets / Ira Steven Behr and Hans Beimler / Allan Kroeker / 17 June 1998

Season Seven

7.01 / Image in the Sand / Ira Steven Behr and Hans Beimler / Les Landau / 30 Sept. 1998

7.02 / Shadows and Symbols / Ira Steven Behr and Hans Beimler / Allan Kroeker / 7 Oct. 1998

7.03 / Afterimage / René Echevarria / Les Landau / 14 Oct. 1998

7.04 / Take Me Out to the Holosuite / Ronald D. Moore / Chip Chalmers / 21 Oct. 1998

7.05 / Chrysalis / René Echevarria / Jonathan West / 28 Oct. 1998

7.06 / Treachery, Faith and the Great River / Philip Kim (story) and David Weddle and Bradley Thompson (teleplay) / Steve Posey / 4 Nov. 1998

7.07 / Once More Unto the Breach / Ronald D. Moore / Allan Kroeker / 11 Nov. 1998

7.08 / The Siege of AR-558 / Ira Steven Behr and Hans Beimler / Winrich Kolbe / 18 Nov. 1998

7.09 / Covenant / René Echevarria / John Kretchmer / 25 Nov. 1998

7.10 / It's Only a Paper Moon / David Alan Mack and John J. Ordover (story) and Ronald D. Moore (teleplay) / Anson Williams / 30 Dec. 1998

7.11 / Prodigal Daughter / Bradley Thompson and David Weddle / Victor Lobl / 6 Jan. 1999

7.12 / The Emperor's New Cloak / Ira Steven Behr and Hans Beimler / LeVar Burton / 3 Feb. 1999

7.13 / Field of Fire / Robert Hewitt Wolfe / Tony Dow / 10 Feb. 1999

7.14 / Chimera / René Echevarria / Steve Posey / 17 Feb. 1999

7.15 / Badda-Bing Badda-Bang / Ira Steven Behr and Hans Beimler / Mike Vejar / 24 Feb. 1999

7.16 / Inter Arma Enim Silent Leges / Ronald D. Moore / David Livingston / 3 Mar. 1999

7.17 / Penumbra / René Echevarria / Steve Posey / 7 Apr. 1999

7.18 / 'Til Death Do Us Part / David Weddle and Bradley Thompson / Winrich Kolbe / 14 Apr. 1999

7.19 / Strange Bedfellows / Ronald D. Moore / René Auberjonois / 21 Apr. 1999

7.20 / The Changing Face of Evil / Ira Steven Behr and Hans Beimler / Mike Vejar / 28 Apr. 1999

7.21 / When It Rains… / Spike Steingasser (story) and René Echevarria (story & teleplay) / Michael Dorn / 5 May 1999

7.22 / Tacking Into the Wind / Ronald D. Moore / Mike Vejar / 12 May 1999

7.23 / Extreme Measures / Bradley Thompson and David Weddle / Steve Posey / 19 May 1999

7.24 / The Dogs of War / Peter Allan Fields (story) and René Echevarria and Ronald D. Moore (teleplay) / Avery Brooks / 26 May 1999

7.25 / What You Leave Behind / Ira Steven Behr and Hans Beimler / Allan Kroeker / 2 June 1999

Notes

1. The episodes listed herein are the episodes that were filmed and/or broadcast for each season. Dates listed are for the first syndicated broadcast of the episode in the United States. We have listed the episodes in the order in which they are indicated on the respective DVD. All information in this list was verified by the DVDs for each series, Erdmann and Block's Deep Space Nine *Companion Guide*, and the internet sites Wikipedia, IMDb, and *Star Trek: Deep Space Nine* Memory Alpha. In some cases, the order of the writers' names was reversed on one site compared to the others. In these instances, we verified the order against credits on the episode in question. Note that Siddig El Fadil is director of "Business as Usual" on the episode's opening credit. His credit for "Profit and Lace" is Alexander Siddig.

2. Episodes are numbered by season and order of broadcast. Thus "Past Prologue" is 1.03: season 1, episode 3. That might not reflect the order in which the episode was filmed.

Appendix B

List of Non-Deep Space Nine
Star Trek *Episodes Cited in Text*

"All Good Things…." *The Next Generation*, season 7, episodes 25 and 26, syndicated, 23 May 1994.

"The Best of Both Worlds." *The Next Generation*, season 3, episode 26, syndicated, 18 June 1990.

"The Cage." *The Original Series*, season 1, episode 0 (original pilot), NBC, 27 Nov. 1998.

"Charlie X." *The Original Series*, season 1, episode 2, NBC, 15 Sept. 1966.

"Descent." *The Next Generation*, season 6, episode 26, syndicated, 19 June 1993.

"Devil's Due." *The Next Generation*, season 4, episode 13, syndicated, 2 Feb. 1991.

"Emanations." *Voyager*, season 1, episode 9, UPN, 13 Mar. 1995.

"Encounter at Farpoint." *The Next Generation*, season 1, episodes 1 and 2, syndicated, 28 September 1987.

"Ensign Ro." *The Next Generation*, season 5, episode 3, syndicated, 7 Oct. 1991.

"Family." *The Next Generation*, season 4, episode 2, syndicated, 29 Sept. 1990.

"Is There in Truth No Beauty?" *The Original Series*, season 3, episode 5, NBC, 18 Oct. 1968.

"Journey's End." *The Next Generation*, season 7, episode 20, syndicated, 28 Mar. 1994.

"Let That Be Your Last Battlefield." *The Original Series*, season 3, episode 15, NBC, 10 January 1969.

"Live Fast and Prosper." *Voyager*, season 6, episode 21, UPN, 19 Apr. 2000.

"The Man Trap." *The Original Series*, season 1, episode 1, NBC, 8 Sept. 1966.

"The Menagerie." *The Original Series*, season 1, episodes 11 and 12, NBC, 17 and 24 Nov. 1966.

"No Small Parts." *Lower Decks*, season 1, episode 10, CBS All Access, 8 Oct. 2020.

"The Offspring." *The Next Generation*, season 3, episode 16, syndicated, 12 March 1990.

"The Outcast." *The Next Generation*, season 5, episode 17, syndicated, 16 March 1992.

"The Paradise Syndrome." *The Original Series*, season 3, episode 3, NBC, 4 Oct. 1968.

"Plato's Stepchildren." *The Original Series*, season 3, episode 10, NBC, 22 Nov. 1968.

"The Price." *The Next Generation*, season 3, episode 8, syndicated, 13 Nov. 1989.

"Qpid." *The Next Generation*, season 4, episode 20, syndicated, 22 April 1991.

"The Return of the Archons." *The Original Series*, season 1, episode 21, NBC, 9 Feb. 1967.

"Rightful Heir." *The Next Generation*, season 6, episode 23, syndicated, 15 May 1993.

"Someone to Watch Over Me." *Voyager*, season 5, episode 21, UPN, 28 Mar. 1995.

"Time's Arrow." *The Next Generation*, season 5, episode 26, syndicated, 13 Apr. 1999.

"Turnabout Intruder." *The Original Series*, season 3, episode 24, NBC, 3 June 1969.

"Where No Man Has Gone Before." *The Original Series*, season 1, episode 3, NBC, 22 Sept. 1966.

"Who Mourns for Adonais?" *The Original Series*, season 2, episode 2, NBC, 22 Sept. 1967.

"Who Watches the Watchers." *The Next Generation*, season 3, episode 4, syndicated, 14 Oct. 1989.

"Year of Hell." *Voyager*, season 4, episodes 8 and 9, UPN, 5 and 12 Nov. 1997.

"Yesterday's Enterprise." *The Next Generation*, season 3, episode 15, syndicated, 17 Feb. 1990.

Appendix C
Star Trek *Filmography*

Media are presented in chronological order.

Television Series

The Original Series. Created by Gene Roddenberry, NBC, 1966–1969.
The Animated Series. Created by Gene Roddenberry, NBC, 1973–1974.
The Next Generation. Created by Gene Roddenberry, syndicated, 1987–1994.
Deep Space Nine. Created by Rick Berman and Michael Piller, syndicated, 1993–1999.
Voyager. Created by Rick Berman, Michael Piller, and Jeri Taylor, UPN, 1995–2001.
Enterprise. Created by Rick Berman and Brannon Braga, UPN, 2001–2005.
Discovery. Created by Bryan Fuller and Alex Kurtzman, CBS All Access, 2017–present.
Picard. Created by Akiva Goldsman, Michael Chabon, Kirsten Beyer, and Alex Kurtzman, CBS All Access, 2020–present.
Lower Decks. Created by Mike McMahan, CBS All Access, 2020–present.
Strange New Worlds. Created by Akiva Goldsman, Alex Kurtzman, and Jenny Lumet. CBS All Access, 2020, in production.

Motion Pictures

The Motion Picture. Directed by Robert Wise. Paramount Studios, 1979.
The Wrath of Khan. Directed by Nicholas Meyer. Paramount Studios, 1982.
The Search for Spock. Directed by Leonard Nimoy. Paramount Studios, 1984.
The Voyage Home. Directed by Leonard Nimoy. Paramount Studios, 1986.
The Final Frontier. Directed by William Shatner. Paramount Studios, 1989.
The Undiscovered Country. Directed by Nicholas Meyer. Paramount Studios, 1991.
Generations. Directed by David Carson. Paramount Studios, 1994.
First Contact. Directed by Jonathan Frakes. Paramount Studios, 1996.

Insurrection. Directed by Jonathan Frakes. Paramount Studios, 1998.
Nemesis. Directed by Stuart Baird. Paramount Studios, 2002.
Star Trek. Directed by J.J. Abrams. Paramount Studios, 2009.
Star Trek into Darkness. Directed by J.J. Abrams. Paramount Studios, 2013.
Star Trek: Beyond. Directed by Justin Lin. Paramount Studios, 2016.

About the Contributors

Erin **Bell** received a Ph.D. from Wayne State University. Her work has been published in *Short Fiction in Theory and Practice*, *The Explicator*, and *Lilith: A Feminist History Journal,* among others. She is an assistant professor and the program director of English for on-ground campuses of Baker College. Her research interests include short fiction, women's writing, and popular culture.

Rowan **Bell** is a Ph.D. candidate in philosophy at Syracuse University, where they are the recent winner of the Graduate Dean's Award for Excellence in Research and Creative Work and the Outstanding TA Award. They also received the 2020 New York SWIP Graduate Student Essay Prize. They work on feminist theory, metaethics, and trans philosophy.

Drew **Chastain** received a Ph.D. from Tulane University and has published a number of articles on spirituality and meaning in life that have appeared in journals such as *The Journal of Philosophy of Life*, *Sophia*, and *Philosophia*, among others. His work explores what it means to be spiritual but not religious and also how to better understand the subjective, experiential aspect of meaning in life.

Michael G. **Cornelius** received a Ph.D. from the University of Rhode Island. He is the author or editor of over 20 books, and has published 70 critical essays in books and journals, including *Fifteenth-Century Studies*, *Journal of Girlhood Studies*, and the *Pennsylvania Literary Journal*. He is a professor of English and director of the Master of Humanities program at Wilson College.

Florent **Favard** is an associate professor in theory and practice of cinema, audiovisual and transmedia at the Institut Européen de Cinéma et d'Audiovisuel (Lorraine University, France). He has published more than 20 essays in French and international journals, as well as three books, including *Écrire une série TV* and *Le Récit dans les séries de science-fiction.*

Sherry **Ginn** received a Ph.D. from the University of South Carolina and retired in 2018 after 35 years of teaching. She is the author or editor of books on women in science fiction, sex in science fiction, time travel, Black Widow, and television series such as *Farscape*, *Doctor Who*, and *Fringe*. She is the co-chair of the science fiction and fantasy area of the Popular Culture Association.

Franklin R. **Halprin** is a Ph.D. candidate at Rutgers University's Edward J. Bloustein School of Planning & Public Policy. He focuses on institutional, political, and historical forces in American environmental policy conflicts, writing about the ways in which peoples' cultural values, thinking patterns, and perceptions filter into the process.

Dylan Reid **Miller** is a Ph.D. student in Bowling Green State University's American Cultural Studies program, researching the temporal dimension of politics in science and speculative fiction. She received an M.A. from NYU's Gallatin School of Individualized Study, writing her thesis on genderqueer potentiality and posthumanity in the *Star Trek* shows of the 1990s.

Val **Nolan** holds a Ph.D. from National University of Ireland, Galway. He has published articles in *Science Fiction Studies* and *Review of Contemporary Fiction*, among others, while his fiction has appeared in *Year's Best Science Fiction*, *Best of British Science Fiction*, and elsewhere. He is a lecturer in genre fiction and creative writing at Aberystwyth University in Wales.

Douglas **Rasmussen** received an M.A. from the University of Saskatchewan in English literature, where he wrote on the AMC television series *Breaking Bad*. His main area of research is film studies, but his research interests also include television and other forms of contemporary media.

Index